ACCOUNTING PRINCIPLES

THIRD CANADIAN EDITION

Accounting Principles

▶ **JERRY J. WEYGANDT** *Ph.D., C.P.A.*

Arthur Andersen Alumni Professor of Accounting
University of Wisconsin—Madison

▶ **DONALD E. KIESO** *Ph.D., C.P.A.*

KPMG Emeritus Professor of Accountancy
Northern Illinois University

▶ **PAUL D. KIMMEL** *Ph.D., C.P.A.*

University of Wisconsin—Milwaukee

▶ **BARBARA TRENHOLM** *M.B.A., F.C.A.*

University of New Brunswick—Fredericton

IN COLLABORATION WITH

▶ **VALERIE A. KINNEAR** *B.S.W., M.Sc. (Bus. Admin.), C.A.*

Mount Royal College

John Wiley & Sons Canada, Ltd.

To our students — past, present, and future

National Library of Canadian Cataloguing in Publication Data

Jerry J. Weygandt
    Accounting principles

3rd Canadian ed.

Includes index.
ISBN 0-470-83375-0 (pt. 1)

    1. Accounting. I. Weygandt, Jerry J

HF5635.A3778 2003   657'.044   C2003-905260-5

Production Credits

Publisher: John Horne
Publishing Services Director: Karen Bryan
Editorial Manager: Karen Staudinger
Developmental Editor: Zoë Craig
Senior Marketing Manager: Janine Daoust
Manager, Business and Online Marketing: Carolyn J. Wells
New Media Editor: Elsa Passera
Editorial Assistant: Gail Brown
Design & Typesetting: Appleby Color Lab
Cover Design: Interrobang Graphic Design
CD Design & Programming: Ian Koo/Tia Seifert
Printing & Binding: Tri-Graphic Printing Limited

Printed and bound in Canada
10 9 8 7 6 5 4 3 2 1

John Wiley & Sons Canada, Ltd.
22 Worcester Road
Etobicoke, Ontario M9W 1L1
Visit our website at: www.wiley.com/canada

Tejal Govande

Part One

Part Two

Part Three

Part Four

concepts for review >>

Before studying this chapter, you should understand or, if necessary, review:

a. How to record revenue. (Ch. 3, pp. 102–103 and Ch. 5, pp. 222–225)
b. Why adjusting entries are made. (Ch. 3, pp. 103–104)
c. How to calculate interest. (Ch. 3, p. 110)

Personal Touch Helps Keep Receivables Healthy

Whitehill Technologies: www.whitehilltech.com

MONCTON, N.B.—Since its founding in 1997, Whitehill Technologies has grown from just two employees to a staff of 90 and annual sales of $10 million. Today, the company's software—which enables companies in the financial services, legal, and insurance sectors to create business documents from data stored on older systems—is used by more than 500 clients in 45 countries.

Whitehill's revenue comes from software licence sales, services such as installation, training and template customization, and ongoing maintenance. The company usually has about $2 million in accounts receivable at any given time.

"We bill for licence fees up front—they're due upon receipt—and our regular terms for services and maintenance are n/30," explains Paul Gunn, Whitehill's VP of Finance and Administration. "With our resellers, it's a little different—we have some that settle quarterly and others that settle monthly."

Contrary to some large companies, Whitehill does not charge interest for amounts past due; nor does it offer discounts for early payment. As Mr. Gunn points out, the fact that the company has "the ability to cut off support" is usually enough to encourage prompt payment.

The company uses a weekly aging report to keep track of its receivables. "When an invoice is nearing 30 days, we will initiate contact with the client, usually by telephone or e-mail to make sure it's in their system," explains Mr. Gunn. "If it gets on to 45 days, we would talk with our project manager and look for an additional contact in the organization."

An account over 90 days goes on a red flag list. "At that point, senior management would likely get involved," says Mr. Gunn. But by maintaining personal contact every step of the way, he adds, the company usually gets customers to pay well before that happens. Still, the company records an estimate for bad debts every year.

"When Whitehill was starting out and growing, accounts receivable collections provided our lifeblood (cash)," says Mr. Gunn. "As we have grown and become stronger financially, we've continued to manage our receivables with the same level of diligence and attention." With receivables, then, what's important is to keep on top of them at all times by having a process in place to deal with them at whatever stage they're at.

the navigator ✔

- Understand *Concepts for Review*
- Read *Feature Story*
- Scan *Study Objectives*
- Read *Chapter Preview*
- Read text and answer *Before You Go On*
- Work *Demonstration Problem*
- Review *Summary of Study Objectives*
- Answer *Self-Study Questions*
- Complete assignments

chapter 8
Accounting for Receivables

study objectives >>

After studying this chapter, you should be able to:

1. Identify and distinguish between the different types of receivables.
2. Show how accounts receivable are recognized in the accounts.
3. Describe and use the method and bases used to value accounts receivable.
4. Determine the entries to record the disposition of accounts receivable.
5. Show how notes receivable are recognized and valued in the accounts.
6. Determine the entries to record the disposition of notes receivable.
7. Explain the statement presentation and analysis of receivables.

In the feature story, receivables are a significant asset for Whitehill Technologies. Receivables are significant to other companies as well, because a large number of sales are made on credit. Companies must therefore pay close attention to their receivables and manage them carefully. In this chapter, we will first review the journal entries companies make when goods and services are sold on account and when cash is collected from those sales. Next, we will learn how companies estimate, record, and then in some cases, collect, their uncollectible accounts.

This chapter is organized as follows:

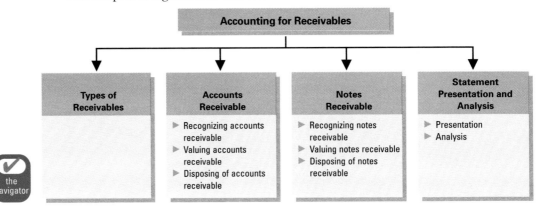

Types of Receivables

study objective 1

Identify and distinguish between the different types of receivables.

The term "receivables" refers to amounts due from individuals and other companies. They are claims that are expected to be collected in cash. Receivables are frequently classified as (1) accounts, (2) notes, and (3) other.

Accounts receivable are amounts owed by customers on account. They result from the sale of goods and services. These receivables generally are expected to be collected within 30 days or so, and are classified as current assets. They are usually the most significant type of claim held by a company.

Notes receivable are claims for which formal instruments of credit are issued as proof of the debt. A note normally requires the debtor to pay interest and extends for periods of 30 days or longer. Notes receivable may be either current assets or long-term assets, depending on their due dates. Notes and accounts receivable that result from sale transactions are often called trade receivables.

Other receivables include nontrade receivables. Examples are accruals (e.g., interest receivable), recoverable GST, loans to company officers, and advances to employees. Accruals and other receivables due within one year are classified as current assets. Loans and advances are generally classified and reported as separate items in the current or noncurrent sections of the balance sheet, according to their due dates.

Accounts Receivable

Three main accounting issues are associated with accounts receivable:

1. Recognizing accounts receivable
2. Valuing accounts receivable
3. Disposing of accounts receivable

Recognizing Accounts Receivable

Recognizing accounts receivable is relatively straightforward. In Chapter 5, we saw how accounts receivable are affected by the sale of merchandise. To illustrate, assume that Adorable Junior Garment sells merchandise on account to Zellers on July 1, for $1,000. On July 5, Zellers returns merchandise worth $100 to Adorable Junior Garment. On July 31, Adorable Junior Garment receives payment from Zellers for the balance due. The journal entries to record these transactions on the books of Adorable Junior Garment are as follows:

study objective 2
Show how accounts receivable are recognized in the accounts.

July 1	Accounts Receivable	1,000	
	Sales		1,000
	To record sale on account.		
5	Sales Returns and Allowances	100	
	Accounts Receivable		100
	To record merchandise returned.		
31	Cash ($1,000 – $100)	900	
	Accounts Receivable		900
	To record collection of accounts receivable.		

A	=	L	+	OE
+1,000				+1,000

Cash flows: no effect

A	=	L	+	OE
−100				−100

Cash flows: no effect

A	=	L	+	OE
+900				
−900				

Cash flows: +900

In a perpetual inventory system, a second journal entry to record the cost of the goods sold (and the cost of the goods returned) would be required for the July 1 and July 5 transactions.

Subsidiary Accounts Receivable Ledger

Adorable Junior Garment does not have only Zellers as a customer. It has hundreds of customers. If it recorded the accounts receivable for each of these customers in only one general ledger account, Accounts Receivable, as we did above, it would be hard to determine the balance owed by any one customer, such as Zellers, at a specific point in time.

Most companies that sell on account use a subsidiary ledger to keep track of individual customer accounts. As we learned in Chapter 5, a subsidiary ledger provides supporting detail to the general ledger. Illustration 8-1 on the next page shows an accounts receivable control account and subsidiary ledger, using assumed data.

Each entry affecting accounts receivable is essentially posted twice—once to the subsidiary ledger and once to the general ledger. Normally entries to the subsidiary ledger are posted daily, while entries to the general ledger are summarized and posted monthly. For example, the $1,000 sale to Zellers was posted to Zellers' account in the subsidiary ledger on July 1. It was also summarized with other sales entries (Kids Online, $6,000 + Snazzy Kids, $3,000 + Zellers, $1,000 = $10,000) in a special sales journal and posted to the accounts receivable control account in the general ledger at the end of the month, on July 31.

Collections on account (Kids Online, $4,000 + Snazzy Kids, $1,000 + Zellers, $900 = $5,900) were also posted individually to the subsidiary ledger accounts and summarized and posted in total to the general ledger account. Non-recurring entries, such as the sales return of $100, are posted to both the subsidiary and general ledgers individually.

Note that the balance of $4,000 in the control account agrees with the total of the balances in the individual accounts receivable accounts in the subsidiary ledger (Kids Online, $2,000 + Snazzy Kids, $2,000 + Zellers, $0). There is more information about how subsidiary ledgers work in Appendix C at the end of this textbook.

GENERAL LEDGER					

Accounts Receivable is a control account.

Accounts Receivable					No. 112
Date	Explanation	Ref.	Debit	Credit	Balance
2004 July 5				100	(100)
31			10,000		9,900
31				5,900	4,000◀

The subsidiary ledger is separate from the general ledger.

ACCOUNTS RECEIVABLE SUBSIDIARY LEDGER					

Kids Online					No. 112-203
Date	Explanation	Ref.	Debit	Credit	Balance
2004 July 11	Invoice 1310		6,000		6,000
19	Payment			4,000	2,000◀

Snazzy Kids Co.					No. 112-413
Date	Explanation	Ref.	Debit	Credit	Balance
2004 July 12	Invoice 1318		3,000		3,000
21	Payment			1,000	2,000◀

Zellers Inc.					No. 112-581
Date	Explanation	Ref.	Debit	Credit	Balance
2004 July 1	Invoice 1215		1,000		1,000
5	Credit memo 1222			100	900
31	Payment			900	0◀

Financing Charges

At the end of each month, the company can easily determine the transactions in each customer's account from the subsidiary ledger and send the customer a statement of transactions that have occurred during the month. If the customer does not pay in full within a specified period (usually 30 days), most retailers add an interest (financing) charge to the balance due. Interest rates vary from company to company, but a common rate for retailers is 18% per year.

When financing charges are added, the seller recognizes interest revenue. If Kids Online still owes $2,000 at the end of the next month, August 31, and Adorable Junior Garment charges 18% on the balance due, the entry that Adorable Junior Garment will make to record interest revenue of $30 ($ 2,000 × 18% × $\frac{1}{12}$) is as follows:

$$A = L + OE$$
$$+30 \qquad +30$$

Cash flows: no effect

Aug. 31	Accounts Receivable		30	
	Interest Revenue			30
	To record interest on amount due.			

Although Whitehill Technologies in our feature story does not charge interest on its overdue accounts, interest revenue is often substantial for service and merchandising companies.

BEFORE YOU GO ON

►Review It

1. What types of receivables does The Forzani Group Ltd. report on its balance sheet? (*Hint:* See Note 5 in addition to looking at the balance sheet.) The answer to this question is at the end of the chapter.
2. How does a subsidiary accounts receivable ledger work?

Related exercise material: BE8–1, BE8–2, and E8–1.

the navigator

Valuing Accounts Receivable

Once receivables are recorded in the accounts, the next question is how these receivables should be reported on the balance sheet. They are reported on the balance sheet as a current asset. But determining the amount to report as an asset is sometimes difficult because some receivables will be uncollectible.

study objective 3

Describe and use the method and bases used to value accounts receivable.

Even if each customer must satisfy the credit requirements of the seller before the credit sale is approved, inevitably, some accounts receivable become uncollectible. For example, a usually reliable customer may suddenly not be able to pay because he has been laid off from his job or is faced with unexpected bills.

Credit losses are debited to bad debts expense. Such losses are considered a normal and necessary risk of doing business on a credit basis. The key issue in valuing accounts receivable is when to recognize these credit losses. If the company waits until it knows for sure that the specific account will not be collected, it could end up recording the bad debts expense in a different period than when the revenue is recorded.

Consider the following example. Assume that in 2004, Quick Buck Computer Company decides it could increase its revenues by offering computers to students without requiring any money down and with no credit approval process. On campuses across the country, it distributes one million computers with a selling price of $1,200 each. This increases Quick Buck's revenues and receivables by $1.2 billion. The promotion is a huge success! The 2004 balance sheet and income statement look great. Unfortunately, during 2005, nearly 40% of the student customers default on their accounts. This makes the year 2005 income statement and balance sheet look terrible. Illustration 8-2 shows that the promotion in 2004 was not such a great success after all.

Year 2004

Huge sales promotions.
Sales increase dramatically.
Accounts receivable increase dramatically.

Year 2005

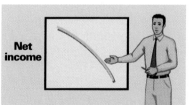

Customers default on loans.
Bad debts expense increases dramatically.
Accounts receivable plummet.

Illustration 8-2 ◄

Effects of mismatching bad debts

If credit losses are not recorded until they occur, no attempt is made to (1) match bad debts expense to sales revenues in the income statement and (2) show the accounts receivable in the balance sheet at the amount actually expected to be received. There is, however, a method that estimates uncollectible accounts receivable and matches expected credit losses against sales in the accounting period in which the sales occur. This method is known as the allowance method.

The allowance method of accounting for bad debts estimates uncollectible accounts at the end of each period. This provides better matching of expenses with revenues on the income statement. It also ensures that receivables are stated at their net realizable value on the balance sheet. Net realizable value is the amount expected to be received in cash. It excludes the amounts that the company estimates it will not collect. With this method, receivables are reduced by estimated uncollectible receivables on the balance sheet.

The allowance method is required for financial reporting purposes when bad debts are material (significant) in amount. Its essential features are as follows:

1. **Recording estimated uncollectibles:** The amount of uncollectible accounts receivable is estimated. This estimate is treated as an expense and is matched against revenues in the accounting period in which the revenues are recorded.
2. **Recording the write-off of an uncollectible account:** Actual uncollectibles are written off at the time each specific account is determined to be uncollectible.
3. **Recovery of an uncollectible account:** When an account previously written off is later collected, the original write-off is reversed and the collection is recorded. Neither the write-off nor the later recovery affect the income statement, and matching is therefore not distorted.

1. Recording Estimated Uncollectibles

To illustrate the allowance method, assume that Adorable Junior Garment has net credit sales of $1.2 million in 2004. Of this amount, $200,000 remains uncollected at December 31. The credit manager estimates (using techniques we'll discuss in the next section) that $24,000 of these receivables will be uncollectible. The adjusting entry to record the estimated uncollectible accounts follows:

A = L + OE			
−24,000 −24,000	Dec. 31	Bad Debts Expense	24,000	
		Allowance for Doubtful Accounts		24,000
Cash flows: no effect		To record estimate of uncollectible accounts.		

Note that a new account, Bad Debts Expense, is used instead of setting up a new contra sales account, as we did for sales returns and allowances. An expense account is used because the responsibilities for granting credit and collecting accounts are normally separated from sales and marketing. Consequently, Bad Debts Expense is reported in the income statement as an operating expense. Thus, the estimated uncollectibles are **matched** with sales in 2004. The expense is recorded in the year the sales are made.

Allowance for Doubtful Accounts is a contra asset account that shows the receivables that are expected to become uncollectible in the future. This contra account is used instead of a direct credit to Accounts Receivable for two reasons. First, we do not know which individual customers will not pay. If the company uses a subsidiary ledger, we are therefore unable to credit specific accounts. Recall that subsidiary ledger accounts must balance with Accounts Receivable, the control account. This would not happen if the control account were credited and the subsidiary ledger accounts were not. Second, the estimate for uncollectibles is just an estimate. A contra account helps to separate estimates from actual amounts, such as those found in Accounts Receivable.

The account balance Allowance for Doubtful Accounts is deducted from Accounts Receivable in the current assets section of the balance sheet. Assuming that Adorable Junior Garment has an opening balance of $1,000 in Allowance for Doubtful Accounts, its ending balance of $25,000 ($1,000 + $24,000) would be reported as follows:

ADORABLE JUNIOR GARMENT
Balance Sheet (partial)
December 31, 2004

Current assets		
Cash		$ 14,800
Accounts receivable	$200,000	
Less: Allowance for doubtful accounts	25,000	175,000
Merchandise inventory		310,000
Prepaid expenses		25,000
Total current assets		$524,800

The amount $175,000 represents the expected net realizable value of the accounts receivable at the statement date.

Illustration 8-3 shows the formula to calculate the net realizable value of accounts receivable.

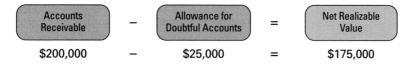

Illustration 8-3 ◄

Formula for calculating net realizable value

Estimating the Allowance. For Adorable Junior Garment, the amount of the expected uncollectibles ($24,000) was given.

In real practice, companies must estimate that amount if they use the allowance method. Two bases are used to determine this amount: (1) **percentage of sales**, and (2) **percentage of receivables**.

Both bases are generally accepted. The choice is a management decision. It depends on the relative emphasis that management wishes to give to expenses and revenues on the one hand, and to net realizable value of the accounts receivable on the other. Illustration 8-4 compares the two bases.

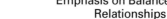

Emphasis on Income Statement   Emphasis on Balance Sheet
Relationships   Relationships

Illustration 8-4 ◄

Comparison of bases for estimating uncollectibles

The percentage of sales basis results in a better matching of expenses with revenues—an income statement viewpoint. The percentage of receivables basis produces the better estimate of net realizable value—a balance sheet viewpoint. Under both bases, it is necessary to determine the company's past experience with bad debt losses.

Percentage of Sales Basis. In the percentage of sales basis, management indicates the percentage of credit sales that will be uncollectible. This percentage is based on past experience and likely credit policy.

The percentage is applied to net credit sales of the current year. To illustrate, assume that Adorable Junior Garment decides to use the percentage of sales basis. It concludes that 2% of net credit sales will become uncollectible. Recall that net credit sales for the calendar year 2004 are $1.2 million. The estimated bad debts expense is $24,000 (2% × $1,200,000). The adjusting entry follows:

A	=	L	+	OE
−24,000				−24,000

Cash flows: no effect

Dec. 31	Bad Debts Expense	24,000	
	Allowance for Doubtful Accounts		24,000
	To record estimate of uncollectible accounts.		

After the adjusting entry is posted, assuming the allowance account has an opening credit balance of $1,000, the accounts will show the following:

Bad Debts Expense		Allowance for Doubtful Accounts	
Dec. 31 Adj. 24,000		Jan. 1 Bal. 1,000	
		Dec. 31 Adj. 24,000	
		Dec. 31 Bal. 25,000	

Helpful hint Because of matching, the balance in the allowance account is *not* involved in the adjusting entry under the percentage of sales approach.

This basis of estimating uncollectibles emphasizes the matching of expenses with revenues. As a result, Bad Debts Expense will show a direct percentage relationship to the sales amount on which it is calculated. **When the adjusting entry is made, the existing balance in Allowance for Doubtful Accounts is disregarded.** The adjusted balance in this account should be a reasonable approximation of the realizable value of the receivables. If actual write-offs differ significantly from the amount estimated, the percentage for future years should be modified.

The percentage of sales basis is quick and easy to use. This is why it is often used to update bad debts for interim reporting purposes.

Percentage of Receivables Basis. Under the percentage of receivables basis, management estimates what percentage of receivables will result in losses from uncollectible accounts. This percentage can be assigned to receivables in total, or stratified (divided further) by age of receivable. Stratifying the percentage classifies customer balances by the length of time they have been unpaid, which can improve the reliability of the estimate. Because of its emphasis on time, this is called aging the accounts receivable.

An aging schedule is an example of output that can be easily obtained from a computerized accounts receivable system. While preparing this schedule by hand is a time-consuming task, the schedule can be done in minutes on a computer.

ACCOUNTING IN ACTION ▶ @–Business

Companies that provide services and bill on an hourly basis spend considerable time tracking their hours and preparing detailed bills. OpenAir.com created the first on-line service delivery product to simplify time management and billing. It can be accessed anywhere there's an Internet connection—your office, your client's office, or your hotel room, for example. This "virtual office" provides a Web-based invoicing, time, and expense tracking service that manages and records data.

To use the service, you create an electronic record that lists the type of project, customer name, product dates, and billing rate. By clicking on the "timer" function, you can automatically track time spent on a particular project as the work is being performed. OpenAir.com will either mail or e-mail invoices to customers. It also keeps track of collections and provides an aging schedule. Its services allow companies to concentrate on generating revenue through their core businesses by cutting down on time-consuming administrative tasks.

After the accounts are arranged by age, the expected bad debt losses are determined. This is done by applying percentages, based on past experience, to the totals in each category. The longer a receivable is past due, the less likely it is to be collected. So, the estimated percentage of uncollectible debts increases with the number of days past due. An aging schedule for Adorable Junior Garment is shown in Illustration 8-5.

Illustration 8-5 ◄

Aging schedule

Customer	Total	Number of Days Outstanding				
		0–30	31–60	61–90	91–120	Over 120
Bansal Garments	$ 6,000		$ 3,000	$ 3,000		
Bortz Clothing	3,000	$ 3,000				
Kids Online	4,500				$ 2,000	$ 2,500
Snazzy Kids Co.	17,000	2,000	5,000	5,000	5,000	
Tykes n' Tots	26,500	10,000	10,000	6,000	500	
Zellers	42,000	32,000	10,000			
Wal-mart	61,000	48,000	12,000	1,000		
Others	40,000	5,000	10,000	10,000	5,000	10,000
	$200,000	$100,000	$50,000	$25,000	$12,500	$12,500
Estimated percentage uncollectible		5%	10%	20%	30%	50%
Estimated bad debts	$25,000	$5,000	$5,000	$5,000	$3,750	$6,250

Note the increasing percentages from 5% to 50%. An important aspect of accounts receivable management is simply keeping a close watch on the accounts.

The $25,000 total for Adorable Junior Garment's estimated bad debts (or uncollectible accounts) represents the amount of existing receivables expected to become uncollectible in the future. This amount is also the required balance in Allowance for Doubtful Accounts at the balance sheet date. **The amount of the bad debt adjusting entry is the difference between the required balance and the existing balance in the allowance account.** If the trial balance shows Allowance for Doubtful Accounts with a credit balance of $1,000, an adjusting entry for $24,000 ($25,000 − $1,000) is necessary, as shown below:

Dec. 31	Bad Debts Expense	24,000	
	Allowance for Doubtful Accounts		24,000
	To adjust allowance account to total estimated uncollectibles.		

A = L + OE
−24,000   −24,000

Cash flows: no effect

After the adjusting entry is posted, Adorable Junior Garment's accounts will show the following:

Bad Debts Expense		Allowance for Doubtful Accounts	
Dec. 31 Adj. 24,000		Jan. 1 Bal.	1,000
		Dec. 31 Adj.	24,000
		Dec. 31 Bal.	25,000

Occasionally, the allowance account will have a debit balance prior to adjustment. This occurs when write-offs during the year exceed previous estimates for bad debts. (We'll discuss write-offs in the next section.) If an opening debit balance exists, **the debit balance** is added to the required balance when the adjusting entry is made. If there had been a $500 debit balance in the Adorable Junior Garment allowance account before adjustment, the adjusting entry would have been for $25,500 to arrive at a credit balance in the allowance account of $25,000.

The percentage of receivables method will normally give a better approximation of net realizable value than the percentage of sales basis. Most companies prefer using the percentage of receivables basis. Within this basis, an aging schedule, rather than a percentage of total receivables, is normally used in order to enable companies to closely monitor the age of their receivables. As noted in our feature story, Whitehill Technologies prepares an aging schedule every week to closely monitor how collectible its accounts receivable are and to identify problem accounts.

2. Recording the Write-Off of an Uncollectible Account

Companies use various methods of collecting past-due accounts, including a sequence of letters, calls, and legal actions. In the feature story, Whitehill Technologies uses e-mail and telephone calls to follow up accounts that are overdue. Senior management gets involved if an account is 90 days overdue, and the company does not hesitate to cut off technical support in order to encourage payment.

When all means of collecting a past-due account have been tried and collection appears impossible, the account should be written off. To prevent premature write-offs, each write-off should be approved in writing by management. To maintain good internal control, authorization to write off accounts should not be given to someone who also has responsibilities related to cash or receivables.

To illustrate a receivables write-off, assume that the vice-president of finance of Adorable Junior Garment authorizes the write-off of a $4,500 balance owed by a delinquent customer, Kids Online, on March 1, 2005. The entry to record the write-off is as follows:

A	=	L	+	OE
+4,500				
−4,500				

Cash flows: no effect

Mar. 1	Allowance for Doubtful Accounts	4,500	
	Accounts Receivable—Kids Online		4,500
	Write-off of uncollectible account.		

Bad Debts Expense is not increased (debited) when the write-off occurs. **Under the allowance method, every account write-off is debited to the allowance account rather than to Bad Debts Expense.** A debit to Bad Debts Expense would be incorrect. The expense was already recognized when the adjusting entry was made for estimated bad debts in the year in which the sale was made.

Instead, the entry to record the write-off of an uncollectible account reduces both Accounts Receivable and Allowance for Doubtful Accounts. After posting, the general ledger accounts will appear as follows:

Accounts Receivable					Allowance for Doubtful Accounts				
Jan. 1	Bal.	200,000	Mar. 1	4,500	Mar. 1	4,500	Jan. 1	Bal.	25,000
Mar. 1	Bal.	195,500					Mar. 1	Bal.	20,500

The allowance account can sometimes end up in a debit balance position after the write-off of an uncollectible account. This can happen if the write-offs during the period exceed the opening balance. This is normally only a temporary situation: it will be corrected when the adjusting entry for estimated uncollectible accounts is made at the end of the period.

A write-off affects only balance sheet accounts. The write-off of the account reduces both Accounts Receivable and Allowance for Doubtful Accounts. Net realizable value in the balance sheet remains the same, as illustrated below:

	Before Write-Off	After Write-Off
Accounts receivable	$200,000	$195,500
Less: Allowance for doubtful accounts	25,000	20,500
Net realizable value	$175,000	$175,000

3. Recovery of an Uncollectible Account

Occasionally, a company collects from a customer after the account has been written off. Two entries are required to record the recovery of a bad debt: (1) The entry made in writing off the account is reversed to restore the customer's account. (2) The collection is journalized in the usual manner.

To illustrate, assume that on July 1, 2005, Kids Online pays the $4,500 amount that had been written off on March 1. The entries are as follows:

	(1)		
July 1	Accounts Receivable—Kids Online	4,500	
	Allowance for Doubtful Accounts		4,500
	To reverse the write-off of Kids Online account.		

A	=	L	+	OE
+4,500				
−4,500				

Cash flows: no effect

	(2)		
July 1	Cash	4,500	
	Accounts Receivable—Kids Online		4,500
	To record collection from Kids Online.		

A	=	L	+	OE
+4,500				
−4,500				

⬆ Cash flows: +4,500

Note that the recovery of a bad debt, like the write-off of a bad debt, affects only balance sheet accounts. The net effect of the two entries is a debit to Cash and a credit to Allowance for Doubtful Accounts for $4,500. Accounts Receivable is debited and later credited, for two reasons. First, the company must reverse the write-off. Second, Kids Online did pay, and the accounts receivable account in the general ledger and Kids Online's account in the subsidiary ledger, if a subsidiary ledger is used, should show this payment as it will need to be considered for future credit purposes.

Summary of Allowance Method

In summary, there are three types of transactions that you may record when valuing accounts receivable using the allowance method:

1. Uncollectible accounts receivable are recorded at the end of the period by debiting Bad Debts Expense and crediting Allowance for Doubtful Accounts. The amount to record can be determined using either the percentage of sales basis or the percentage of receivables basis.
2. Actual uncollectibles, or write-offs, are subsequently debited to Allowance for Doubtful Accounts and credited to Accounts Receivable.
3. Later recoveries, if any, are recorded in two separate entries. The first reverses the write-off by debiting Accounts Receivable and crediting Allowance for Doubtful Accounts. The second records the normal collection of the account by debiting Cash and crediting Accounts Receivable.

These entries are summarized in T accounts below:

Accounts Receivable		Allowance for Doubtful Accounts	
Beginning balance	Collections	Write-offs	Beginning balance
Credit sales	Write-offs		Subsequent recoveries
Subsequent recoveries			Bad debt adjusting entry
Ending balance			Ending balance

BEFORE YOU GO ON . . .

►Review It

1. What are the essential features of the allowance method?
2. Explain the difference between the percentage of sales and the percentage of receivables bases.

►Do It

The unadjusted trial balance for Woo Wholesalers Co. reveals the following selected information:

	Debit	Credit
Accounts receivable	$120,000	
Allowance for doubtful accounts		$ 2,000
Net credit sales		820,000

Prepare the journal entry to record bad debts expense for each of the following *independent* situations:

1. Using the percentage of sales approach, Woo estimates uncollectible accounts to be 1% of net credit sales.
2. Using the percentage of receivables approach, Woo estimates uncollectible accounts to be as follows: 0–30 days, $85,000, 5% uncollectible; 31–60 days, $25,000, 15% uncollectible; and 61–90 days, $10,000, 25% uncollectible.

Action Plan

- % of sales: Apply the percentage to net credit sales to determine estimated bad debts—the adjusting entry amount.
- % of receivables: Apply percentages to the receivables in each age category to determine total estimated uncollectible accounts. The total amount determined in the aging schedule is the ending balance required in the allowance account, not the amount of the adjustment.
- Do not use the existing balance in the allowance account to determine the required adjusting entry when the percentage of sales basis is used. Use the existing balance in the allowance account to determine the required adjusting entry when the percentage of receivables basis is used.

Solution

1.	Bad Debts Expense ($820,000 × 1%)	8,200	
	Allowance for Doubtful Accounts		8,200
	To record estimate of uncollectible accounts.		

2.	Bad Debts Expense ($10,500[1] − $2,000)	8,500	
	Allowance for Doubtful Accounts		8,500
	To record estimate of uncollectible accounts.		

[1] ($85,000 × 5%) + ($25,000 × 15%) + ($10,000 × 25%) = $10,500

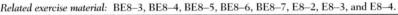

Related exercise material: BE8–3, BE8–4, BE8–5, BE8–6, BE8–7, E8–2, E8–3, and E8–4.

Disposing of Accounts Receivable

study objective 4

Determine the entries to record the disposition of accounts receivable.

In the normal course of events, accounts receivable are collected in cash and removed from the books. However, as credit sales and receivables increase in size, the normal course of events changes. Companies often sell their receivables to another company for cash, and thus shorten the cash-to-cash operating cycle.

Receivables are sold for three major reasons. The first is their size. For competitive reasons, **sellers often provide financing to purchasers of their goods**. For example, many major companies in the automobile, truck, equipment, computer, and appliance industries have created companies that accept responsibility for accounts receivable financing. Bombardier has Bombardier Capital, Ford has Ford Credit Canada, and Hudson's Bay Company has Hudson's Bay Company Acceptance Limited. These companies are referred to as captive finance companies because they are wholly owned by the company selling the product.

The purpose of captive finance companies is to encourage the sale of the product by assuring financing to buyers but without the parent companies having to hold large amounts of receivables. Retailers in Canada depend heavily on their financial divisions to support their bottom line. For example, 82% of Hudson's Bay Co.'s operating profit in 2002 came from its financial services unit.

Second, **receivables may be sold because they are the only reasonable source of cash.** When money is tight, companies may not be able to borrow money in the usual credit markets. Even if credit is available, the cost of borrowing may be too high.

A final reason for selling receivables is that billing and collection are often time-consuming and costly. It is often easier for a retailer to sell its receivables to another party with expertise in billing and collection matters. Credit card companies, such as Visa and MasterCard, specialize in billing and collecting accounts receivable.

Factored Receivables

A common kind of sale of receivables is to a factor. A **factor** is a finance company or bank that buys receivables from businesses for a fee. If the customer does not pay, the company is usually responsible for reimbursing the factor for the uncollected amounts. This is known as selling receivables on a recourse basis.

Companies such as Sears Canada regularly sell their accounts receivable to speed up collection. For example, Sears sold more than half of its receivables in 2002.

Factoring arrangements vary widely, but, typically, the factor (purchaser of the receivables) will advance up to 90% of the net realizable value of approved invoices, less the factor's fee. Fees are negotiable and often range from 16% to 36% of the amount of receivables purchased.

Accounting for factored receivables becomes quite complex, as the receivables can be sold with or without recourse (risk). Further discussion of factored receivables is left for a future accounting course.

Credit Card Sales

More than 75 million credit cards were recently estimated to be in use in Canada. Of these, about 65% are bank cards, such as Visa or MasterCard. The other 35% are cards issued by large department stores, gasoline companies, and other issuers such as American Express and Diners Club/enRoute.

Three parties are involved when credit cards are used in making retail sales: (1) the credit card issuer, who is independent of the retailer, (2) the retailer, and (3) the customer. The major advantages of credit cards to the retailer are shown in Illustration 8-6.

Issuer does credit investigation of customer   **Issuer maintains customer accounts**

Credit card issuer   Customer   Retailer

**Issuer undertakes collection
process and absorbs any losses**   **Retailer receives cash more
quickly from credit card issuer**

Illustration 8-6 ◄

Advantages of credit cards
to the retailer

In exchange for these advantages, the retailer pays the credit card issuer a fee (a percentage of the invoice price) for its services.

Cash Sales: Bank Credit Cards. As discussed in Chapter 7, sales using credit cards issued by banks, such as Visa and MasterCard, are considered cash sales by the retailer. When a credit card sale occurs, the bank immediately adds the amount to the seller's bank balance, less a service fee. Banks generally charge a fee of about 3.5% of the credit card sales slip, or a transaction fee, for this service. In addition, a rental charge for use of the equipment is likely to be incurred.

To illustrate, suppose on October 21 Kerr Music Co. sells $1,000 of compact discs to a customer who pays the bill with a RBC Financial Group Visa card. The service fee that RBC charges Kerr Music for credit card sales is 3.5%. The entry made to record this transaction by Kerr Music is:

	A	=	L	+	OE
	+965				−35
					+1,000

⬆ Cash flows: +965

Oct. 21	Cash	965	
	Credit Card Expense ($1,000 × 3.5%)	35	
	Sales		1,000
	To record Visa credit card sale.		

Credit Sales: Nonbank Credit Cards. Sales that involve nonbank cards such as American Express, Diners Club/enRoute, Sears, and Petro-Canada Card are reported as credit sales, not cash sales. Conversion into cash does not occur until these companies remit the net amount to the seller.

To illustrate, assume that Kerr Music accepts an American Express card on October 24 for a $500 bill. The entry for the sale by Kerr Music (assuming a 5% service fee) is:

	A	=	L	+	OE
	+475				−25
					+500

Cash flows: no effect

Oct. 24	Accounts Receivable—American Express	475	
	Credit Card Expense ($500 × 5%)	25	
	Sales		500
	To record American Express credit card sales.		

American Express will pay Kerr Music $475. The music store will record this collection as follows:

	A	=	L	+	OE
	+475				
	−475				

⬆ Cash flows: +475

Nov. 17	Cash	475	
	Accounts Receivable—American Express		475
	To record redemption of credit card billing.		

Credit Card Expense is reported as an operating expense in the income statement.

ACCOUNTING IN ACTION ▶ Business Insight

The average interest rate on a bank credit card in Canada is 18%. Interest on nonbank cards, such as The Bay, can be as high as 21%. The Bank of Canada interest rate is 2%. Why are credit card rates so much higher than other interest rates?

The Bank of Canada interest rate is called the "risk free" rate. This means that, theoretically, money can be borrowed at 2% if there is no other credit risk. The difference between the Bank of Canada rate and credit card rates is called a "risk premium." Banks justify this higher interest rate by saying that credit cards pose a greater risk. They argue that they have to cover their losses from fraud as well as their administrative costs.

Debit Card Sales

In Chapter 7 we learned the difference between a debit card and a credit card. Debit cards allow customers to spend only what is in their bank account. Credit cards give access to money made available to a customer by a bank or other financial institution, like a loan. Credit cards are issued with the understanding that the amount charged will be repaid, plus interest, if the account is not paid in full each month.

When a debit card sale occurs, the bank immediately deducts the cost of the purchase from the customer's bank account. This amount is electronically transferred into the retailer's bank account, less a service fee. Banks usually charge a transaction fee for this service. The entries to record a debit card sale are identical to those illustrated earlier for bank credit card sales except that the expense account used is Debit Card Expense, not Credit Card Expense.

Loans Secured by Receivables

Rather than selling receivables, a common way to speed up cash flow from accounts receivable is to go to a bank and borrow money using accounts receivable as collateral. While this does have a cost (interest has to be paid to the bank on the loan), the company gets the use of its cash sooner. The loan can then be repaid as the receivables are collected. Generally, banks are willing to provide financing of up to 75% of receivables that are less than 90 days old. Quite often, these arrangements occur through an **operating line of credit**, which is discussed in a later chapter.

BEFORE YOU GO ON . . .

►Review It

1. Why do companies sell their receivables?
2. What is the journal entry made to record bank credit card sales? Nonbank credit card sales? Debit card sales?

►Do It

Prepare journal entries to record the following selected debit and credit card transactions for the Bulk Department Store:

July 22 A customer paid for a $1,200 purchase with her Visa credit card. The bank charges a service fee of 3%.
   25 A customer paid for a $500 purchase with his Bulk Department Store credit card.
   28 A customer used her debit card to pay for a $650 purchase. The company was charged a 2% service fee.

Action Plan

- Bank credit cards are recorded as cash sales, less the service charge.
- Nonbank credit cards are recorded as receivables. There is no service charge for a company credit card.
- Debit cards are recorded as cash sales, less the service charge.

Solution

July 22	Cash	1,164	
	Credit Card Expense ($1,200 x 3%)	36	
	Sales		1,200
	To record Visa credit card sale.		
25	Accounts Receivable	500	
	Sales		500
	To record company credit card sale.		
28	Cash	637	
	Debit Card Expense ($650 × 2%)	13	
	Sales		650
	To record debit card sale.		

Related exercise material: BE8–8, E8–5, and E8–6.

the navigator

Notes Receivable

Helpful hint Note the similarities and differences between a note receivable and an account receivable.

Similarities: Both are credit instruments. Both are valued at their net realizable values. Both can be sold to another party.

Differences: An account receivable is an informal promise to pay. A note receivable is secured by a formal, written promise to pay. An account receivable results from a credit sale. A note receivable arises from financing a purchase, lending money, or extending an account receivable beyond normal amounts or due dates. An account receivable is usually due within a short period of time (e.g., 30 days), while a note can extend for longer periods of time (e.g., 30 days to many years). An account receivable does not incur interest unless the account is overdue. A note usually bears interest for the entire period.

Credit may also be granted in exchange for a promissory note. A promissory note is a written promise to pay a specified amount of money on demand or at a definite time. Promissory notes may be used (1) when individuals and companies lend or borrow money, (2) when the amount of the transaction and the credit period exceed normal limits, or (3) in settlement of accounts receivable.

In a promissory note, the party making the promise to pay is called the maker. For the maker of the promissory note, this is a note payable. The party to whom payment is to be made is called the payee. The payee may be specifically identified by name, or may be designated simply as the bearer of the note. For the payee of the promissory note, this is a note receivable.

The promissory note details the names of the parties, the amount of the loan, the loan period, the interest rate, and whether interest is repayable monthly or at maturity (the note's due date) along with the principal. Other details might include whether any security is pledged as collateral for the loan and what happens if the maker defaults (does not pay).

Notes receivable give the payee a stronger legal claim to assets than accounts receivable. Like accounts receivable, notes receivable can be readily sold to another party. Promissory notes are negotiable instruments (as are cheques). This means that they can be transferred to another party by endorsement (signature of the payee).

The majority of notes originate from loans. However, notes receivable are also accepted from customers who need to extend the payment of an account receivable. They are often required from high-risk customers. In some industries (such as the heavy equipment industry), all credit sales are supported by notes.

The basic issues in accounting for notes receivable are the same as those for accounts receivable, as follows:

1. Recognizing notes receivable
2. Valuing notes receivable
3. Disposing of notes receivable

Recognizing Notes Receivable

study objective 5

Show how notes receivable are recognized and valued in the accounts.

To illustrate the basic entry for notes receivable, we will assume that Wolder Company (the payee) lends Higly Inc. (the maker) $10,000 on May 31. The note is due in four months, on September 30, at which time 4.5% interest is also due. Assuming that the note was written to settle an open account, the entry for the receipt of the note by Wolder Company is as follows:

A	=	L	+	OE
+10,000				
−10,000				

Cash flows: no effect

May 31	Notes Receivable—Higly	10,000	
	Accounts Receivable—Higly		10,000
	To record acceptance of Higly note.		

The note receivable is recorded at its **face value**, the value shown on the face of the note. No interest revenue is reported when the note is accepted. The revenue recognition principle does not recognize revenue until it is earned. Interest is earned (accrued) as time passes.

If a note is exchanged for cash instead of an account receivable, the entry is a debit to Notes Receivable and a credit to Cash for the amount of the loan.

Calculating Interest

As we learned in Chapter 3, the basic formula for calculating interest on an interest-bearing note is the following:

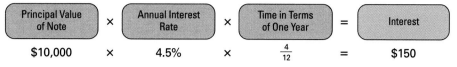

Principal Value of Note	×	Annual Interest Rate	×	Time in Terms of One Year	=	Interest
$10,000	×	4.5%	×	$\frac{4}{12}$	=	$150

Illustration 8-7 ◄

Formula for calculating interest

The interest rate specified in a note is an **annual** rate of interest. The time factor in the above formula gives the fraction of a year the note is outstanding. The calculation of interest revenue for Wolder Company and interest expense for Higly Inc. is also shown in Illustration 8-7. As we did in Chapter 3, to keep it simple, we will assume that interest is calculated in months rather than days.

If the Wolder Company's year end was June 30, the following adjusting journal entry would be required to accrue interest for the month of June:

June 30	Interest Receivable	37.50	
	Interest Revenue ($10,000 × 4.5% × $\frac{1}{12}$)		37.50
	To accrue interest on Higly note receivable.		

A	=	L	+	OE
+37.50				+37.50

Cash flows: no effect

Some notes are due on demand rather than at a specified date. For these notes, interest is calculated for the length of time from the issue date until the note is called in for repayment. If it is necessary to accrue interest for an interim period, interest is calculated for the period that the note has been outstanding.

Valuing Notes Receivable

Valuing notes receivable is the same as valuing accounts receivable. Like accounts receivable, notes receivable are reported at their net realizable value. The notes receivable allowance account is called Allowance for Doubtful Notes. In some companies, only one allowance account is used for both accounts and notes, called Allowance for Doubtful Accounts. The estimates involved in determining net realizable value and in recording the bad debts expense and related allowance are similar.

Disposing of Notes Receivable

Notes may be held to their maturity date, at which time the principal plus any unpaid interest is due. Sometimes, the maker of the note defaults and an appropriate adjustment to the accounts must be made. At other times, the holder of the note speeds up the conversion to cash by selling the note. The entries for honouring (paying) and dishonouring (not paying) notes are shown on the following pages.

> **study objective 6**
>
> Determine the entries to record the disposition of notes receivable.

Honouring of Notes Receivable

A note is honoured when it is paid in full at its maturity date. For an interest-bearing note, the amount due at maturity is the principal of the note plus interest for the length of time the note is outstanding (assuming interest is due at maturity rather than monthly).

To illustrate, refer again to the situation described earlier where Wolder Company lent Higly Inc. $10,000 on May 31, accepting a note due on September 30 at 4.5% interest. The entry by Wolder to record the collection on September 30, the maturity date, is as follows:

A	=	L	+	OE
+10,150.00				+112.50
−10,000.00				
−37.50				

↑ Cash flows: +10,150

Sept. 30	Cash	10,150.00	
	Notes Receivable—Higly		10,000.00
	Interest Revenue		112.50
	Interest Receivable		37.50
	To record collection of Higly note.		

Recall that one month of interest, $37.50 ($10,000 \times 4.5\% \times \frac{1}{12}$), has previously been accrued on June 30, Wolder's year end. Consequently, only three months of interest revenue, $112.50 ($10,000 \times 4.5\% \times \frac{3}{12}$), are recorded in this period.

Dishonouring of Notes Receivable

A **dishonoured note** is a note that is not paid in full at maturity. A dishonoured note receivable is no longer negotiable. However, the payee still has a claim against the maker of the note. Therefore, the notes receivable account is usually transferred to an accounts receivable account.

To illustrate, assume that on September 30, Higly Inc. says that it cannot pay at the present time. The entry to record the dishonouring of the note depends on whether eventual collection is expected. If Wolder Company expects eventual collection, the amount due on the note (principal and interest) is debited to Accounts Receivable. Wolder would make the following entry at the time the note is dishonoured:

A	=	L	+	OE
+10,150.00				+112.50
−10,000.00				
−37.50				

Cash flows: no effect

Sept. 30	Accounts Receivable—Higly	10,150.00	
	Notes Receivable—Higly		10,000.00
	Interest Revenue		112.50
	Interest Receivable		37.50
	To record dishonouring of Higly note.		

If there is no hope of collection, the principal of the note would be written off by debiting the allowance account. No interest revenue would be recorded, because collection will not occur. Any interest which had previously been accrued must also be written off.

Sale of Notes Receivable

Notes receivable may be sold to a third party before the maturity date in order to immediately receive cash on the note. The proceeds that a company receives for discounting the note are equal to the maturity value of the note less the third party's discount fee. Since these notes are purchased at a discount, the sale of notes receivable is commonly called **discounting** notes receivable. The accounting entries for the sale of notes receivable are more complicated and are left for a more advanced course.

BEFORE YOU GO ON . . .

▶ **Review It**

1. What is the basic formula for calculating interest?
2. At what value are notes receivable reported on the balance sheet?
3. Explain the difference between honouring and dishonouring a note receivable.

▶ **Do It**

On May 10, Gambit Stores accepts from J. Nyznyk a $3,400, three-month, 6% note in settlement of Nyznyk's overdue account. Interest is due at maturity. What are the entries made by Gambit on May 10 and on August 10, the maturity date, assuming Nyznyk does not pay the note at that time and that no accruals are made in the intervening period. Eventual collection is expected in the next month.

Action Plan

- Calculate the accrued interest. The formula is face value × annual interest rate × time in terms of one year.
- Prepare the entry to record the transfer of the note and any interest earned to an accounts receivable account if eventual collection is expected, or to an allowance account if collection is not expected.

Solution

May 10	Notes Receivable—J. Nyznyk	3,400	
	Accounts Receivable—J. Nyznyk		3,400
	To replace account receivable with a 6% note receivable, due August 10.		
Aug. 10	Accounts Receivable—J. Nyznyk	3,451	
	Notes Receivable—J. Nyznyk		3,400
	Interest Revenue ($3,400 × 6% × $\frac{3}{12}$)		51
	To record dishonouring of the Nyznyk note.		

Related exercise material: BE8–9, BE8–10, BE8–11, BE8–12, E8–7, E8–8, and E8–9.

Statement Presentation and Analysis

Presentation

Each of the major types of receivables should be identified in the balance sheet or in the notes to the financial statements. Short-term receivables are reported in the current assets section of the balance sheet, following cash and temporary investments. Although only the net amount of receivables less any allowance must be disclosed, it is helpful to report both the gross amount of receivables and the allowance for doubtful accounts either in the statement or in the notes to the financial statements.

> **study objective 7**
>
> Explain the statement presentation and analysis of receivables.

The following shows the current assets presentation of receivables for Bell Canada International Inc. Note that notes receivable are often listed before accounts receivable because notes are more easily converted to cash.

BELL CANADA INTERNATIONAL INC.
Balance Sheet (partial)
December 31, 2002
(in thousands)

Current assets		
Cash and cash equivalents		$ 2,617
Temporary investments		146,488
Notes receivable		268,532
Accounts receivable	$1,989	
Less: Allowance for doubtful accounts	429	1,560
Prepaid expenses and other current assets		1,317
		$420,514

In the income statement, Bad Debts Expense, Credit Card Expense, and Debit Card Expense are reported in the operating expenses section. Interest Revenue is shown under other revenues in the non-operating section of the income statement.

Analysis

Managers keep a watchful eye on the relationship between sales, accounts receivable, and cash collections. If sales increase, then accounts receivable are also expected to increase. But a disproportionate increase in accounts receivable might signal trouble. Perhaps the company increased its sales by loosening its credit policy, and these receivables may be difficult to collect.

The receivables turnover is a useful measure for assessing a company's efficiency in converting its credit sales into cash. It is calculated by dividing net credit sales by average gross accounts receivable. Unfortunately, companies seldom report the amount of net sales made on credit in their financial statements. In such instances, net sales (including both cash and credit sales) is used as a substitute. Gross accounts receivable are normally used in the denominator of the receivables turnover ratio. However, few companies publicly report this figure, in which case net accounts receivable must be used. As long as one is consistent in choosing the components of any ratio, the resulting ratio will be useful for comparison purposes.

These proxy figures—total revenue and net accounts receivable were used to calculate the receivables turnover for Forzani in Illustration 8-8.

Illustration 8-8 ▶

Receivables turnover

$$\text{Net Credit Sales} \div \text{Average Gross Accounts Receivable} = \text{Receivables Turnover}$$

$$\$923{,}795 \div \frac{\$38{,}275 + \$35{,}988}{2} = 24.9 \text{ times}$$

The result indicates an accounts receivable turnover ratio of 24.9 times per year for Forzani. The higher the turnover ratio is, the more liquid the company's receivables are.

It is informative to convert the receivables turnover ratio into the number of days it takes the company to collect its receivables. This ratio, called the **collection period**, is calculated by dividing 365 days by the receivables turnover, as illustrated for Forzani in Illustration 8-9.

Illustration 8-9 ▶

Collection period

$$\text{Days in Year} \div \text{Receivables Turnover} = \text{Collection Period}$$

$$365 \text{ days} \div 24.9 = 15 \text{ days}$$

This means that Forzani collects its receivables, on average, in approximately 15 days.

The collection period is frequently used to assess the effectiveness of a company's credit and collection policies. The general rule is that the collection period should not be much longer than the credit term period (i.e., the time allowed for payment).

ACCOUNTING IN ACTION ▶ Business Insight

In some cases, receivables turnover may be misleading. Some companies, especially large retail chains, encourage credit and revolving charge sales. They slow collections in order to earn a healthy return on the outstanding receivables in the form of interest at rates of up to 28.8%. This may explain why Sears Canada's receivables turnover is only 7.4 times (an average collection period of 49 days), for example. In general, the faster the turnover, the greater the reliance that can be placed on the current ratio for assessing liquidity.

BEFORE YOU GO ON . . .

►Review It

1. Explain where and how accounts and notes receivable are reported on the balance sheet.
2. Where are bad debts expense, credit card expense, debit card expense, and interest revenue reported on the income statement?
3. What do the receivables turnover and collection period reveal?

Related exercise material: BE8–13, BE8–14, E8–10, E8–11, E8–12, and E8–13.

Demonstration Problem

Selected transactions for Dylan Co. are presented below. Dylan's year end is June 30.

Mar. 1 Sold $20,000 of merchandise to Potter Company, terms n/30.

　　1 Accepted Juno Company's $16,500, six-month, 6% note for the balance due on account.

　　11 Potter Company returned $600 worth of goods.

　　13 Made Dylan Co. credit card sales for $13,200.

　　15 Made MasterCard credit sales that totalled $6,700. A 3% service fee is charged by MasterCard.

　　30 Received payment in full from Potter Company.

Apr. 13 Received collections of $8,200 on Dylan Co. credit card sales. Added interest charges of 18% to the remaining balance.

May 10 Wrote off as uncollectible $16,000 of accounts receivable.

June 30 Dylan uses an aging schedule to estimate bad debts. Estimated uncollectible accounts are determined to be $20,000 at June 30. The credit balance in the allowance account before adjustment is $3,500.

　　30 Recorded the interest accrued on the Juno Company note.

July 16 One of the accounts receivable written off in May pays the amount due, $4,000, in full.

Instructions

Prepare the journal entries for the transactions.

Additional
Demonstration
Problems

Solution to Demonstration Problem

Mar. 1	Accounts Receivable—Potter	20,000	
	Sales		20,000
	To record sale on account.		
1	Notes Receivable—Juno	16,500	
	Accounts Receivable—Juno		16,500
	To record acceptance of Juno Company note.		
11	Sales Returns and Allowances	600	
	Accounts Receivable—Potter		600
	To record return of goods.		
13	Accounts Receivable	13,200	
	Sales		13,200
	To record company credit card sales.		
15	Cash	6,499	
	Credit Card Expense (3% × $6,700)	201	
	Sales		6,700
	To record bank credit card sales.		
30	Cash ($20,000 − $600)	19,400	
	Accounts Receivable—Potter		19,400
	To record collection of accounts receivable.		

Action Plan

- Record accounts receivable at the invoice price.
- Recognize that sales returns and allowances reduce the amount received on accounts receivable.
- Record a service charge expense when credit cards are used.
- Calculate interest by multiplying the interest rate by the face value, adjusting for the portion of the year that has passed.
- Consider any existing balance in the allowance account when making the adjustment for uncollectible accounts.
- Record write-offs of accounts receivable only in balance sheet accounts.

Apr. 13	Cash		8,200	
	Accounts Receivable			8,200
	To record collection of accounts receivable.			
13	Accounts Receivable [($13,200 − $8,200) × 18% × $\frac{1}{12}$]		75	
	Interest Revenue			75
	To record interest on amount due.			
May 10	Allowance for Doubtful Accounts		16,000	
	Accounts Receivable			16,000
	To record write-off of accounts receivable.			
June 30	Bad Debts Expense ($20,000 − $3,500)		16,500	
	Allowance for Doubtful Accounts			16,500
	To record estimate of uncollectible accounts.			
30	Interest Receivable ($16,500 × 6% × $\frac{4}{12}$)		330	
	Interest Revenue			330
	To record interest earned.			
July 16	Accounts Receivable		4,000	
	Allowance for Doubtful Accounts			4,000
	To reverse write-off of accounts receivable.			
16	Cash		4,000	
	Accounts Receivable			4,000
	To record collection of accounts receivable.			

the navigator

Summary of Study Objectives

1. *Identify and distinguish between the different types of receivables.* Receivables are frequently classified as (1) accounts, (2) notes, and (3) other. Accounts receivable are amounts owed by customers on account. Notes receivable are formal instruments of credit. Other receivables include nontrade receivables such as accruals, GST recoverable, loans to company officers, and advances to employees.

2. *Show how accounts receivable are recognized in the accounts.* Accounts receivable are recorded at the invoice price. They are reduced by Sales Returns and Allowances. When interest is charged on a past-due receivable, this interest is added to the accounts receivable balance and is recognized as interest revenue.

3. *Describe and use the method and bases used to value accounts receivable.* The allowance method is used to match expected bad debts against sales, in the period in which the sales occur. There are two bases that can be used to estimate the bad debts: (1) percentage of sales, or (2) percentage of receivables. The percentage of sales basis emphasizes the matching principle. The percentage of receivables basis emphasizes the net realizable value of the accounts receivable. An aging schedule is usually used with this basis.

4. *Determine the entries to record the disposition of accounts receivable.* When an account receivable is col-

lected or written off, Accounts Receivable is credited. Accounts receivable can also be sold to a factor in advance of collection, for a reduced value. Credit and debit card sales and using receivables as security for a loan help speed up collection.

5. *Show how notes receivable are recognized and valued in the accounts.* Notes receivable are recorded at their principal, or face, value. It is necessary to record or accrue interest prior to maturity. In these cases, Cash or Interest Receivable is debited and Interest Revenue is credited.

Like accounts receivable, notes receivable are reported at their net realizable value. The notes receivable allowance account is called Allowance for Doubtful Notes. The calculations and estimates involved in valuing notes receivable at net realizable value, and in recording the proper amount of bad debts expense and related allowance, are similar to those required for accounts receivable.

6. *Determine the entries to record the disposition of notes receivable.* Notes are normally held to maturity. At that time, the principal plus any unpaid interest is due and the note is removed from the accounts. If a note is not paid at maturity, it is said to be dishonoured. If eventual collection is still expected, an account receivable replaces the note receivable and any unpaid interest. Otherwise, the note must be written off.

7. *Explain the statement presentation and analysis of receivables.* Each major type of receivable should be identified in the balance sheet or in the notes to the financial statements. It is desirable to report the gross amount of receivables and the allowance for doubtful accounts/notes. Bad debts and credit and debit card expenses are reported in the income statement as operating expenses. Interest expense is shown as other expenses, and interest revenue is shown as other revenues in the non-operating section of the statement.

The liquidity of receivables can be evaluated by calculating the receivables turnover and collection period ratios. The receivables turnover is calculated by dividing net credit sales by average gross accounts receivable. This ratio measures how efficiently the company is converting its receivables into sales. The collection period converts the receivables turnover into days, dividing 365 days by the receivables turnover ratio. It shows the number of days, on average, it takes a company to collect its accounts receivable.

Glossary

Key Term Matching Activity

Aging the accounts receivable Analysing customer balances by the length of time they have been unpaid. (p. 390)

Allowance method A method of accounting for bad debts that involves estimating uncollectible accounts at the end of each period. (p. 388)

Bad debts expense An expense account to record uncollectible receivables. (p. 387)

Collection period The result of 365 days divided by the receivables turnover. Determines the average number of days that receivables are outstanding. (p. 402)

Dishonoured note A note that is not paid in full at maturity. (p. 400).

Factor A finance company or bank that buys receivables from businesses and then collects the payments directly from the customers. (p. 395).

Net realizable value Gross receivables less allowance for doubtful accounts. The net amount of receivables expected to be received in cash. (p. 388)

Percentage of receivables basis Management establishes a percentage relationship between the amount of receivables and the expected losses from uncollectible accounts. (p. 390).

Percentage of sales basis Management establishes a percentage relationship between the amount of credit sales and the expected losses from uncollectible accounts. (p. 389)

Promissory note A written promise to pay a specified amount of money on demand or at a definite time. (p. 398)

Receivables turnover A measure of the liquidity of receivables. Calculated by dividing net credit sales by average gross accounts receivable. (p. 402)

Self-Study Questions

Chapter 8 Self-Test

Answers are at the end of the chapter.

(SO 2) AP 1. On June 15, Patel Company sells merchandise on account to Bullock Co. for $1,000, terms n/30. On June 20, Bullock returns merchandise worth $300 to Patel. On July 14, payment is received from Bullock for the balance due. What is the amount of the receivable reported at the end of June?
(a) $0   (c) $1,300
(b) $700   (d) None of the above

(SO 3) AP 2. Sanderson Company has a credit balance of $5,000 in Allowance for Doubtful Accounts before any adjustments are made. Based on a review and aging of its accounts receivable at the end of the period, the company estimates that $60,000 of its receivables are uncollectible. The amount of bad debts expense which should be reported for this accounting period is:
(a) $5,000.   (c) $60,000.
(b) $55,000.   (d) $65,000.

(SO 3) AP 3. Assume Sanderson Company has a debit balance of $5,000 in Allowance for Doubtful Accounts before any adjustments are made. Based on a review and aging of its accounts receivable at the end of the period, the company estimates that $60,000 of its receivables are uncollectible. The amount of bad debts expense which should be reported for this accounting period is:
(a) $5,000.   (c) $60,000.
(b) $55,000.   (d) $65,000.

(SO 3) AP 4. Net sales for the month are $800,000 and bad debts are expected to be 1.5% of net sales. The company uses the percentage of sales basis. If Allowance for Doubtful Accounts has a credit balance of $15,000 before adjustment, what is the balance in the allowance account after adjustment?
(a) $15,000   (c) $27,000
(b) $23,000   (d) $31,000

(SO 3) AP 5. In 2005, Lawrence Company had accounts receivable of $750,000. On January 1, 2005, Allowance for Doubtful Accounts had a credit balance of $18,000. During 2005, $30,000 of uncollectible accounts receivable were written off. Past experience indicates that 3% of total receivables will become uncollectible. What should the adjusted balance of Allowance for Doubtful Accounts be at December 31, 2005?
   (a) $4,500   (c) $22,500
   (b) $10,500   (d) $70,500

(SO 4) AP 6. Morgan Retailers accepted $50,000 of TD Bank Visa credit card charges for merchandise sold on July 1. TD Bank charges 4% for its credit card use. The entry to record this transaction by Morgan Retailers will include a credit to sales of $50,000 and debit(s) to:
   (a) Cash for $48,000, and Credit Card Expense for $2,000.
   (b) Accounts Receivable for $48,000, and Credit Card Expense for $2,000.
   (c) Cash for $50,000.
   (d) Accounts Receivable for $50,000.

(SO 5) K 7. Sorenson Co. accepts a $1,000, three-month, 8% promissory note in settlement of an account with Parton Co. The entry to record this transaction is:

(a) Notes Receivable	1,020	
Accounts Receivable		1,020
(b) Notes Receivable	1,000	
Accounts Receivable		1,000
(c) Notes Receivable	1,000	
Sales		1,000
(d) Notes Receivable	1,080	
Accounts Receivable		1,080

8. Schlicht Co. holds Osgrove Inc.'s $10,000, four-month, 9% note. If no interest has been accrued when the note is collected, the entry made by Schlicht Co. is: (SO 6) K

(a) Cash	10,300	
Notes Receivable		10,300
(b) Cash	10,900	
Interest Revenue		900
Notes Receivable		10,000
(c) Accounts Receivable	10,300	
Notes Receivable		10,000
Interest Revenue		300
(d) Cash	10,300	
Notes Receivable		10,000
Interest Revenue		300

9. Accounts and notes receivable are reported in the current assets section of the balance sheet at: (SO 7) K
   (a) net realizable value.
   (b) net book value.
   (c) lower of cost and market value.
   (d) invoice cost.

10. Moore Company had net credit sales during the year of $800,000 and a cost of goods sold of $500,000. The balance in accounts receivable at the beginning of the year was $100,000 and at the end of the year it was $150,000. What were the receivables turnover and collection period ratios, respectively? (SO 7) AP
   (a) 4.0 and 91 days   (c) 6.4 and 57 days
   (b) 5.3 and 69 days   (d) 8.0 and 46 days

the navigator ✔

Questions

(SO 1) C 1. Identify the three major types of receivables. Where is each type of receivable generally classified on a balance sheet?

(SO 1) K 2. What are some common types of receivables other than accounts receivable and notes receivable?

(SO 2) C 3. (a) What are the advantages of using an accounts receivable subsidiary ledger? (b) Describe the relationship between the general ledger control account and the subsidiary ledger.

(SO 3) K 4. What are the essential features of the allowance method of accounting for bad debts?

(SO 3) C 5. What is the purpose of the account Allowance for Doubtful Accounts? Although the normal balance of this account is a credit balance, it sometimes has a debit balance. Explain how this can happen.

(SO 3) C 6. Soo Eng cannot understand why net realizable value does not decrease when an uncollectible account is written off under the allowance method. Clarify this point for Soo Eng.

(SO 3) C 7. Distinguish between the two bases that may be used in estimating uncollectible accounts under the allowance method.

(SO 3) C 8. Kyoto Company has a credit balance of $3,500 in Allowance for Doubtful Accounts. The estimated uncollectible amount under the percentage of sales basis is $4,100. The total estimated uncollectible amount under the percentage of receivables basis is $5,800. Describe the similarities and the differences in preparing the adjusting journal entry to record the estimated uncollectible accounts under each basis.

(SO 3) C 9. Why is the bad debt expense in the income statement typically not the same amount as the allowance for doubtful accounts amount in the balance sheet?

(SO 4) C 10. When an account receivable that was written off is later collected, two journal entries are usually made. Explain why.

(SO 4) K 11. Why do companies sometimes sell their receivables?

(SO 4) C 12. Sears accepts debit cards, bank credit cards, and its own nonbank Sears credit card. What are the advantages of accepting each type of card? Explain how the accounting for sales differs for each type of card.

(SO 5) C 13. Compare the characteristics of a note receivable with those of an account receivable.

(SO 5) C 14. Why might a company prefer to have a note receivable instead of an account receivable?

(SO 7) C 15. Saucier Company has accounts receivable, notes receivable, allowances for doubtful accounts, and allowances for doubtful notes. How should the receivables be reported on the balance sheet?

(SO 7) C 16. The president proudly announces her company's improved liquidity. Its current ratio increased substantially this year. Does an increase in the current ratio always indicate improved liquidity? What other ratio(s) might you review to determine whether or not the increase in the current ratio represents an improvement in financial health?

(SO 7) AN 17. Does an increase in the receivables turnover indicate faster or slower collection of receivables? An increase or decrease in the collection period?

Brief Exercises

BE8–1 Presented below are three receivables transactions. Indicate whether these receivables are reported as accounts receivable, notes receivable, or other receivables on a balance sheet.

(a) Advanced $10,000 to an employee.
(b) Received a promissory note of $57,000 for services performed.
(c) Sold merchandise on account to a customer for $60,000.

Identify types of receivables. (SO 1) K

BE8–2 Record the following transactions on the books of Essex Co.:

(a) On July 1, Essex Co. sold merchandise on account to Cambridge Inc. for $14,000, terms n/30.
(b) On July 8, Cambridge Inc. returned merchandise worth $2,400 to Essex Co.
(c) On July 31, Cambridge Inc. paid for the merchandise.

Record accounts receivable transactions. (SO 2) AP

BE8–3 Qinshan Co. uses the percentage of sales basis to record bad debts expense. It estimates that 1.5% of net credit sales will become uncollectible. Credit sales are $800,000 for the year ended April 30, 2005, sales returns and allowances are $50,000, and the allowance for doubtful accounts has a credit balance of $12,000. Prepare the adjusting entry to record bad debts expense in 2005.

Prepare bad debts adjusting entry using percentage of sales basis. (SO 3) AP

BE8–4 Groleskey Co. uses the percentage of receivables basis to record bad debts expense. It estimates that 4% of total accounts receivable will become uncollectible. Accounts receivable are $500,000 at the end of the year. The allowance for doubtful accounts has a credit balance of $3,000.

(a) Prepare the adjusting journal entry to record bad debts expense for the year ended December 31.
(b) If the allowance for doubtful accounts had a debit balance of $800 instead of a credit balance of $3,000, determine the amount to be reported for bad debts expense.

Prepare bad debts adjusting entry using percentage of receivables basis. (SO 3) AP

BE8–5 Refer to BE8–4. Groleskey Co. decides to refine its estimate of uncollectible accounts by preparing an aging schedule. Complete the following schedule and prepare the adjusting journal entry using this estimate. Assume Allowance for Doubtful Accounts has a credit balance of $3,000.

Prepare bad debts adjusting entry using aging schedule. (SO 3) AP

Number of Days Outstanding	Accounts Receivable	% Estimated Uncollectible	Estimated Bad Debts
0–30 days	$315,000	1%	
31–60 days	91,000	4%	
61–90 days	59,000	10%	
Over 90 days	35,000	20%	
Total	$500,000		

Prepare entry for write-off; determine net realizable value.
(SO 3) AP

BE8–6 At the end of 2004, Searcy Co. has accounts receivable of $700,000 and an allowance for doubtful accounts of $54,000. On January 24, 2005, it is learned that the company's $18,000 receivable from Hutley Inc. is not collectible. Management authorizes a write-off.

(a) Prepare the journal entry to record the write-off.
(b) What is the net realizable value of the accounts receivable (1) before the write-off, and (2) after the write-off?

Prepare entry for subsequent collection of write-off.
(SO 3) AP

BE8–7 Assume the same information as in BE8–6. Hutley's financial difficulties are over. On March 4, 2005, Searcy Co. receives an $18,000 payment in full from Hutley Inc. Prepare the journal entries to record this transaction.

Prepare entries to record credit and debit card transactions.
(SO 4) AP

BE8–8 St. Pierre Restaurant accepted a Visa card in payment of a $100 lunch bill on July 27. The bank charges a 3.5% fee. What entry should St. Pierre make? How would this entry change if the payment had been made with an American Express card instead of a Visa card? A debit card instead of a Visa card?

Calculate interest on notes receivable.
(SO 5) AN

BE8–9 Presented below are data on three promissory notes. Determine the missing amounts.

Date of Note	Terms	Principal	Interest Rate	Total Interest
(a) April 1	2 months	$900,000	10%	?
(b) July 2	1 month	79,000	?%	$526.67
(c) March 7	6 months	?	6%	$1,680.00

Calculate interest accrued on notes receivable.
(SO 5) AN

BE8–10 Rocky Ridge Co. has three outstanding notes receivable at its December 31, 2004, fiscal year end. Calculate total interest revenue for each note. How much of the interest revenue should be recorded for each note (a) in 2004 and (b) in 2005?

Date of Note	Terms	Principal	Interest Rate
(a) September 1	6 months	$40,000	8.25%
(b) July 31	1 year	16,000	7.50%
(c) November 1	5 months	39,000	6.75%

Prepare entries for note receivable.
(SO 5, 6) AP

BE8–11 On February 1, 2005, Raja Co. sold merchandise on account to Opal Co. for $12,000, terms n/30. On March 2, 2005, Opal gave Raja a 7%, five-month promissory note in settlement of the account. Interest is to be paid at maturity. On August 1, Opal paid the note and accrued interest. Prepare the journal entries for Raja Co. for the above transactions. Raja Co. has a June 30 fiscal year end and adjusts its accounts on an annual basis.

Record acceptance, honouring, and dishonouring of note.
(SO 5, 6) AP

BE8–12 Lee Company accepts a $9,000, 7%, three-month note receivable in settlement of an account receivable on April 1, 2005. Interest is to be paid at maturity.

(a) Prepare the journal entries to record the issue of the note on April 1 and the settlement of the note on July 1, assuming the note is honoured. No interest has previously been accrued.
(b) Repeat part (a) assuming that the note is dishonoured but eventual collection is expected.
(c) Repeat part (a) assuming that the note is dishonoured and eventual collection is not expected.

Prepare bad debts adjusting entry using percentage of receivables basis; show balance sheet presentation and calculate ratios.
(SO 3, 7) AP

BE8–13 During its first year of operations, WAF Company had credit sales of $3 million. At year end, February 28, 2005, $600,000 remained uncollected. The credit manager estimates that $35,000 of these receivables will become uncollectible.

(a) Prepare the journal entry to record the estimated uncollectibles.
(b) Prepare the current assets section of the balance sheet for WAF Company, assuming that in addition to the receivables, it has cash of $90,000, merchandise inventory of $130,000, and prepaid expenses of $10,000.
(c) Calculate the receivables turnover and collection period. (*Hint:* Remember that this is the end of the first year of business.)

Calculate ratios to analyse receivables.
(SO 7) AP

BE8–14 The financial statements of **Maple Leaf Foods Inc.** report sales of $5,075,879 thousand for the year ended December 31, 2002. Accounts receivable are $243,122 thousand at the end of fiscal 2002, and $248,064 thousand at the end of fiscal 2001. Calculate Maple Leaf's receivables turnover and collection period.

Exercises

E8–1 Presented below are the transactions for the Discovery Sports Co. store and four of its customers during the company's first month of business:

Feb. 2 Andrew Noren used his Discovery Sports credit card to purchase $570 of merchandise.
 4 Andrew returned $75 of merchandise for credit.
 5 Sold $380 of merchandise to Elaine Davidson, who used her Discovery Sports credit card.
 8 Erik Smistad purchased $421 of merchandise and paid for it in cash.
 9 Madison Canuel used her Discovery Sports credit card to purchase $869 in merchandise.
 15 Elaine Davidson made a $100 payment on her credit card account.
 17 Andrew Noren used his Discovery Sports credit card to purchase an additional $348 of merchandise.
 28 Madison Canuel paid her account in full.
 28 Erik Smistad used his Discovery Sports credit card to purchase $299 of merchandise.

Instructions
(a) Prepare journal entries for each of the above transactions.
(b) Set up general ledger accounts for the accounts receivable control account and for the accounts receivable subsidiary ledger accounts. Post the journal entries to these accounts.
(c) Prepare a list of customers and the balances of their accounts from the subsidiary ledger. Prove the total of the subsidiary ledger is equal to the control account balance.

Prepare entries for accounts receivable and post to subsidiary and general ledgers.
(SO 2) AP

E8–2 The ledger of Patillo Company at the end of the current year shows Accounts Receivable $80,000, Sales $940,000, and Sales Returns and Allowances $40,000.

Instructions
(a) If Allowance for Doubtful Accounts has a credit balance of $800 in the trial balance, journalize the adjusting entry at December 31, assuming bad debts are estimated to be (1) 1% of net sales, and (2) 10% of accounts receivable.
(b) If Allowance for Doubtful Accounts has a debit balance of $500 in the trial balance, journalize the adjusting entry at December 31, assuming bad debts are estimated to be (1) 0.5% of net sales, and (2) 5% of accounts receivable.

Prepare bad debts adjusting entries using two bases.
(SO 3) AP

Interactive Homework

E8–3 Grevina Company has accounts receivable of $92,500 at March 31. An analysis of the accounts shows the following:

Month of Sale	Balance
March	$65,000
February	12,600
January	8,500
October, November, and December	6,400
	$92,500

Prepare aging schedule and bad debts adjusting entry.
(SO 3) AP

Interactive Homework

Credit terms are n/30. At March 31, Allowance for Doubtful Accounts has a credit balance of $2,200, prior to adjustment. The company uses the percentage of receivables basis and an aging schedule to estimate uncollectible accounts. The company's percentage estimates of bad debts are as follows:

Age of Accounts	Estimated Percentage Uncollectible
0–30 days outstanding	2%
31–60 days outstanding	10%
61–90 days outstanding	30%
Over 90 days outstanding	50%

Instructions
(a) Prepare an aging schedule to determine the total estimated uncollectible amount at March 31.
(b) Prepare the adjusting entry at March 31 to record bad debts expense.

Prepare bad debts adjusting entry using percentage of sales basis; prepare entries for write-off and recovery.
(SO 3) AP

E8–4 On December 31, 2004, when its Allowance for Doubtful Accounts had a debit balance of $1,000, Ceja Co. estimated that 2% of its $420,000 of accounts receivable would become uncollectible and recorded the bad debts adjusting entry. On May 11, 2005, Ceja Co. determined that Robert Worthy's account was uncollectible and wrote off $950. On June 12, 2005, Worthy paid the amount previously written off.

Instructions

Prepare the journal entries on December 31, 2004, May 11, 2005, and June 12, 2005.

Prepare entries for credit card sales.
(SO 4) AP

E8–5 Presented below are two independent situations:

(a) On December 15, Guy Benicoeur uses his Visa Desjardins bank credit card to purchase artwork for $1,150 from the Galerie d'art Bégin located in the Marché Bonsecours. Le Mouvement Desjardins charges the gallery a 3.5% credit card transaction fee. Prepare the entries on the Galerie d'art Bégin's books to record this sale on December 15.

(b) On April 2, P. Zachos uses her Hudson's Bay credit card to purchase merchandise from The Bay for $1,450. On May 1, Zachos is billed for the $1,450 due. Zachos pays $800 on the balance due on May 3. On June 1, Zachos receives a bill for the amount due, including interest of 28.8% on the unpaid balance for the month. Prepare the entries on The Bay's books for the transactions that occurred on April 2, May 3, and June 1.

Identify reason for sale of receivables.
(SO 4) C

E8–6 The Canadian National Railway Company, in the notes to its financial statements, states that it has a five-year revolving agreement to sell eligible freight trade receivables up to a maximum of $350 million of receivables outstanding at any point in time.

Instructions

Explain why CN, a financially stable company, might choose to sell its receivables.

Prepare entries for notes receivable transactions.
(SO 5, 6) AP

E8–7 Passera Supply Co. has the following transactions for notes receivable during the last two months of the year:

Nov. 1 Loaned $24,000 cash to A. Morgan on a one-year, 8% note.
Dec. 1 Sold goods to Wright, Inc., receiving a $4,200, three-month, 6% note.
15 Received an $8,000, six-month, 7% note on account from Barnes Company.
31 Accrued interest revenue on all notes receivable. Interest is due at maturity.

Instructions

Journalize the transactions for Passera Supply Co. Round your answers to the nearest dollar.

Prepare entries for notes receivable.
(SO 5, 6) AP

Interactive Homework

E8–8 Record the following transactions for Prejear Co. in its general journal:

Mar. 1 Received a $10,500, nine-month, 10% note on account from Jones Bros.
June 30 Accrued interest on the Jones note.
Dec. 1 Received principal plus interest on the Jones note. (No interest has been accrued since June 30.)

Prepare entries for dishonouring of notes receivable.
(SO 5, 6) AP

E8–9 On May 2, Ni Co. lends $5,000 to Fein Inc., issuing a six-month, 10% note. At the maturity date, November 1, Fein indicates that it cannot pay.

Instructions

(a) Prepare the entry to record the dishonouring of the note, assuming that Ni Co. expects that there will be collection in full in the future.

(b) Prepare the entry to record the dishonouring of the note, assuming that Ni Co. does not expect any collection for this note.

Prepare entries for credit and debit card sales and indicate statement presentation.
(SO 4, 7) AP

E8–10 Kasko Stores accepts both its own and national credit cards, in addition to debit cards. During the year, the following selected summary transactions occurred:

Jan. 15 Made Kasko credit card sales totalling $17,000.
20 Made Visa credit card sales (service charge fee, 3.25%) totalling $4,500.
30 Made debit card sales (service charge fee, 2.25%) totalling $1,000.
Feb. 10 Collected $12,000 on Kasko credit card sales.
15 Added finance charges of 18% to Kasko credit card balances.

Instructions

(a) Journalize the transactions for Kasko Stores.
(b) Indicate the statement presentation of the financing charges and the credit card and debit card expense for Kasko Stores.

E8–11 Indicate whether the following transactions would increase (+), decrease (−), or have no effect (NE) on the Bakbone Co.'s receivables turnover ratio of 8 times:

(a) _____ Recorded sales on account.
(b) _____ Collected amounts owing from customers.
(c) _____ Recorded bad debts expense for the year.
(d) _____ Wrote off an account from a customer as uncollectible.

Indicate effect of transactions on receivables turnover.
(SO 7) AN

E8–12 Drost Company reports the following balances in its receivables accounts at October 31, 2005 (in thousands): Accounts Receivable, $2,907; Advances to Employees, $5; Allowance for Doubtful Accounts, $31; Notes Receivable, $228; and HST Recoverable, $25.

Prepare balance sheet presentation of receivables.
(SO 7) AP

Instructions

Prepare the balance sheet presentation of Drost Company's receivables as at October 31, 2005.

E8–13 The following information was taken from the December 31 financial statements of the Canadian National Railway Company:

Calculate ratios.
(SO 7) AN

(in millions)	2002	2001	2000
Accounts receivable, gross	$ 781	$ 726	$ 800
Allowance for doubtful accounts	59	81	63
Accounts receivable, net	722	645	737
Revenues	6,110	5,652	5,446
Total current assets	1,163	1,164	1,125
Total current liabilities	2,134	1,638	1,915

Instructions

(a) Calculate the 2002 and 2001 current ratios.
(b) Calculate the receivables turnover and average collection period for 2002 and for 2001.
(c) Are accounts receivable a material component of the company's current assets?
(d) Comment on any improvement or deterioration in CN's management of its receivables.

Problems: Set A

P8–1A At December 31, 2004, Bordeaux Co. reported the following information on its balance sheet:

Prepare entries for accounts receivable and bad debts.
(SO 2, 3) AP

Accounts receivable	$960,000
Less: Allowance for doubtful accounts	70,000

During the first quarter of 2005, the company had the following transactions related to receivables:

1. Sales on account, $3,200,000
2. Sales returns and allowances, $50,000
3. Collections of accounts receivable, $3,000,000
4. Write-offs of accounts receivable deemed uncollectible, $90,000
5. Recovery of accounts previously written off as uncollectible, $21,000

Instructions

(a) Prepare the summary journal entries to record each of these five transactions.
(b) Enter the January 1, 2005, balances in the Accounts Receivable and Allowance for Doubtful Accounts general ledger accounts. Post the entries to the two accounts and determine the balances.
(c) Prepare the journal entry to record bad debts expense for the first quarter of 2005. An aging of accounts receivable indicates that expected bad debts are $110,000.
(d) Calculate the net realizable value of accounts receivable at the end of the first quarter.

Calculate bad debts using various bases.
(SO 3) AP

P8–2A Information on Hohenberger Company for 2005 is summarized below:

Total credit sales	$2,000,000
Accounts receivable at December 31	800,000
Bad debts written off during 2005	35,000

Instructions

(a) Assume that Hohenberger Company estimates its bad debts expense at 3% of credit sales. What amount of bad debts expense will Hohenberger Company record if it has an Allowance for Doubtful Accounts credit balance of $4,000 before making the adjustment?

(b) Assume that Hohenberger Company estimates its bad debts expense based on 6% of total accounts receivable. What amount of bad debts expense will Hohenberger Company record if it has an Allowance for Doubtful Accounts credit balance of $3,000 before making the adjustment?

(c) Assume the same facts as in (b) except that there is a $3,000 debit balance in Allowance for Doubtful Accounts. What amount of bad debts expense will Hohenberger record?

(d) Assume Hohenberger Company used an aging schedule and estimated uncollectible accounts will be $52,000. What amount of bad debts expense will Hohenberger Company record if there is a debit balance of $4,000 in Allowance for Doubtful Accounts before making the adjustment?

(e) How does the write-off of an uncollectible account affect the bad debt expense for the current period?

(f) How does the write-off of an uncollectible account affect the net realizable value of accounts receivable?

Prepare entries for bad debts using aging schedule.
(SO 3) AP

P8–3A Presented below is an aging schedule for the Hagiwara Company for the year ended December 31, 2004:

Customer	Total	Number of Days Outstanding			
		0–30	31–60	61–90	91–120
Hayashi	$ 20,000		$ 9,000	$11,000	
Tanaka	30,000	$ 30,000			
Takahashi	52,000	15,000	7,000		$30,000
Yamada	39,000				39,000
Others	120,000	92,000	15,000	13,000	
	$261,000	$137,000	$31,000	$24,000	$69,000
Estimated percentage uncollectible		1.5%	6%	15%	36%
Estimated bad debts	$ 32,355	$ 2,055	$ 1,860	$ 3,600	$24,840

At December 31, 2004, the unadjusted balance in Allowance for Doubtful Accounts is a credit of $14,000.

Instructions

(a) Journalize and post the adjusting entry for bad debts at December 31, 2004.

(b) Journalize and post the following events and transactions for 2005 to the allowance account:
   1. March 1, a $1,000 customer balance originating in 2004 is judged uncollectible.
   2. May 1, a cheque for $1,000 is received from the customer whose account was written off as uncollectible on March 1.

(c) Journalize the adjusting entry for bad debts on December 31, 2005, assuming that the unadjusted balance in Allowance for Doubtful Accounts is $4,070 (credit) and the 2005 aging schedule indicates that total estimated bad debts will be $37,100.

P8–4A The following is selected information taken from a company's aging schedule to esti-mate uncollectible accounts receivable at year end:

Calculate bad debts and prepare entries using aging schedule. (SO 3) AP

	Total	Number of Days Outstanding			
		0–30	31–60	61–90	91–120
Accounts receivable	$260,000	$120,000	$60,000	$50,000	$30,000
Percentage uncollectible		1%	5%	10%	20%
Estimated bad debts					

Instructions

(a) Calculate the total estimated bad debts based on the above information.
(b) Prepare the year-end adjusting journal entry to record the bad debts using the allowance method and the aged uncollectible accounts receivable determined in (a). Assume the unadjusted balance in Allowance for Doubtful Accounts is a $10,000 credit.
(c) In the next fiscal year, $2,000 is determined to be uncollectible. Prepare the journal entry to write off the uncollectible accounts.
(d) The company collects $850 of the $2,000 on the account that was determined to be uncol-lectible in (c). Prepare the journal entry (or entries) necessary to restore the $2,000 account receivable and record the partial cash collection. Collection of the remaining amount due is anticipated in the near future.
(e) Explain how establishing an allowance satisfies the matching principle.

P8–5A At the beginning of the current period, Huang Co. had accounts receivable of $200,000 and an allowance for doubtful accounts of $14,000 (credit). During the period, it had net credit sales of $800,000 and collections of $723,000. It wrote off accounts receivable of $21,750 as uncollectible. However, $3,500 of one of the accounts written off as uncollectible was recov-ered before the end of the current period.

Prepare entries for accounts receivable and bad debts using various bases. (SO 3) AP

Instructions

(a) Prepare the entries to record sales and collections during the period.
(b) Prepare the entries to record the write-off of uncollectible accounts and the recovery of accounts written off as uncollectible during the period.
(c) Prepare the entry to record bad debt expense for the period if Huang Co. estimates that 2% of net sales will become uncollectible.
(d) Determine the ending balances in Accounts Receivable and Allowance for Doubtful Accounts.
(e) What is the net realizable value of receivables at the end of the period?
(f) What is bad debt expense on the income statement for the period?
(g) Assume that Huang Co. uses the percentage of receivables basis instead of the percentage of sales basis to estimate uncollectible accounts. Repeat (c) through (f) assuming Huang esti-mates 5% of the ending accounts receivable will become uncollectible.

P8–6A The balance sheets of Watson & Company on December 31, Year 1 and Year 2, showed gross accounts receivable of $8,450 thousand and $9,275 thousand, respectively. The balances in Allowance for Doubtful Accounts at the end of Year 1 and Year 2—after adjusting entries—were $725 thousand and $796 thousand, respectively.

Analyse accounts and prepare entries for accounts receivable and bad debts. (SO 2, 3) AN

The income statements for Year 1 and Year 2 showed bad debts expense of $402 thousand and $455 thousand, respectively, which was equal to 1% of sales. All sales were on account.

Instructions

Prepare summary journal entries for Year 2 to record the bad debts expense, sales, write-offs, and col-lections. (*Hint:* You may find the use of T accounts helpful in determining the amounts involved.)

P8–7A Bassano Company uses the percentage of sales basis to record bad debts expense for its monthly financial statements and the percentage of receivables basis for its year-end finan-cial statements. Bassano Company has an October 31 fiscal year end and closes temporary accounts annually.

Prepare entries for accounts receivable and bad debts. Show statement presentation. (SO 2, 3, 4, 7) AN

On August 31, 2005, after completing its month-end adjustments, it had accounts receivable of $742,500, a credit balance of $27,570 in Allowance for Doubtful Accounts, and bad debts expense of $85,680. During September and October, the following occurred:

September

1. Sold $546,300 of merchandise on credit.
2. Sold $172,900 of merchandise for cash.
3. A total of $9,170 of the merchandise sold on credit was returned. These customers were issued credit memos.
4. Refunded $1,425 cash to customers for returns of cash purchases of merchandise.
5. Collected $592,750 cash on account from customers.
6. In addition to the cash collected in (5) above, collected $2,520 cash from a customer whose account had been written off in July.
7. Wrote off as uncollectible $17,410 of accounts receivable.
8. As part of the month-end adjusting entries, recorded bad debt expense of 2% of net credit sales for the month.

October

1. Credit sales during the month were $639,900.
2. Cash sales in October were $154,950.
3. Customers returned $10,480 of merchandise purchased on credit and $2,190 of merchandise purchased with cash. Issued credit memos to credit customers and refunded cash to cash customers.
4. Received $3,450 cash from a customer whose account had been written off in September.
5. Collected $585,420 cash, in addition to the cash collected in (4) above, from customers on account.
6. Wrote off $29,440 of accounts receivable as uncollectible.
7. Recorded the year-end adjustment for bad debts. Uncollectible accounts were estimated to be 3% of accounts receivable.

Instructions

(a) Prepare journal entries to record the above transactions and adjustments. Round all calculations to the nearest dollar.
(b) Show how Accounts Receivable will appear on the October 31, 2005, balance sheet.
(c) What amount will be reported as bad debts expense on the income statement for the year ended October 31, 2005?

Prepare entries for receivables.
(SO 2, 4, 5, 6) AP

P8–8A Bleumortier Company has a March 31 fiscal year end. Selected transactions during the year included the following:

Jan.   5 Sold $9,000 of merchandise to Brooks Company, terms n/30.
Feb.   1 Accepted a $9,000, four-month, 8% promissory note from Brooks Company for the balance due. Interest must be paid monthly.
      18 Sold $4,000 of merchandise to Mathias Co., terms n/10.
      28 Sold $6,700 of merchandise to Gage Company and accepted Gage's $6,700, two-month, 10% note for the balance due. Interest is to be paid at maturity.
Mar.   1 Collected the monthly interest payment from Brooks Company.
       2 Accepted a $4,000, three-month, 7.5% note from Mathias Co. for its balance due, interest payable at maturity.
      31 Accrued interest on any outstanding notes.
Apr.   1 Collected the monthly interest payment from Brooks Company.
      30 Collected Gage Company note in full.
May   1 Collected the monthly interest payment from Brooks Company.
June   1 Collected Brooks Company note in full.
       2 Mathias Co. dishonours its note of March 2. It is expected that Mathias will eventually pay the amount owed.
July 13 Sold $5,000 of merchandise to Tritt Inc. and accepted Tritt's $5,000, three-month, 9% note for the amount due, interest payable at maturity.
Oct. 13 The Tritt Inc. note was dishonoured. Tritt Inc. is bankrupt and there is no hope of future settlement.

Instructions

Journalize the transactions. Round your answers to the nearest dollar.

P8–9A Tardif Company adjusts its books monthly. On September 30, 2005, selected ledger account balances are as follows:

Prepare entries for notes receivable. Show balance sheet presentation. (SO 4, 5, 6, 7) AP

Notes Receivable	$25,200
Interest Receivable	155

Notes receivable include the following:

Date	Maker	Principal	Interest	Term
Aug. 1	Foran Inc.	$ 9,000	7%	2 months
Aug. 31	Drexler Co.	6,000	10%	2 months
Sept. 30	MGH Corp.	10,200	9%	6 months

Interest is due at maturity. During October, the following transactions were completed:

Oct. 1 Received payment in full from Foran Inc. on the amount due.
    7 Made sales of $5,800 on Tardif credit cards.
  12 Made sales of $750 on Visa credit cards. The credit card service charge is 3%.
  15 Added $485 to Tardif charge-customer balances for finance charges on unpaid balances.
  31 Received notice that the Drexler note had been dishonoured. (Assume that Drexler is expected to pay in the future.)

Instructions

(a) Journalize the October transactions and the October 31 adjusting entry for accrued interest receivable.
(b) Enter the balances at October 1 in the receivables accounts, and post the entries to all of the receivables accounts.
(c) Show the balance sheet presentation of the receivables accounts at October 31.
(d) How would the journal entry on October 31 differ if Drexler were not expected to pay in the future?

P8–10A Presented here is basic financial information (in millions) from the 2002 financial statements of **Rogers Communications Inc.** and **Shaw Communications Inc.**:

Calculate and interpret ratios. (SO 7) AN

	Rogers	Shaw
Sales	$4,323.0	$1,888.6
Allowance for doubtful accounts, Jan. 1	63.4	19.2
Allowance for doubtful accounts, Dec. 31	65.5	19.3
Accounts receivable balance (gross), Jan. 1	558.8	208.8
Accounts receivable balance (gross), Dec. 31	577.6	206.8

Instructions

Calculate the receivables turnover and average collection period for both companies. Comment on the difference in their collection experiences.

Problems: Set B

P8–1B At December 31, 2004, Underwood Imports reported the following information on its balance sheet:

Prepare entries for accounts receivable and bad debts. (SO 2, 3) AP

Accounts receivable	$995,000
Less: Allowance for doubtful accounts	62,500

During 2005, the company had the following transactions related to receivables:

1. Sales on account, $2,600,000
2. Sales returns and allowances, $40,000
3. Collections of accounts receivable, $2,700,000
4. Write-offs of accounts deemed uncollectible, $75,000
5. Recovery of bad debts previously written off as uncollectible, $30,000

Instructions

(a) Prepare the summary journal entries to record each of these five transactions.

(b) Prepare the journal entry to record bad debts expense for 2005. Bad debts are estimated at 2.5% of net credit sales.

(c) Enter the January 1, 2005, balances in the Accounts Receivable and Allowance for Doubtful Accounts general ledger accounts. Post the entries to the two accounts and determine the balances at December 31, 2005.

(d) Calculate the net realizable value of Accounts Receivable at December 31, 2005.

Calculate bad debts using
various bases.
(SO 3) AP

P8–2B Information related to Tisipai Company for 2005 is summarized below:

Total credit sales	$1,650,000
Accounts receivable at December 31	625,000
Accounts receivable written off during 2005	24,000
Accounts receivable recovered later during 2005	4,000

Instructions

(a) Assume that Tisipai Company estimates its bad debts expense to be 2.5% of credit sales. What amount of bad debts expense will the company record if Allowance for Doubtful Accounts has a credit balance of $3,500?

(b) Assume that Tisipai Company estimates its bad debts expense to be 6% of total accounts receivable. What amount of bad debts expense will the company record if Allowance for Doubtful Accounts has a credit balance of $3,500?

(c) Assume the same facts as in (b), except that there is a $2,250 debit balance in Allowance for Doubtful Accounts. What amount of bad debts expense will the company record?

(d) Assume Tisipai Company used an aging schedule and estimated uncollectible accounts will be $52,000. What amount of bad debts expense will Tisipai Company record if there is a debit balance of $2,750 in the Allowance for Doubtful Accounts before making the adjustment?

(e) How does the later recovery of an account previously written off affect the net realizable value of accounts receivable?

(f) How does the later recovery of an account previously written off affect the bad debts expense for the current period?

Prepare entries for bad
debts using aging
schedule.
(SO 3) AP

P8–3B Presented below is an aging schedule for Hake Company for the year ended December 31, 2004:

Customer	Total	Number of Days Outstanding			
		0–30	31–60	61–90	91–120
Benson	$ 22,000		$10,000	$12,000	
Ripper	40,000	$ 40,000			
Bilck	57,000	16,000	6,000		$35,000
Freeland	30,000				30,000
Others	136,000	106,000	16,000	14,000	
	$285,000	$162,000	$32,000	$26,000	$65,000
Estimated percentage uncollectible		4%	8%	12%	25%
Estimated bad debts					

At December 31, the unadjusted balance in Allowance for Doubtful Accounts is a credit of $7,500.

Instructions

(a) Calculate the estimated bad debts on December 31, 2004, from the above information.

(b) Journalize and post the adjusting entry for bad debts at December 31, 2004.

(c) Journalize and post the following transactions in the year 2005 to the allowance account:

1. On March 31, an $1,800 customer balance originating in 2004 is judged uncollectible.

2. On May 31, a cheque for $800 is received in partial settlement from the customer whose account was written off as uncollectible on March 31. The remainder is anticipated to be collected in the near future.

(d) Journalize the adjusting entry for bad debts on December 31, 2005. Assume that the unadjusted balance in Allowance for Doubtful Accounts is a credit balance of $3,770. The 2005 aging schedule indicates that total estimated bad debts in 2005 will be $38,500.

P8–4B Imagine Co. uses the allowance method to estimate uncollectible accounts receivable. The computer produced the following aging of the accounts receivable at year end:

Calculate bad debts and prepare entries using aging schedule.
(SO 3) AP

Customer	Total	Number of Days Outstanding			
		0–30	31–60	61–90	91–120
Accounts receivable	$385,000	$220,000	$100,000	$40,000	$25,000
Percentage uncollectible		1%	4%	8%	25%
Estimated bad debts					

Instructions

(a) Calculate the total estimated bad debts based on the above information.
(b) Prepare the year-end adjusting journal entry to record the bad debts using the aged uncollectible accounts receivable determined in (a). Assume the opening balance in Allowance for Doubtful Accounts is a $9,500 debit.
(c) Of the above accounts, $6,500 is determined to be uncollectible. Prepare the journal entry to write off the uncollectible accounts.
(d) The company collects $3,000 of the $6,500 account receivable that was determined to be uncollectible in (c). No further amounts are anticipated to be collected. Prepare the journal entry (or entries) necessary to restore the account and record the cash collection.
(e) Comment on how your answers to parts (a) to (d) would change if Imagine Co. used a percentage of total accounts receivable of 3% rather than aging the accounts receivable.
(f) What are the advantages for the company of aging the accounts receivable rather than applying a percentage to total accounts receivable?

P8–5B At the beginning of the current period, Hong Co. had balances in Accounts Receivable of $400,000 and in Allowance for Doubtful Accounts of $22,000 (credit). During the period, it had net credit sales of $950 thousand and collections of $1,021 thousand. It wrote off accounts receivable of $29,250 as uncollectible. However, $1,750 of one of the accounts written off as uncollectible was recovered before the end of the current period.

Prepare entries for accounts receivable and bad debts using various bases.
(SO 3) AP

Instructions

(a) Prepare the entries to record sales and collections during the period.
(b) Prepare the entries to record the write-off of uncollectible accounts and the recovery of accounts written off as uncollectible during the period. Determine the unadjusted ending balance in Accounts Receivable and Allowance for Doubtful Accounts.
(c) Prepare the entry to record bad debts expense for the period if Hong Co. estimates that 6% of total accounts receivable will become uncollectible.
(d) Determine the ending balances in Accounts Receivable and Allowance for Doubtful Accounts.
(e) What is the net realizable value of receivables at the end of the period?
(f) What is the bad debts expense on the income statement for the period?
(g) Now assume that Hong Co. uses the percentage of sales basis instead of the percentage of receivables basis to estimate uncollectible accounts. Repeat (c) through (f) assuming Hong estimates 1.5% of the net credit sales will become uncollectible.

P8–6B The balance sheets of Beancounter and Company on December 31, Year 1 and Year 2, showed gross accounts receivable of $3,250 thousand and $3,760 thousand, respectively. The credit balances in Allowance for Doubtful Accounts at the end of Year 1 and Year 2—after adjusting entries—were $227,500 and $263,500, respectively. Accounts receivable written off amounted to $195,000 during Year 1 and $215,500 during Year 2.

All sales were made on account. Bad debts expense for each year was estimated as 1% of sales.

Analyse accounts and prepare entries for accounts receivable and bad debts.
(SO 2, 3) AN

Instructions

Show (in summary form) all the journal entries made during Year 2 that had an effect on Accounts Receivable or Allowance for Doubtful Accounts. (*Hint:* You may find T accounts helpful in analysing this problem.)

Prepare entries for
accounts receivable
and bad debts. Show
statement presentation.
(SO 2, 3, 4, 7) AN

P8–7B Assiniboia Co. uses the percentage of sales basis to record bad debts expense for its monthly financial statements and the percentage of receivables basis for its year-end financial statements. Assiniboia Co. has a May 31 fiscal year end and closes temporary accounts annually.

On March 31, 2005, after completing its month-end adjustments, it had accounts receivable of $892,500, a credit balance of $47,750 in Allowance for Doubtful Accounts, and bad debts expense of $115,880. During April and May the following occurred:

April

1. Sold $646,900 of merchandise on credit.
2. Sold $197,500 of merchandise for cash.
3. Accepted returns of $10,900 of the merchandise sold on credit. These customers were issued credit memos.
4. Refunded $2,545 cash to customers for returns of cash purchases of merchandise.
5. Collected $696,250 cash on account from customers.
6. In addition to the cash collected in (5) above, collected $3,570 cash from a customer whose account had been written off in July.
7. Wrote off as uncollectible $39,920 of accounts receivable.
8. As part of the month-end adjusting entries, recorded bad debts expense of 3% of net credit sales for the month.

May

1. Credit sales during the month were $763,600.
2. Cash sales in October were $182,550.
3. Customers returned $13,880 of merchandise purchased on credit and $3,910 of merchandise purchased with cash. Issued credit memos to credit customers and refunded cash to cash customers.
4. Received $4,450 cash from a customer whose account had been written off in September.
5. Collected $785,240 cash, in addition to the cash collected in (4) above, from customers on account.
6. Wrote off $32,660 of accounts receivable as uncollectible.
7. Recorded the year-end adjustment for bad debts. Uncollectible accounts were estimated to be 6% of accounts receivable.

Instructions

(a) Prepare journal entries to record the above transactions and adjustments.
(b) Show how Accounts Receivable will appear on the May 31, 2005, balance sheet.
(c) What amount will be reported as bad debts expense on the income statement for the year ended May 31, 2005?

Prepare entries for
receivables.
(SO 2, 4, 5, 6) AP

P8–8B On January 1, 2004, Vu Co. had accounts receivable of $146,000, notes receivable of $12,000, interest receivable of $80, and allowance for doubtful accounts of $13,200. The note receivable is from the Annabelle Company. It is a five-month, 8% note dated November 30, 2003, and the appropriate interest has been accrued. Vu Co. prepares financial statements annually for the year ended December 31. Assume interest is due at maturity unless otherwise specified. During the year, the following selected transactions occurred:

Jan.   5 Sold $16,000 of merchandise to George Company, terms n/15.
       20 Accepted George Company's $16,000, three-month, 9% note for the balance due.
Feb. 18 Sold $8,000 of merchandise to Swaim Company and accepted Swaim's $8,000, six-month, 7% note for the amount due.
Apr. 20 Collected George Company note in full.
       30 Received payment in full from Annabelle Company for the amount due.
May 25 Accepted Avery Inc.'s $6,000, three-month, 8% note in settlement of a past-due balance on account. Interest is payable monthly.
June 25 Received one month's interest from Avery Inc. on its note.
July 25 Received one month's interest from Avery Inc. on its note.
Aug. 18 Received payment in full from Swaim Company for the note due.
       23 The Avery Inc. note was dishonoured. Avery Inc. is bankrupt and future payment is not expected.
Sept. 1 Sold $10,000 of merchandise to Young Company and accepted a $10,000, six-month, 7.25% note for the amount due.

Nov. 22 News reports indicate that several key officers of Young Company have been arrested on charges of fraud and embezzlement, and that the company's operations have been shut down indefinitely.

    30 Gave MRC Corp a $5,000 cash loan and accepted MRC's 12%, four-month note receivable.

Dec. 31 Accrued interest is recorded on any outstanding notes at year end.

Instructions

(a) Journalize the transactions.
(b) If there have been no further reports on the situation regarding Young Company, do you think the note should be written off? If not, do you think interest should be accrued on the note receivable at year end?

P8–9B Ouellette Co. adjusts its books monthly. On June 30, 2005, selected ledger account balances are as follows:

Prepare entries for notes receivable. Show balance sheet presentation.
(SO 4, 5, 6, 7) AP

Notes Receivable	$19,800
Interest Receivable	?

Notes receivable include the following:

Date	Maker	Principal	Term	Interest
May 1	Alder Inc.	$6,000	2 months	6.00%
May 31	Dorn Co.	4,800	2 months	6.75%
June 30	MJH Corp.	9,000	6 months	5.00%

Interest is due at maturity. During July, the following transactions were completed:

July 1 Received payment in full from Alder Inc. on the amount due.
    5 Made sales of $7,800 on Ouellette credit cards.
  14 Made sales of $700 on MasterCard credit cards. The credit card service charge is 3%.
  16 Added $415 to Ouellette credit card customer balances for financing charges on unpaid balances.
  31 Received notice that the Dorn Co. note has been dishonoured. Assume that Dorn Co. is expected to pay in the future.

Instructions

(a) Calculate the interest receivable at June 30.
(b) Journalize the July transactions and the July 31 adjusting entry for accrued interest receivable.
(c) Enter the balances at July 1 in the receivables accounts. Post the entries to all the receivables accounts.
(d) Show the balance sheet presentation of the receivables accounts at July 31, 2005.
(e) How would the journal entry on July 31 differ if Dorn Co. were not expected to pay in the future?

P8–10B Presented here is basic financial information (in U.S. millions) from the 2002 financial statements of **Nike** and **Reebok**:

Calculate and interpret ratios.
(SO 7) AN

	Nike	Reebok
Sales	$9,893.0	$3,127.9
Allowance for doubtful accounts, Jan. 1	72.1	55.2
Allowance for doubtful accounts, Dec. 31	77.4	60.9
Accounts receivable balance (gross), Jan. 1	1,693.5	438.6
Accounts receivable balance (gross), Dec. 31	1,884.5	482.7

Instructions

Calculate the receivables turnover and average collection period for both companies and compare the two companies. Comment on the difference in the two companies' collection experiences.

Continuing Cookie Chronicle

(Note: This is a continuation of the Cookie Chronicle from Chapters 1 through 7.)

Natalie has been approached by one of her friends, Curtis Lesperance. Curtis runs a coffee shop where he sells specialty coffees, and prepares and sells muffins and cookies. He is very anxious to buy one of Natalie's fine European mixers because he would then be able to prepare larger batches of muffins and cookies. Curtis, however, cannot afford to pay for the mixer for at least 30 days. He has asked Natalie if she would be willing to sell him the mixer on credit.

Natalie comes to you for advice and asks the following questions:

1. Curtis has provided me with a set of his most recent financial statements. What calculations should I do with the data from these statements and what questions should I ask him after I have analysed the statements? How will this information help me decide if I should extend credit to Curtis?
2. Is there another alternative other than extending credit to Curtis for 30 days?
3. I am thinking seriously about being able to have my customers use credit cards. What are some of the advantages and disadvantages of letting my customers pay by credit card?

The following transactions occurred in June through August:

June   1 After much thought, Natalie sells a mixer to Curtis on credit, terms n/30, for $1,025 (cost of mixer $566).
    2 Natalie meets with the bank manager and arranges to get access to a credit card account. The terms of credit card transactions are 3% of the sales transaction and a monthly equipment rental charge of $75.
   30 Natalie teaches 12 classes in June. Seven classes were paid for in cash, $875; the other five classes were paid for by credit card, $750.
   30 Natalie receives and reconciles her bank statement. She makes sure that the monthly $75 charge for the rental of the credit card equipment and the 3% fee on the credit card transactions have been correctly processed by the bank.
   30 Curtis calls Natalie. He is unable to pay the amount outstanding for another month, so he signs a one-month, 8.25%, note receivable.
July 15 Natalie sells a mixer to a friend of Curtis'. The friend pays $1,025 for the mixer by credit card (cost of mixer $566).
   30 Natalie teaches 15 classes in July. Eight classes are paid for in cash, $1,000; and seven classes are paid for by credit card, $1,050.
   31 Natalie reconciles her bank statement and makes sure the bank has recorded the correct amounts for the rental of the credit card equipment and the credit card sales.
   31 Curtis calls Natalie. He cannot pay today but hopes to have a cheque for her at the end of the week. Natalie prepares the appropriate journal entry.
Aug. 10 Curtis calls again and promises to pay at the end of August, including interest for two months.
   31 Natalie receives a cheque from Curtis in payment of his balance owing plus interest outstanding.

Instructions:

(a) Answer Natalie's questions.
(b) Prepare journal entries for the transactions that occurred in June, July, and August.

Financial Reporting and Analysis

Practice
Tools

Financial Reporting Problem

BYP8–1 The receivables turnover and collection period for **The Forzani Group Ltd.** were calculated in this chapter, based on its financial statements for the 2003 fiscal year. These financial statements are presented in Appendix A.

Instructions

(a) Calculate Forzani's receivables turnover and average collection period for the 2002 fiscal year. Note that the company's accounts receivable at the end of its 2001 fiscal year amounted to $31,600 thousand.

(b) Comment on any significant differences which you observe between the ratios for 2003 (as calculated in the chapter) and 2002 (as calculated above).

Interpreting Financial Statements

BYP8–2 **Suncor Energy Inc.** reported the following information (in millions) in its financial statements for the fiscal years 2000 through 2002:

	2002	2001	2000
Revenues (assume all credit)	$4,902	$4,194	$3,385
Accounts receivable (gross)	406	309	410
Allowance for doubtful accounts	3	3	3
Total current assets	722	622	665
Total current liabilities	797	773	837

Additional detail about Suncor's receivables includes the following:

> The company has a securitization program in place to sell to a third party, on a revolving, fully serviced, and limited recourse basis, up to $170 million of accounts receivable having a maturity of 45 days or less. As at December 31, 2002, $170 million in outstanding accounts receivable had been sold under the program.

Industry averages for the current ratio, receivables turnover, and average collection period are 1:1, 6.3 times, and 58 days, respectively.

Instructions

(a) Calculate the current ratios, receivables turnover ratios, and average collection periods for fiscal 2002 and 2001. Comment on Suncor's liquidity for each of the years and compared to the industry.

(b) Suncor has not changed the dollar amount of its allowance for doubtful accounts for several years. Comment on the relevance of this as a percentage of accounts receivable.

(c) Suncor regularly sells a portion of its accounts receivable. Comment on this practice as part of Suncor's management of its accounts receivable.

Accounting on the Web

BYP8–3 This case examines the Credit Card Costs Calculator, provided by Industry Canada. Based on how a credit card is used, we will determine which cards cost the least in interest and fees over a year. The cost of borrowing from a bank is then compared to the cost of using a credit card.

Instructions
Specific requirements of this Internet case are available on the Weygandt website.

Critical Thinking

Collaborative Learning Activity

BYP8–4 Johanna and Jake Berkvom own Campus Fashions. Since it opened, Campus Fashions has sold merchandise either for cash or on account. No credit cards have been accepted. During the past several months, the Berkvoms have begun to question their sales policies. First, they have lost some sales because of their refusal to accept credit cards. Second, representatives of two banks have been persuasive, almost convincing them to accept their credit cards. One of these, the National Bank, has stated that its credit card fee is 3%.

The Berkvoms decide that they should determine the cost of issuing their own credit card. From the accounting records of the past three years, they accumulate the following data:

	2005	2004	2003
Net credit sales	$530,000	$650,000	$400,000
Collection agency fees for slow-paying customers	2,450	2,500	2,400
Salary of part-time accounts receivable manager	4,100	4,100	4,100

Credit and collection expenses as a percentage of net credit sales are as follows: uncollectible accounts, 1.6%; billing and mailing costs, 0.5%; and credit investigation fees on new customers, 0.15%.

Johanna and Jake also determine that the average accounts receivable balance outstanding during the year is 5% of net credit sales. The Berkvoms estimate that they could earn an average of 6% annually on cash invested in other business opportunities.

Instructions
With the class divided into groups, do the following:

 (a) Prepare a table showing total credit and collection expenses in dollars and as a percentage of net credit sales for each year.
 (b) Determine the net credit and collection expenses, in dollars and as a percentage of sales, after considering the revenue not earned from other investment opportunities.
 (c) Discuss both the financial and non-financial factors that are relevant to the decision.

Communication Activity

BYP8–5 Toys for Big Boys sells snowmobiles, personal watercraft, ATVs, and the like. Recently, the credit manager of Toys for Big Boys retired. The sales staff threw him a big retirement party—they were glad to see him go, because they felt his credit policies restricted their selling ability. The sales staff convinced management that there was no need to replace the credit manager since they could handle this responsibility in addition to their sales positions.

Management was thrilled at year end when sales doubled. However, accounts receivable quadrupled and cash flow halved. The company's average collection period increased from 30 days to 120 days.

Instructions

In a memo to management, explain the financial impact of allowing the sales staff to manage the credit function. Has the business assumed any additional credit risk? What would you recommend the company do to better manage its increasing accounts receivable?

Ethics Case

BYP8–6 The comptroller of Proust Company has completed an aging schedule, using the following percentages to estimate the uncollectible accounts: 0–30 days, 5%; 31–60 days, 10%; 61–90 days, 30%; 91–120 days, 50%; and over 120 days, 80%. The president of the company, Suzanne Bros, is nervous because the bank expects the company to sustain its current growth rate of at least 5% over the next two years—the remaining term of its bank loan. President Bros suggests that the comptroller increase the percentages, which will increase the amount of the required bad debts expense adjustment. The president thinks that the lower net income (because of the increased bad debts expense) will make it easier next year to show a better growth rate.

Instructions

(a) Who are the stakeholders in this case?
(b) Does the president's request pose an ethical dilemma for the comptroller?
(c) Should the comptroller be concerned with Proust Company's growth rate in estimating the allowance? Explain your answer.

Answers to Self-Study Questions

1. b   2. b   3. d   4. c   5. c   6. a   7. b   8. d   9. a   10. c

Answer to Forzani Review It Question 1

In its balance sheet, Forzani reports accounts receivable of $38,275 thousand in the current assets section and long-term receivables of $950 thousand as other assets (detailed in Note 5).

Remember to go back to the Navigator Box at the beginning of the chapter to check off your completed work.

concepts for review >>

the navigator

Before studying this chapter, you should understand or, if necessary, review:

a. The cost principle (Ch. 1, pp. 7–8) and the matching principle. (Ch. 3, p. 101)
b. The time period assumption. (Ch. 3, p. 101)
c. What amortization is, and how to make adjustments for it. (Ch. 3, p. 113)

On the Books, Your Classroom May Be Worthless

Southern Alberta Institute of Technology: www.sait.ab.ca

CALGARY, Alta.—For a college or university, the buildings where its classes and other activities take place are some of its most important assets. Look around the campus of your own school. Where did the money for these buildings come from? Who pays to maintain them? And how much are they worth?

For the Southern Alberta Institute of Technology (SAIT) in Calgary, the first of these questions is easy. The provincial government originally financed the buildings and turned them over to SAIT.

The second question is a little more complex. SAIT receives government funding, some of which is specially earmarked to keep up the buildings. "We also get donations—from both individuals and companies—which are often designated for specific projects, such as lab and classroom renovations," explains Lisa Pilon, director of corporate reporting for the college. Day-to-day maintenance is financed with general college revenue, which comes both from tuition fees and government grants.

How much the buildings are worth is the trickiest question. For SAIT, the cost of a building is amortized over 40 years, based on its cost at the time SAIT acquired it. The school uses the straight-line method of amortization. "For example, the Heart Building, a new classroom facility we built in 2001 as part of a $176-million general expansion project, and the Clayton Caroll Automotive Centre, which opened in 2002, will not be fully amortized until 2041 and 2042 respectively," says Ms. Pilon.

In addition, SAIT's policy is to amortize major renovations over 25 years. In many organizations, renovations are amortized over the remaining useful life of the asset. But the school finds the fixed 25-year policy easier to capitalize and administer. It also avoids the problem of trying to combine original cost and renovation costs in the same account if the buildings have a remaining useful life of less than 25 years.

The original cost of a few older buildings, such as Heritage Hall, has now been completely amortized. This means that, on the books, this handsome historic building, dating from 1926, had no net book value after 1966. Which is not to say it had no market value! Heritage Hall's book value changed in 2001 when new costs associated with its renovation were added. In accordance with its renovation policy, these costs will be amortized by SAIT over the next 25 years, until 2026.

the navigator ✅

- Understand *Concepts for Review*
- Read *Feature Story*
- Scan *Study Objectives*
- Read *Chapter Preview*
- Read text and answer *Before You Go On*
- Work *Demonstration Problem*
- Review *Summary of Study Objectives*
- Answer *Self-Study Questions*
- Complete assignments

c h a p t e r   9
Long-Lived Assets

study objectives >>

the navigator

After studying this chapter, you should be able to:

1. Demonstrate how the cost principle applies to property, plant, and equipment.
2. Explain the concept of, and be able to calculate, amortization.
3. Describe and demonstrate the procedure for revising periodic amortization.
4. Distinguish between operating and capital expenditures, and prepare the entries for these expenditures.
5. Explain and demonstrate how to account for the disposal of property, plant, and equipment.
6. Calculate the periodic amortization of natural resources.
7. Contrast the accounting for intangible assets with the accounting for tangible assets.
8. Illustrate how long-lived assets are reported and analysed.

The accounting for campus buildings at the Southern Alberta Institute of Technology has important implications for the school's reported results. In this chapter, we explain the application of the cost principle of accounting to property, plant, and equipment, as well as to natural resources and intangible assets. We describe the methods that may be used to allocate the cost of an asset over its useful life. In addition, we discuss the accounting for expenditures which occur during the useful life of assets, such as the cost of renovations incurred by SAIT. We also discuss the disposition of these assets during and at the end of their useful lives.

The chapter is organized as follows:

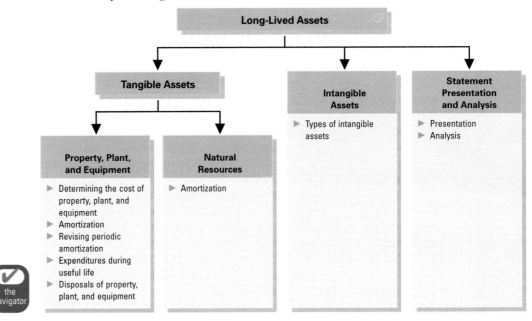

Tangible Assets

Long-lived **tangible assets** are resources that have physical substance (a definite size and shape), are used in the operations of a business, and are not intended for sale to customers. Contrary to current assets, which are used or consumed in the current accounting period, long-lived tangible assets provide benefits over many accounting periods.

Tangible assets can be subdivided into two categories: (1) property, plant, and equipment, and (2) natural resources. A key distinction between property, plant, and equipment and natural resources is that natural resources physically lose substance, or deplete, as they are used. For example, there is less of a tract of timberland (a natural resource) as the timber is cut and sold. When we use equipment, its physical substance remains the same regardless of the product it produces. We discuss each category of tangible asset in the next two sections of the chapter.

Property, Plant, and Equipment

Property, plant, and equipment are long-lived assets the company owns to support the production and sale of goods or services to consumers. Property, plant, and equipment are often subdivided into four classes:

Alternative terminology
Property, plant, and equipment are also commonly known as *fixed assets*; *land, building, and equipment*; or *capital assets*.

1. Land, such as a building site
2. Land improvements, such as driveways, parking lots, fences, and underground sprinkler systems
3. Buildings, such as stores, offices, factories, and warehouses
4. Equipment, such as store checkout counters, cash registers, coolers, office furniture, factory machinery, and delivery equipment

Except for land, these assets decline in service potential over their useful lives.

We will now learn how to determine and allocate the cost of these long-lived assets.

Determining the Cost of Property, Plant, and Equipment

Property, plant, and equipment are recorded at historical cost, in accordance with the **cost principle** of accounting. The buildings at the Southern Alberta Institute of Technology are recorded at cost. Cost includes all expenditures made to acquire the asset and **make it ready for its intended use**. For example, the cost of factory machinery includes the purchase price, freight costs paid by the purchaser, and any installation costs. All of these costs are **capitalized** (recorded as property, plant, and equipment), rather than expensed, because they will provide benefits over future periods.

study objective 1

Demonstrate how the cost principle applies to property, plant, and equipment.

Cost is measured by the cash paid in a cash transaction or by the cash equivalent price paid when noncash assets are used in payment. **The cash equivalent price is equal to the fair market value of the asset given up.** Or, if that value cannot be clearly determined, the cash equivalent price is the fair market value of the asset received. Once cost is established, it becomes the basis of accounting for the asset over its useful life. Current market or replacement values are not used after an asset is acquired unless the values permanently decline below net book value (cost less accumulated amortization). If an asset's fair market value falls below its net book value, an impairment loss should be recorded. An impairment loss recognizes the decline in value, reducing the asset's net book value to its fair market value. If the fair market value later increases, the book value is *not* adjusted for any recovery in value.

Unlike inventories, the lower of cost and market rule does not apply automatically to property, plant, and equipment. Because inventory is expected to be converted into cash within the year, it is important to value it annually at the lesser of its cost and saleable, or market, value. In contrast, property, plant, and equipment are used in operations over a longer term and are not available for resale. The going concern assumption assumes that a company will recover at least the cost of its long-lived assets. So it is only when a permanent impairment occurs in their value that these assets are written down to market.

Write-downs do not happen often, and are subject to certain recoverability tests before recording any decrease in value. Fewer than 2% of the companies surveyed by *Financial Reporting in Canada* in a recent year wrote down any property, plant, and equipment.

The application of the cost principle to each of the major classes of property, plant, and equipment is explained in more detail in the following sections.

Land

The cost of land includes (1) the purchase price and (2) closing costs such as survey and legal fees. All the costs to prepare land for its intended use are debited to the land account. When vacant land is acquired, these might include costs for clearing, draining, filling, and grading the land. Sometimes the land has a building on it that must be removed before construction of a new building begins. In this case, all demolition and removal costs (less any proceeds from salvaged materials) are debited to the land account.

To illustrate, assume that the Budovitch Manufacturing Company acquires real estate for $100,000 cash. The property contained an old warehouse that is removed at a net cost of $6,000 ($7,500 in costs less $1,500 of proceeds from salvaged materials). Additional expenditures include the legal fee of $3,000. The cost of the land is $109,000, calculated as follows:

Land

Cash price of property	$100,000
Net cost of removing warehouse	6,000
Legal fee	3,000
Cost of land	$109,000

In recording the acquisition, Land is debited for $109,000 and Cash is credited for $109,000.

Land Improvements

Land is a unique long-lived asset. Its cost is not amortized—allocated over its useful life—because land has an unlimited useful life. However, there are costs to improve the land with structures that do have limited useful lives. Land improvements are structural additions made to land, such as driveways, parking lots, fences, and landscaping. Land improvements decline in service potential over time and require maintenance and replacement to maintain their value. Because of this, these costs are recorded separately from land and amortized over their useful lives.

Buildings

All costs related to the purchase or construction of a building are debited to the buildings account. When a building is purchased, such costs include the purchase price and closing costs (e.g., legal fees). Costs to make the building ready for its intended use can include expenditures for remodelling, and for replacing or repairing the roof, floors, electrical wiring, and plumbing.

When a new building is built, at your school, for example, cost includes the contract price for construction of the building plus payments for architects' fees, building permits, and excavation costs. Interest costs incurred to finance the project are also included in the cost of the asset when a significant period of time passes before the building is ready for use. In these circumstances, interest costs are considered as necessary as materials and labour. Only the interest costs which occur during the construction period are included. After construction is finished, future interest payments on funds borrowed to finance the cost of the constructed building are debited to Interest Expense.

Equipment

The cost of equipment includes the cash purchase price and other related costs. These costs include freight charges and insurance during transit if they are paid by the purchaser. They also include costs to assemble, install, and test the unit. Costs such as motor vehicle licences and insurance on company trucks and cars are not capitalized as equipment. They are annual recurring expenditures that do not benefit future periods. Two criteria apply in determining the cost of the equipment: (1) the frequency of the cost—one-time or recurring—and (2) the benefit period—life of asset or one year.

To illustrate, assume that O'Reilly Company purchases a used delivery truck on August 1 for $22,000 cash. Related expenditures include painting and lettering, $500; a motor vehicle licence, $80; and an insurance policy, $2,600. The cost of the delivery truck is $22,500, calculated as follows:

	Delivery Truck
Cash price	$22,000
Painting and lettering	500
Cost of delivery truck	$22,500

The cost of the motor vehicle licence is expensed when its cost is incurred and the cost of the insurance policy is recorded as a prepaid asset. The entry to record the purchase of the truck and related expenditures is as follows:

Aug. 1	Delivery Truck	22,500	
	Licence Expense	80	
	Prepaid Insurance	2,600	
	Cash		25,180
	To record purchase of delivery truck and		
	related expenditures.		

```
 A     =   L   +   OE
+22,500             -80
 +2,600
-25,180
```
Cash flows: -25,180

Basket Purchase

Property, plant, and equipment are often purchased together for a single price. This is known as a **basket purchase**. We need to know the cost of each individual asset in order to journalize the purchase, and later to calculate amortization. When a basket purchase occurs, we determine individual costs by allocating the total price paid for the group of assets to each individual asset based on their relative fair market values.

Alternative terminology
A basket purchase is also known as a *lump-sum purchase*.

To illustrate, assume Sega Company acquired a building and a parcel of land on July 31 for $150,000, paying $25,000 in cash and incurring a mortgage payable for the balance. The land was recently appraised at $60,000. The building was appraised at $100,000. The $150,000 cost should be allocated on the basis of fair market (appraised) values as shown in Illustration 9-1.

	Fair Market Value	Allocated Percentage	Allocated Cost
Land	$ 60,000	37.5% ($60,000 ÷ $160,000)	$ 56,250 ($150,000 × 37.5%)
Building	100,000	62.5% ($100,000 ÷ $160,000)	93,750 ($150,000 × 62.5%)
Totals	$160,000	100.0%	$150,000

Illustration 9-1 ◄

Allocating cost in a basket purchase

The journal entry to record this purchase is as follows:

July 31	Land	56,250	
	Building	93,750	
	Cash		25,000
	Mortgage Payable		125,000
	To record purchase of land and building, with costs		
	allocated based on appraised values of $60,000 and		
	$100,000, respectively.		

```
 A     =    L     +   OE
+56,250   +125,000
+93,750
-25,000
```
Cash flows: -25,000

BEFORE YOU GO ON . . .

▶Review It

1. What are long-lived assets? What are the major classes of property, plant, and equipment?
2. How is the cost principle applied to accounting for property, plant, and equipment?
3. What is a basket purchase?
4. What is the cost of each type of capital asset The Forzani Group Ltd. reports in Note 3 to its balance sheet? The answer to this question is at the end of the chapter.

▶Do It

Assume that factory machinery is purchased on November 6 for $10,000 cash and a $40,000 note payable. Related cash expenditures include insurance during shipping, $500; the annual insurance policy, $750; and installation and testing, $1,000. Prepare the journal entry to record these expenditures.

Action Plan

- Identify which expenditures are made to get the machinery ready for its intended use. Capitalize these costs because they benefit future periods.
- Expense the operating costs that benefit only the current period, or which are recurring costs.

Solution

Factory Machinery

Purchase price	$50,000
Insurance during shipping	500
Installation and testing	1,000
Cost of machinery	$51,500

The entry to record the purchase and related expenditures is:

Nov. 6	Factory Machinery	51,500	
	Prepaid Insurance	750	
	Cash ($10,000 + $500 + $750 + $1,000)		12,250
	Note Payable		40,000
	To record purchase of factory machinery and related expenditures.		

the navigator

Related exercise material: BE9–1, BE9–2, BE9–3, E9–1, and E9–2.

Amortization

study objective 2

Explain the concept of, and be able to calculate, amortization.

Alternative terminology
Amortization is also commonly known as *depreciation*.

As explained in Chapter 3, **amortization is the allocation of the cost of a long-lived asset to expense over its useful (service) life in a rational and systematic manner.** The allocation of cost matches expenses with revenues, in accordance with the matching principle.

As also learned in Chapter 3, amortization is allocated through an adjusting journal entry which debits Amortization Expense and credits Accumulated Amortization. Amortization Expense is an income statement account. Accumulated Amortization appears on the balance sheet as a contra account to the related asset account. This contra asset account is similar in purpose to the one used in Chapter 8 for the allowance for doubtful accounts. Both contra accounts reduce assets to their respective carrying values (*net realizable value* for accounts receivable and *net book value* for long-lived assets).

Recognizing amortization for an asset does not result in the accumulation of cash for the replacement of the asset. The balance in Accumulated Amortization represents the total amount of the asset's cost that has been allocated to expense—it is not a cash fund. The Cash account is not affected by the adjusting entry to record amortization described above.

It is important to understand that **amortization is a process of cost allocation, not a process of asset valuation**, as shown in Illustration 9-2. Accountants do not measure the change in an asset's market value during ownership, because property, plant, and equipment are not for resale. Current market values are not relevant (unless a permanent impairment loss has occurred). So, the net book value of property, plant, or equipment (cost less accumulated amortization) may differ significantly from its market value. This is why Heritage Hall in our feature story can have a low book value and still have a substantial market value.

Illustration 9-2 ◄
Amortization as an allocation concept

Amortization applies to three classes of property, plant, and equipment: land improvements, buildings, and equipment. Each of these classes is considered an amortizable asset. Why? Because the usefulness to the company and the revenue-producing ability of each class declines over the asset's useful life. Amortization does not apply to land, because its usefulness and revenue-producing ability generally remain the same over time. In fact, in many cases, the usefulness of land increases because of the scarcity of good land sites. Thus, land is not an amortizable asset.

During an amortizable asset's useful life, its revenue-producing ability declines because of **physical factors** such as wear and tear. A delivery truck that has been driven 100,000 kilometres is less useful to a company than one driven only 1,000 kilometres.

Revenue-producing ability may also decline because of **economic factors** such as obsolescence. Obsolescence means being out of date before the asset physically wears out. For example, the rapid pace of technological change forces frequent computer and other electronic upgrades long before the equipment wears out. It is important to understand that amortization only approximates the decline in revenue-producing ability. It does not exactly measure the true effects of physical or economic factors.

Factors in Calculating Amortization

Three factors affect the calculation of amortization:

1. Cost. The factors that affect the cost of an amortizable asset were explained earlier in this chapter. Recall that property, plant, and equipment are recorded at cost, in accordance with the cost principle. This includes all costs incurred to get the asset ready for use.
2. Useful life. **Useful life** is an estimate of the expected productive life, also called the *service life*, of the asset. Useful life may be expressed in terms of time, units of activity (such as machine hours), or units of output. Useful life is an estimate. In making the estimate, management considers factors such as the intended use of the asset, its expected need for repair and maintenance, and its vulnerability to obsolescence. Past experience with similar assets is often helpful in estimating expected useful life.
3. Residual value. **Residual value** is an estimate of the asset's value at the end of its useful life. This value may be based on the asset's worth as scrap or on its expected trade-in value. Residual value is not amortized, since the amount is expected to be recovered at the end of the asset's useful life. Like useful life, residual value is an estimate. In making the estimate, management considers how it plans to dispose of the asset and its experience with similar assets.

Alternative terminology
Another term sometimes used for residual value is *salvage value*.

Illustration 9-3 summarizes these three factors.

Illustration 9-3 ▶

Three factors in calculating amortization

Cost: All expenditures necessary to acquire the asset and make it ready for its intended use

Useful life: Estimate of the expected life based on need for repair, service life, and vulnerability to obsolescence

Residual value: Estimate of the asset's value at the end of its useful life

Amortization Methods

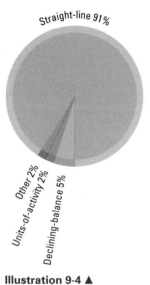

Straight-line 91%

Other 2%
Units-of-activity 2%
Declining-balance 5%

Illustration 9-4 ▲

Use of amortization methods in Canadian public companies

Amortization is generally calculated using one of the following methods:

1. Straight-line
2. Declining-balance
3. Units-of-activity

Each method is acceptable under generally accepted accounting principles. Management selects the method it believes to be appropriate in the circumstances. The goal is to choose the amortization method that best measures an asset's contribution to revenue over its useful life. Once a method is chosen, it should be applied consistently over the useful life of the asset. Consistency makes the comparison of financial statements easier.

Illustration 9-4 shows the distribution of these three amortization methods in Canadian public companies. Many companies use more than one method—for example, straight-line amortization for buildings and declining-balance for equipment. Regardless of how many methods are used, nearly every company uses the straight-line method of amortization.

We will learn how to calculate the three amortization methods and will compare them, using the following data for a small delivery truck bought by 1 Stop Florists on January 1, 2005:

Cost	$25,000
Expected residual value	$2,000
Estimated useful life (in years)	5
Estimated useful life (in kilometres)	200,000

Straight-Line. Under the straight-line method, amortization expense is the same for each year of the asset's useful life. To calculate amortization expense, we must first determine the amortizable cost. Amortizable cost is the cost of the asset less its residual value. It is the total amount that can be amortized. Amortizable cost is divided by the asset's useful life to determine the annual amortization expense. The calculation of amortization expense in the first year for 1 Stop Florists' delivery truck is shown in Illustration 9-5.

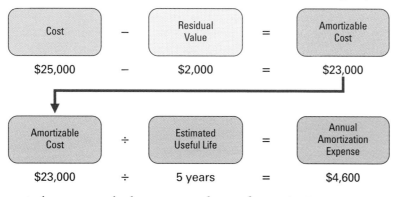

Illustration 9-5 ◄

Formula for straight-line method

Alternatively, we can calculate an annual rate of amortization:

Illustration 9-6 ◄

Straight-line amortization rate

Another way to calculate the straight-line rate of amortization is to divide amortization expense by the amortizable cost. For 1 Stop Florists, this would be as follows: $4,600 ÷ $23,000 = 20% per year. When an annual rate is used, the straight-line percentage rate is applied to the amortizable cost of the asset, as shown in the following amortization schedule:

Illustration 9-7 ◄

Straight-line amortization schedule

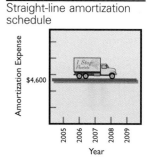

	1 STOP FLORISTS				
Year	Amortizable Cost	× Amortization Rate	= Amortization Expense	Accumulated Amortization	Net Book Value
					$25,000
2005	$23,000	20%	$ 4,600	$ 4,600	20,400
2006	23,000	20%	4,600	9,200	15,800
2007	23,000	20%	4,600	13,800	11,200
2008	23,000	20%	4,600	18,400	6,600
2009	23,000	20%	4,600	23,000	2,000
			$23,000		

Note that the amortization expense of $4,600 is the same each year. The Amortization Expense column total is the amortizable cost of the asset over its accounting life. The book value at the end of the useful life is equal to the estimated $2,000 residual value.

What happens when an asset is purchased during the year, rather than on January 1 as in our example? Most companies **prorate the annual amortization** for the time used. If 1 Stop Florists had purchased the delivery truck on April 1, 2005, the amortization for 2005 would be $3,450 ($23,000 × 20% × $\frac{9}{12}$). Note that amortization is normally rounded to the nearest month. Since amortization is an estimate only, calculating it to the nearest day offers a false sense of accuracy.

Some companies establish a simple convention for partial period amortization, rather than calculating amortization monthly. Companies may choose to charge a full year's amortization in the year of acquisition and none in the year of disposal. Others may charge a half year's amortization in the year of acquisition and a half year's amortization in the year of disposal. Whatever the policy chosen for partial-year acquisitions, the impact is not significant over time if the policy is applied consistently.

As indicated earlier, the straight-line method of amortization is the most popular. Many large companies, including Bell Canada, Bombardier, Canadian Pacific, Domtar, and Loblaw, use the straight-line method. It is simple to apply, and it matches expenses with revenues when the asset is used in a consistent way throughout its service life. In the feature story, SAIT uses the straight-line method of amortization for its buildings.

Declining-Balance.   The **declining-balance method** produces a decreasing annual amortization expense over the asset's useful life. The method has this name because the periodic amortization is based on a **declining book value** of the asset. The annual amortization expense is calculated by multiplying the book value at the beginning of the year by the straight-line amortization rate. The amortization rate remains constant from year to year, but the book value the rate is applied to declines each year.

Book value for the first year is the cost of the asset. This is because the balance in accumulated amortization at the beginning of the asset's useful life is zero. In the following years, the book value is the difference between cost and accumulated amortization at the beginning of the year. Unlike the other amortization methods, the declining-balance method does not use amortizable cost. **Residual value is ignored in determining the amount the rate of amortization is applied to.** Residual value does, however, limit the total amortization that can be taken. Amortization stops when the asset's book value equals its expected residual value.

Varying rates of amortization may be used, depending on how fast the company wishes to accelerate amortization. You will find rates such as 1 time (single), 1.5 times, 2 times (double), and even 3 times (triple) the straight-line rate of amortization. An amortization rate that is often used is double the straight-line rate. This method is referred to as the **double declining-balance method**. If 1 Stop Florists uses the double declining-balance method, the amortization rate is 40% (2 × the straight-line rate of 20%). The calculation of amortization for the first year on the delivery truck follows:

Illustration 9-8 ▶

Formula for double declining-balance method

Net Book Value at Beginning of Year	×	Straight-Line Rate × 2	=	Annual Amortization Expense
$25,000	×	40%	=	$10,000

Illustration 9-9 shows the amortization schedule under this method:

Illustration 9-9 ▶

Double declining-balance amortization schedule

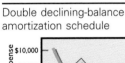
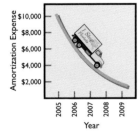

	1 STOP FLORISTS				
Year	Net Book Value Beginning of Year	× Amortization Rate	= Amortization Expense	Accumulated Amortization	Net Book Value
					$25,000
2005	$25,000	40%	$10,000	$10,000	15,000
2006	15,000	40%	6,000	16,000	9,000
2007	9,000	40%	3,600	19,600	5,400
2008	5,400	40%	2,160	21,760	3,240
2009	3,240	40%	1,240*	23,000	**2,000**
			$23,000		

* Calculation of $1,296 ($3,240 × 40%) is adjusted to $1,240 in order for net book value to equal residual value.

You can see that the delivery truck is 70% amortized ($16,000 ÷ $23,000) at the end of the second year. Under the straight-line method it would be amortized 40% ($9,200 ÷ $23,000) at that time. Because the declining-balance method produces a higher amortization expense in the early years than the later years, it is considered an accelerated amortization method.

The declining-balance method respects the matching principle. The higher amortization expense in early years is matched with the higher benefits received in these years. A lower amortization expense is recognized in later years when the asset's contribution to revenue is less. Also, some assets lose their usefulness rapidly because of obsolescence. In these cases, the declining-balance method provides a more appropriate amortization amount.

When an asset is purchased during the year, the first year's declining-balance amortization must be prorated. For example, if 1 Stop Florists had purchased the delivery truck on April 1, 2005, the amortization for the partial year would be $7,500 ($25,000 × 40% × $\frac{9}{12}$). The net book value for calculating amortization in 2006 would then become $17,500 ($25,000 − $7,500). The amortization for 2006 would be $7,000 ($17,500 × 40%). Future calculations would follow from these amounts until the net book value equalled the residual value.

While the declining-balance method is not as popular as the straight-line method, it is still used by many companies, including Canadian Tire, Cara Operations, Le Château, and Maclean Hunter. In some cases, this method is chosen because it provides the best match of cost and benefit. In other cases, declining-balance is chosen because it must be used for income tax purposes (discussed later in this chapter), and it is simpler to use the same method for both accounting and tax purposes.

Units-of-Activity. Under the units-of-activity method, useful life is expressed as the total units of activity or production expected from the asset, rather than as a time period. The units-of-activity method is ideally suited to factory machinery where production is measured in units of output or machine hours. This method can also be used for assets such as delivery equipment (kilometres driven) and airplanes (hours in use). The units-of-activity method is generally not suitable for buildings or furniture, because amortization of these assets is more a function of time than of use.

In this method, the total units of activity for the entire useful life are estimated. This amount is divided into the amortizable cost to determine the amortization cost per unit. The amortization cost per unit is then applied to the units of activity during the year to determine the annual amortization expense.

To illustrate, assume that the 1 Stop Florist delivery truck is driven 30,000 kilometres in the first year of a total estimated life of 200,000 kilometres. Illustration 9-10 shows the calculation of amortization expense in the first year.

Alternative terminology
The units-of-activity method is often called the *units-of-production* method.

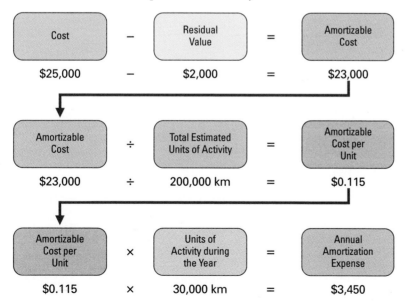

Illustration 9-10 ◀
Formula for units-of-activity method

The units-of-activity amortization schedule, using assumed kilometres, follows in Illustration 9-11:

Illustration 9-11 ▶

Units-of-activity amortization
schedule

1 STOP FLORISTS

Year	Units of Activity	×	Amortizable Cost/Unit	=	Amortization Expense	Accumulated Amortization	Net Book Value
							$25,000
2005	30,000		$0.115		$ 3,450	$ 3,450	21,550
2006	60,000		$0.115		6,900	10,350	14,650
2007	40,000		$0.115		4,600	14,950	10,050
2008	50,000		$0.115		5,750	20,700	4,300
2009	20,000		$0.115		2,300	23,000	**2,000**
	200,000				$23,000		

This method is easy to apply when assets are purchased during the year. When this happens, the productivity of the asset for the partial year is used in calculating the amortization. The units of activity, therefore, do not need to be adjusted for partial periods as they already reflect how much the asset was used during the specific period.

The units-of-activity method is not nearly as popular as the other methods, mostly because it is often difficult to make a reasonable estimate of total activity. However, this method is used by some very large companies such as Boise Cascade, Imperial Metals, Imperial Oil, and Pan-Canadian. When the productivity of the asset varies significantly from one period to another, the units-of-activity method results in the best matching of expenses with revenues.

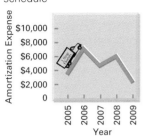

ACCOUNTING IN ACTION ▶ Business Insight

Why does Gingiss Formalwear have 70 amortization accounts and use the units-of-activity method for its tuxedos? The reason is that Gingiss wants to track wear and tear on each of its 16,000 tuxedos individually. Each tuxedo has a bar code, like a box of cereal at the grocery store. When a tux is rented, a clerk runs its code across an electronic scanner. At year end, the computer adds up the total rentals for each of the tuxedos, then divides this number by expected total use to calculate the rate. For instance, on one dolphin-grey tux, Gingiss expects a life of 30 rentals. In one year, the tux was rented 13 times. The amortization rate for that period was 43% (13 ÷ 30) of the amortizable cost.

Comparison of Amortization Methods

Illustration 9-12 presents a comparison of annual and total amortization expense for 1 Stop Florists under each of the three amortization methods. In addition, if we assume for simplicity that net income before deducting amortization expense is $50,000 for each of the five years, we can clearly see the impact the choice of method has on net income.

Illustration 9-12 ▶

Comparison of amortization
methods

Year	Straight-Line Amortization Expense	Straight-Line Net Income	Double Declining-Balance Amortization Expense	Double Declining-Balance Net Income	Units-of-Activity Amortization Expense	Units-of-Activity Net Income
2005	$4,600	$ 45,400	$10,000	$ 40,000	$ 3,450	$ 46,550
2006	4,600	45,400	6,000	44,000	6,900	43,100
2007	4,600	45,400	3,600	46,400	4,600	45,400
2008	4,600	45,400	2,160	47,840	5,750	44,250
2009	4,600	45,400	1,240	48,760	2,300	47,700
	$23,000	$227,000	$23,000	$227,000	$23,000	$227,000

Straight-line amortization results in a constant amount of amortization expense and net income each year. Declining-balance results in a higher amortization expense in early years, and lower income. This method results in a lower amortization expense in later years, with higher income. Results with the units-of-activity method vary depending on actual usage each year. While the annual amortization expense and net income vary each year among the methods, *total* amortization expense and total net income are the same over the five-year period.

Each method is acceptable because each recognizes the decline in service potential of the asset in a rational and systematic manner. Which method is preferable? There is no easy answer to this question.

GAAP requires businesses to match the cost of a long-lived asset to the revenue produced by that asset. Since the pattern of revenue production is different for each type of asset, each amortization method should be chosen based on the revenue pattern of the specific asset. For an asset that generates revenues fairly consistently over time, the straight-line method is appropriate. The declining-balance method best fits assets that are more productive—generating greater revenues—in the earlier years of their life. The units-of-activity method applies well to assets whose usage varies substantially over time.

► **Ethics note**
Practical considerations, rather than theoretical ones, often influence a manager's choice of amortization method—ease of use, convenience, tradition.

Amortization and Income Tax

The Canada Customs and Revenue Agency (CCRA) allows taxpayers to deduct amortization expense when calculating taxable income. For accounting purposes, a company should choose the amortization method that best matches revenues to expenses. However, the CCRA does not permit a choice among the three amortization methods. Income tax regulations require the taxpayer to use the single declining-balance method on the tax return.

In addition, the CCRA does not permit taxpayers to estimate the useful lives, or amortization rates, of assets. It groups assets into various classes and provides maximum amortization rates for each class. Amortization allowed for income tax purposes is calculated on a class (group) basis and is called **capital cost allowance (CCA)**. Selected asset classes and CCA rates are shown below:

Class	Asset Group	CCA Rate
Class 1	Buildings	4%
Class 8	Office equipment	20%
Class 10.1	Automobiles	30%
Class 10	Computers	30%
Class 12	Computer software	100%
Class 43	Manufacturing and processing equipment	30%

As part of its policy to minimize alternative treatments, the CCRA also sets partial-year amortization rules. Only one-half of the CCA is allowed in the year of acquisition. Capital cost allowance is an optional deduction from taxable income. While businesses must deduct amortization for accounting purposes (to fulfill the matching principle), they may choose to deduct varying amounts of CCA for tax purposes, ranging from none to the maximum specified amount for the class.

Helpful hint Guideline useful lives (amortization rates) for specific types of assets are provided by the CCRA for income tax purposes. However, the useful life chosen for accounting purposes must be based on management's own expectations.

BEFORE YOU GO ON . . .

►Review It

1. What is the relationship, if any, of amortization to (a) cost allocation, (b) asset valuation, and (c) cash accumulation?
2. What are the formulas for calculating annual amortization under each of the amortization methods—straight-line, declining-balance, and units-of-activity?
3. How do annual amortization and net income under each method differ over the useful life of the asset?

►Do It

On January 1, 2005, the Iron Mountain Ski Company purchases a new snow grooming machine for $50,000. The machine is estimated to have a five-year life with a $2,000 residual value. It is also expected to have a total useful life of 6,000 hours. It is used 1,000 hours during 2005 and 1,200 hours during 2006. How much amortization expense should Iron Mountain Ski record in each of 2005 and 2006 using each of the following methods of amortization: (a) straight-line, (b) double declining-balance, and (c) units-of-activity?

Action Plan

- Amortization is an allocation concept.
- Under straight-line amortization, an equal amount of the amortizable cost (cost less residual value) is allocated to each period.
- Under declining-balance amortization, more amortization is allocated in the early years than in the later years. Apply double the straight-line rate of amortization to the net book value. Residual values are ignored in this method.
- Under units-of-activity amortization, first determine an amortizable cost per unit. Then multiply this amount by the actual usage in each period to determine amortization expense.

Solution

	2005	2006
Straight-line	$ 9,600	$ 9,600
Double declining-balance	20,000	12,000
Units-of-activity	8,000	9,600

(a) Straight-line: ($50,000 − $2,000) ÷ 5 years = $9,600

(b) Double declining-balance: 100% ÷ 5 years = 20% straight-line rate

    2005: $50,000 × 20% × 2 = $20,000
    2006: ($50,000 − $20,000) × 20% × 2 = $12,000

(c) Units-of-activity: ($50,000 − $2,000) ÷ 6,000 hours = $8.00 per hour

    2005: 1,000 × $8.00 = $8,000
    2006: 1,200 × $8.00 = $9,600

the navigator

Related exercise material: BE9–4, BE9–5, BE9–6, BE9–7, BE9–8, E9–3, E9–4, and E9–5.

Revising Periodic Amortization

study objective 3

Describe and demonstrate the procedure for revising periodic amortization.

Amortization is one example of the use of estimates in the accounting process. The factors (useful life and residual value) affecting amortization calculations should be reviewed periodically by management. If physical or economic factors indicate that the estimates are too low or too high, a change should be made.

When a change in an estimate is required, the change is made for current and future years. It is not made retroactively for prior periods. In other words, there is no correction of previously recorded amortization expense. Instead, amortization expense for current and future years is revised. The rationale is that the estimate made in the past was based on the best information available at that time. Estimates are necessary in the accounting process. Continually restating prior periods because of changes in estimates could adversely affect the reader's confidence in financial statements.

To determine the new annual amortization expense, we first calculate the asset's net book value at the time of the change in estimate. We then deduct any revised residual value to determine the amortizable cost at the time of the revision. Next, the revised amortizable cost is allocated over the **remaining** useful life.

To illustrate, assume that 1 Stop Florists decides on January 1, 2008, to extend the useful life of the truck an additional year (to December 31, 2010) because of its good condition. The estimated residual value is expected to decline from its original estimate of $2,000 to $700. The company has used the straight-line method to amortize the asset to date. The book value at January 1, 2008, is $11,200 (refer to the net book value at December 31, 2007, in Illustration 9-7). The new annual amortization is $3,500, calculated as in Illustration 9-13 below:

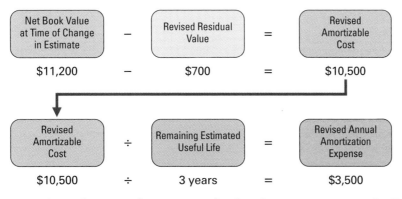

Illustration 9-13 ◄

Formula for revised amortization

At this time, 1 Stop Florists makes no entry for the change in estimate. On December 31 of 2008, 2009, and 2010, during the preparation of adjusting entries, it records an amortization expense of $3,500.

If the units-of-activity amortization method is used, the calculation is as shown above except that the remaining useful life is expressed in terms of units rather than years. If the declining-balance method is used, the revised straight-line rate would be applied to the net book value at the time of the change in estimate. The straight-line rate must be revised because the useful life has changed.

Expenditures during Useful Life

During the useful life of a long-lived asset, a company may incur costs for ordinary repairs, additions, or improvements. Ordinary repairs are costs to *maintain* the operating efficiency and expected productive life of the unit. They are usually fairly small amounts that occur frequently. Motor tune-ups and oil changes, painting of buildings, and replacement of worn-out gears on machinery are examples. Such repairs are debited to Repair (or Maintenance) Expense as they occur. Because they are immediately charged as an expense against revenues, these costs are referred to as operating expenditures.

Additions and improvements are costs incurred to *increase* the operating efficiency, productive capacity, or expected useful life of the asset. These costs are usually substantial and occur less often. Additions and improvements increase the company's investment in productive facilities and are generally debited to the appropriate property, plant, or equipment account affected. They are called capital expenditures. They are amortized over the remaining life of the original structure or the useful life of the addition, if it is not dependent on the original asset.

As discussed in the feature story, SAIT amortizes its building renovations over 25 years, regardless of the remaining life of the building. Using a fixed life like this does not always provide the best match of expenses to revenues. SAIT argues that this practice is simpler and that any mismatch is likely not material.

study objective 4

Distinguish between operating and capital expenditures, and prepare the entries for these expenditures.

 ACCOUNTING IN ACTION ► Ethics Insight

In what will likely be heralded as one of the largest accounting frauds in history, World-Com, a global communications company operating in more than 65 countries, improperly capitalized US$7.2 billion of expenses. This accounting fraud artificially boosted WorldCom's net earnings by US$5 billion for fiscal 2001 and the first quarter of 2002. If these expenses had been recorded properly as operating expenditures, WorldCom would have reported a net loss for

2001, as well as for the first quarter of 2002. Instead, WorldCom reported net earnings of $1.4 billion for 2001 and $130 million for the first quarter of 2002. As a result of these and other problems, WorldCom declared bankruptcy, to the dismay of its investors and creditors. Several WorldCom executives have since been indicted for fraud.

BEFORE YOU GO ON...

▶Review It

1. Are revisions of periodic amortization made to prior periods, future periods, or both? Explain.
2. Distinguish between operating and capital expenditures.

▶Do It

On August 1, 1990, just after its year end, The Fine Furniture Company purchased a building for $500,000. The company used straight-line amortization to allocate the cost of this building, estimating a residual value of $50,000 and a useful life of 30 years. After 15 years of use, on August 1, 2005, the company was forced to replace the roof at a cash cost of $25,000. The residual value was expected to remain at $50,000 but the total useful life was now expected to increase to 40 years. Prepare journal entries to record (1) amortization for the year ended July 31, 2005; (2) the cost of the addition on August 1, 2005; and (3) amortization for the year ended July 31, 2006.

Action Plan

- Understand the difference between an operating expenditure (benefits only current period) and a capital expenditure (benefits future periods).
- Capital expenditures are normally recorded in the same asset account, not in a separate asset account.
- To revise annual amortization, calculate the net book value (cost less accumulated amortization) at the revision date. Note that the cost of any capital expenditure will increase the book value of the asset to be amortized.
- Subtract any revised residual value from the net book value at the time of the change in estimate (plus the capital expenditure in this case) to determine the amortizable cost.
- Allocate the revised amortizable cost over the remaining (not total) useful life.

Solution

(1)

July 31, 2005	Amortization Expense [($500,000 − $50,000) ÷ 30]	15,000	
	Accumulated Amortization—Building		15,000
	To record annual amortization expense.		

(2)

Aug. 1, 2005	Building	25,000	
	Cash		25,000
	To record replacement of roof.		

(3)

Net book value before replacement of roof, August 1, 2005	
($500,000 − $50,000) ÷ 30 × 15	$225,000
Add: Capital expenditure (roof)	25,000
Net book value after replacement of roof, August 1, 2005	250,000
Less: Revised residual value	50,000
Revised amortizable cost	200,000
Divide by: Remaining useful life (40 − 15)	÷25 years
Revised annual amortization	$ 8,000

July 31, 2006	Amortization Expense	8,000	
	Accumulated Amortization—Building		8,000
	To record revised annual amortization expense.		

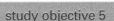

Related exercise material: BE9–9, BE9–10, E9-6, and E9–7.

Disposals of Property, Plant, and Equipment

Property, plant, and equipment may be disposed of in one of three ways—retirement, sale, or exchange—as shown in Illustration 9-14.

study objective 5

Explain and demonstrate how to account for the disposal of property, plant, and equipment.

Retirement
Equipment is scrapped or discarded

Sale
Equipment is sold to another party

Exchange
Existing equipment is traded for new equipment.

Illustration 9-14 ◄

Methods of property, plant, and equipment disposal

There are four steps to record the retirement, sale, or exchange of a long-lived asset:

Step 1: Update amortization

Update any unrecorded amortization for the portion of the year to the date of the disposal. Note that the update period will never be more than one year, since adjusting entries are made at least annually.

    Dr. Amortization Expense
       Cr. Accumulated Amortization

Step 2: Calculate the net book value

    net book value = cost − accumulated amortization

Step 3: Calculate the gain or loss

Determine the amount of the gain or loss on disposal, if any, by comparing the proceeds received to the net book value:

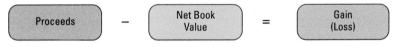

If the proceeds of the sale are more than the net book value of the property, plant, or equipment, there is a gain on disposal. If the proceeds of the sale are less than the net book value of the asset sold, there is a loss on disposal.

Step 4: Record the disposal

Record the disposal, removing the cost of the asset and the accumulated amortization from these two separate accounts. Record the proceeds (if any) and the gain or loss on disposal (if any):

    Dr. Cash (or other account)
    Dr. Accumulated Amortization
    Dr. Loss on Disposal or Cr. Gain on Disposal
       Cr. Property, plant, or equipment account

    In the following section, we will illustrate the accounting for each of the three disposal methods described in Illustration 9-14, using these four steps.

Retirement of Property, Plant, and Equipment

Some assets are retired at the end of their useful lives rather than sold or exchanged. For example, some productive assets used in manufacturing may have highly specialized uses and consequently have no general market when their useful life expires. In such cases, the asset is simply retired.

When an asset is retired, there are no proceeds for the company. The accumulated amortization account is decreased (debited) for the full amount of amortization taken over the life of the asset. The asset account is reduced (credited) for the original cost of the asset. Quite often the net book value will equal zero; however, a journal entry is still required to remove the asset and its related amortization account from the books.

To illustrate the retirement of a piece of property, plant, and equipment, assume that on August 1, 2005, Baseyev Enterprises retires its computer printers, which cost $32,000. At the time of purchase, the printers were expected to have a four-year useful life. The balance in the account Accumulated Amortization at Baseyev's year end, December 31, 2004, was $27,333. Straight-line amortization for the seven months ended August 1 is $4,667.

To update the amortization since the last time adjusting journal entries were made, which would have been at Baseyev's year-end, December 31, 2004, a journal entry to record the seven months of amortization is made as follows:

A	=	L	+	OE
-4,667				-4,667

Cash flows: no effect

Aug. 1	Amortization Expense		4,667	
	Accumulated Amortization—Printing Equipment			4,667
	To record amortization expense for seven months.			

After this journal entry is posted, the balance in Accumulated Amortization is $32,000 ($27,333 + $4,667). The printers are now fully amortized with a net book value of zero (cost of $32,000 − accumulated amortization of $32,000).

The entry to record the retirement of the computer printers is:

A	=	L	+	OE
+32,000				
-32,000				

Cash flows: no effect

Aug. 1	Accumulated Amortization—Printing Equipment		32,000	
	Printing Equipment			32,000
	To record retirement of fully amortized printing equipment.			

What happens if a company is still using a fully amortized asset? In this case, the asset and its accumulated amortization continue to be reported on the balance sheet, without further amortization, until the asset is retired. Reporting the asset and related amortization on the balance sheet informs the reader of the financial statements that the asset is still being used by the company. Once an asset is fully amortized, even if it is still being used, no additional amortization should be taken. Accumulated amortization on a piece of property, plant, and equipment can never be more than the asset's cost.

If a piece of property, plant, and equipment is retired before it is fully amortized and no residual value is received, a loss on disposal occurs (a gain is not possible on retirement). Assume that Baseyev Enterprises retires its printing equipment on January 1, 2005. The loss on disposal is calculated by subtracting the net book value of the asset from the proceeds received. In this case, there are no proceeds and the net book value is $4,667 (cost of $32,000 − accumulated amortization of $27,333), resulting in a loss of $4,667.

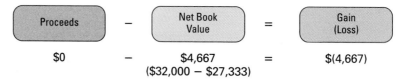

Proceeds	−	Net Book Value	=	Gain (Loss)
$0	−	$4,667 ($32,000 − $27,333)	=	$(4,667)

The entry to record the retirement of equipment is as follows:

Jan.	1	Accumulated Amortization—Printing Equipment	27,333	
		Loss on Disposal	4,667	
		Printing Equipment		32,000
		To record retirement of printing equipment at a loss.		

A = L + OE
+27,333   −4,667
−32,000

Cash flows: no effect

This loss is reported in the other expenses section of a multiple-step income statement.

Sale of Property, Plant, and Equipment

In a disposal by sale, the four steps listed previously are followed. While a gain is not possible when an asset is retired, and a loss does not always occur, both gains and losses on disposal are common when an asset is sold. Only by coincidence will the net book value and the fair market value (the proceeds) of the asset be the same when the asset is sold.

We will illustrate the sale of office furniture at both a gain and a loss in the following sections.

Gain on Disposal. To illustrate a gain, assume that on July 1, 2005, Baseyev Enterprises sells office furniture for $16,000 cash. The office furniture originally cost $60,000. As at December 31, 2004, it had accumulated amortization of $41,000. Annual amortization using the straight-line method is $16,000.

The first step is to update any unrecorded amortization. The entry to record amortization expense and update accumulated amortization for the first six months of 2005 is as follows:

July	1	Amortization Expense	8,000	
		Accumulated Amortization—Office Furniture		8,000
		To record amortization expense for the first		
		six months of 2005.		

A = L + OE
−8,000   −8,000

Cash flows: no effect

After the accumulated amortization balance is updated to $49,000 ($41,000 + $8,000), the net book value of the office furniture is $11,000 (cost of $60,000 − accumulated amortization of $49,000). A $5,000 gain on disposal is therefore calculated as follows:

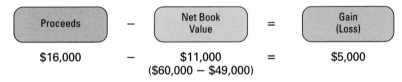

Proceeds	−	Net Book Value	=	Gain (Loss)
$16,000	−	$11,000	=	$5,000
		($60,000 − $49,000)		

The entry to record the sale of the office furniture is:

July	1	Cash	16,000	
		Accumulated Amortization—Office Furniture	49,000	
		Office Furniture		60,000
		Gain on Disposal		5,000
		To record the sale of office furniture at a gain.		

A = L + OE
+16,000   +5,000
+49,000
−60,000

↑ Cash flows: +16,000

The gain on disposal is reported in the other revenues section of a multiple-step income statement.

Loss on Disposal. Assume that instead of selling the office furniture for $16,000 Baseyev sells it for $9,000. In this case, a loss of $2,000 is calculated as follows:

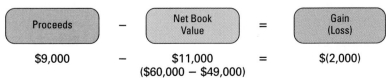

Proceeds	−	Net Book Value	=	Gain (Loss)
$9,000	−	$11,000	=	$(2,000)
		($60,000 − $49,000)		

The entry to record the sale of the office furniture is as follows:

A	=	L	+	OE
+9,000				−2,000
+49,000				
−60,000				

Cash flows: +9,000

July	1	Cash	9,000	
		Accumulated Amortization—Office Furniture	49,000	
		Loss on Disposal	2,000	
		Office Furniture		60,000
		To record the sale of office furniture at a loss.		

As noted earlier in the chapter, the loss on disposal is reported in the other expenses section of the income statement.

Exchanges of Property, Plant, and Equipment

Some long-lived assets are sold for cash when they are no longer needed. Others are exchanged for new assets. In an exchange of assets, the new asset is typically purchased by trading in an old asset, and a **trade-in allowance** is given to partially offset the purchase price of the new asset. Cash may also be involved. It is usually a payment for the difference between the trade-in allowance and the purchase price of the new asset.

Instead of being sold for cash, therefore, the old asset is sold for a trade-in allowance on the purchase of the new asset. The new asset is seen as being purchased for cash plus the value of the old asset.

Trade-in allowances, however, often contain price concessions related to the new asset and rarely reflect the fair market value of the asset given up. Consequently, trade-in allowances are ignored for accounting purposes.

The accounting for exchange transactions depends on whether the exchange is a **nonmonetary exchange of assets** or a **monetary exchange of assets**. A nonmonetary exchange is an exchange of similar assets, such as trading in a photocopier for a larger photocopier, with little or no cash included in the transaction. A monetary exchange is either an exchange of similar assets with a significant amount of cash included (more than 10% of the total consideration) or an exchange of dissimilar assets, such as exchanging a parcel of land for a piece of equipment.

The accounting differs for each type of exchange transaction as explained in the following sections.

Nonmonetary Exchanges of Assets.
An exchange of nonmonetary, or **similar**, assets involves assets of the same type, where the new asset performs the same function as the old asset. Currently, generally accepted accounting principles require a new asset in a nonmonetary exchange situation to be recorded at the **net book value of the old asset given up plus any cash paid (or less any cash received)**. Net book value is used not because it represents the *worth* of the asset given up; fair market value is actually the best measure of worth in this case. Rather, net book value is used because the new asset is simply substituted or swapped for the old asset. Because the operations of the business are not significantly changed by the exchange, the earnings process is not considered complete.

At the time of writing, new rules are anticipated to be promulgated in 2004 that will require nonmonetary exchanges to be recorded at fair market value, except in certain circumstances. These changes will harmonize the accounting for nonmonetary exchanges of assets with international financial reporting standards and with proposed changes to US accounting standards. They will also move the accounting for nonmonetary exchanges closer to that of monetary exchanges, explained in the next section.

However, until these rules are finalized, the accounting for nonmonetary exchanges of assets is complex. This type of exchange is also uncommon. Further discussion of nonmonetary assets is left for an intermediate accounting course.

Monetary Exchanges of Assets.
If the assets exchanged are **dissimilar**—a delivery truck for office furniture, for example—or a significant amount of cash (more than 10%

of the total consideration) is involved in the exchange of similar assets, the exchange is a monetary asset exchange.

The exchange is viewed as both a sale of the old asset and a purchase of the new asset. The new asset is recorded at the cash equivalent price paid, which is the **fair market value of the asset given up plus any cash paid (or less any cash received)**. The old asset is seen as having been sold for proceeds equivalent to its fair market value. Accounting for the exchange of assets in these situations allows the recognition of gains and losses, since the earnings process is complete.

Gains and losses from an exchange are determined just as they are for the sale of a piece of property, plant, and equipment. The gain or loss is the difference between the net book value and the fair market value of the asset given up. When the book value is more than the market value, a loss results. When the book value is less than the market value, a gain results.

In summary, the procedure to account for monetary exchanges is as follows:

Step 1: Update any unrecorded amortization expense to the date of the exchange.
Step 2: Calculate net book value (cost − accumulated amortization).
Step 3: Calculate any gain or loss on disposal [fair market value − net book value = gain (loss)].
Step 4: Record the disposal: remove the cost of the asset given up and the accumulated amortization and record any gain or loss on disposal. Record the new asset at the fair market value of the old asset plus any cash paid (or less any cash received).

To illustrate an exchange of monetary assets, assume that Chilko Company exchanged old computers for new computers on October 1, 2005. The original cost of the old computers was $61,000 on January 1, 2003. Amortization is calculated using the straight-line method, over a three-year useful life, with an estimated residual value of $1,000. The fair market value of the old computers on October 1 is $5,000.

The list price of the new computers was $51,000. In addition to receiving an $8,000 trade-in allowance from the computer retailer for the old computers, Chilko paid $43,000 cash for the new computers. Chilko's year end is December 31.

The first step is to update the amortization for the nine months ended October 1, 2005. Annual amortization expense is $20,000 [($61,000 − $1,000) ÷ 3], so amortization for the nine months is $15,000 ($20,000 × $\frac{9}{12}$).

Oct. 1	Amortization Expense	15,000	
	Accumulated Amortization—Computers		15,000
	To record amortization expense for 9 months.		

A = L + OE
−15,000   −15,000

Cash flows: no effect

After this entry is posted, the balance in Accumulated Amortization on October 1, 2005, is $55,000 [$20,000 (in 2003) + $20,000 (in 2004) + $15,000 (in 2005)]. The accumulated amortization can also be calculated as follows: $20,000 × 2.75 years = $55,000. Be sure to watch the dates and time periods carefully when calculating partial period amortization.

On October 1, 2005, the net book value is $6,000 (cost of $61,000 − accumulated amortization of $55,000). The loss on disposal on the old computers is determined by comparing the net book value to the fair market value, which represents proceeds in this situation.

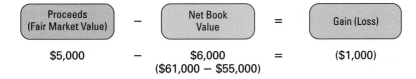

| Proceeds (Fair Market Value) | − | Net Book Value | = | Gain (Loss) |
| $5,000 | − | $6,000 ($61,000 − $55,000) | = | ($1,000) |

The entry to record the exchange of computers is as follows:

A	=	L	+	OE
+48,000				−1,000
+55,000				
−61,000				
−43,000				

Cash flows: −43,000

Oct. 1	Computers (new)	48,000	
	Accumulated Amortization—Computers	55,000	
	Loss on Disposal	1,000	
	Computers (old)		61,000
	Cash		43,000
	To record exchange of computers, plus cash.		

Note that the exchange of computers is not netted; rather, it is shown as a separate increase and decrease to the general ledger account Computers. The cost of the new computers ($48,000) is determined by the fair market value of the old computers ($5,000) plus the cash paid ($43,000). The list price of $51,000 and the trade-in allowance of $8,000 are ignored in determining the real cost of the new computers.

BEFORE YOU GO ON . . .

▶Review It

1. What is the proper accounting for the retirement, sale, and exchange of a piece of property, plant, and equipment?
2. What is the formula to calculate a gain or loss on disposal?
3. When is an exchange of assets considered a nonmonetary exchange? A monetary exchange?

▶Do It

Overland Trucking has an old truck that originally cost $75,000. The truck currently has accumulated amortization of $70,000. Assume each of the following four independent situations:

1. Overland retires the truck.
2. Overland sells the truck for $6,500 cash.
3. Overland sells the truck for $4,500 cash.
4. Overland exchanges the old truck, plus $53,000 cash, for a new truck. The old truck has a fair market value of $7,500. The new truck has a list price of $63,000, but the dealer will give Overland a $10,000 trade-in allowance on the old truck.

Prepare the journal entry to record each of these situations.

Action Plan

- Update any unrecorded amortization for partial-year dispositions.
- Compare the proceeds with the asset's net book value to determine whether any gain or loss has occurred.
- Record any proceeds received and any gain or loss. Remove both the asset and any related accumulated amortization from the accounts.
- Determine the cash paid in an exchange situation as the difference between the list price and the trade-in allowance.
- Record the cost of the new asset in an exchange situation as the fair market value of the asset given up plus the cash paid.

Solution

(1) Retirement of truck:

	Loss on Disposal [($0 − ($75,000 − $70,000)]	5,000	
	Accumulated Amortization—Truck	70,000	
	Truck		75,000
	To record retirement of truck.		

(2) Sale of truck for $6,500:

	Cash	6,500	
	Accumulated Amortization—Truck	70,000	
	Truck		75,000
	Gain on Disposal [($6,500 − ($75,000 − $70,000)]		1,500
	To record sale of truck at a gain.		

(3) Sale of truck for $4,500:

Cash	4,500	
Loss on Disposal [($4,500 − ($75,000 − $70,000)]	500	
Accumulated Amortization—Truck	70,000	
Truck		75,000
To record sale of truck at a loss.		

(4) Exchange of truck:

Truck (new) ($7,500 + $53,000)	60,500	
Accumulated Amortization—Truck	70,000	
Gain on Disposal [$7,500 − ($75,000 − $70,000)]		2,500
Truck (old)		75,000
Cash ($63,000 − $10,000)		53,000
To record exchange of trucks, plus cash.		

Related exercise material: BE9–11, BE9–12, BE9–13, E9–8, and E9–9.

Natural Resources

Natural resources consist of standing timber and underground deposits of oil, gas, and minerals. Canada is rich in natural resources, ranging from the towering rainforests in coastal British Columbia to the world's largest nickel deposits in Voisey's Bay, Labrador. These long-lived productive assets have two distinguishing characteristics: (1) They are physically extracted in operations such as mining, cutting, or pumping. (2) They are replaceable only by an act of nature. Because of these characteristics, natural resources are frequently called **wasting assets**.

Similar to property, plant, and equipment, the acquisition cost of a natural resource is the cash or cash equivalent price of acquiring the resource and preparing it for its intended use. The cost of a natural resource can also be increased by future removal and site restoration cleanup costs, which are often significant. These costs, known as **asset retirement obligations**, are usually required to return the resource as closely as possible to its natural state at the end of its useful life.

The accounting for asset retirement obligations and the allocation of these obligations over the useful life of the natural resource is complicated. Further discussion of these concepts is left to an intermediate accounting course. We will, however, look at how the acquisition cost of a natural resource is allocated over its useful life in the next section.

Amortization

The units-of-activity method (learned earlier in the chapter) is generally used to calculate the amortization of wasting assets. It is used because natural resource amortization is, most often, a function of the units extracted during the year. Under the units-of-activity method, the total cost of the natural resource minus its residual value is divided by the number of units estimated to be in the resource. The result is an amortizable cost per unit of product. The amortizable cost per unit is then multiplied by the number of units extracted and sold, to determine the annual amortization expense.

To illustrate, assume that the Rabbit Lake Company invests $5.5 million in a mine estimated to yield 10 million tonnes of uranium. It has a $200,000 residual value. In the first year, 800,000 tonnes of uranium are extracted and sold. Using the formulas shown in Illustration 9-15, the calculations are as follows:

study objective 6

Calculate the periodic amortization of natural resources.

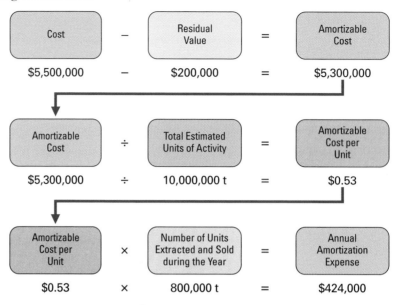

Alternative terminology
Amortization for natural resources is also known as *depletion,* because the assets physically deplete with extraction of the resource.

The amortization expense for the resource extracted is initially charged (debited) to an inventory account. Note that this differs from how we record amortization for property, plant, and equipment. In the case of natural resources, the amortization expense is recorded initially as a current asset, not as an expense.

Natural resources are accounted for in this way because the resource extracted is available for sale—similar to merchandise purchased or manufactured for sale as we learned in Chapter 5. Therefore the cost of extracting the natural resource—both current period costs such as labour and the allocation of the long-term cost of the asset such as amortization—is recorded as inventory. Subsequently, the inventory account is reduced (credited) for the cost of the resource sold during the year. In other words, the amortization is charged to the income statement only in the period in which the related goods are sold. The amount not sold remains in inventory and is reported as a current asset.

The entry to record amortization expense for the Rabbit Lake Company's first year of operation, ended December 31, 2005, is as follows:

A = L + OE
+424,000
−424,000

Cash flows: no effect

Dec. 31	Inventory ($0.53 × 800,000 t)	424,000	
	Accumulated Amortization—Uranium Mine		424,000
	To record amortization expense on uranium mine.		

In some companies, an accumulated amortization account is not used. In such cases, the amount of amortization is credited directly to the natural resource account.

Since all of the resource extracted was sold, Rabbit Lake would also make the following entry:

A = L + OE
−424,000   −424,000

Cash flows: no effect

Dec. 31	Cost of Goods Sold (Amortization Expense)		
	($0.53 × 800,000 t)	424,000	
	Inventory		424,000
	To charge amortization expense on uranium mine		
	to cost of goods sold.		

More often, however, some of the natural resource extracted in one accounting period will not be sold until a later period. To illustrate, assume that the Rabbit Lake Company does not sell all of the 800,000 tonnes of uranium extracted in 2005. It sells 700,000 tonnes and stores 100,000 tonnes for later sale. The journal entries to record the amortization expense for the year would be as follows:

Dec. 31	Inventory ($0.53 x 800,000 t)	424,000	
	Accumulated Amortization—Uranium Mine		424,000
	To record amortization expense on uranium mine.		
31	Cost of Goods Sold (Amortization Expense) ($0.53 × 700,000 t)	371,000	
	Inventory		371,000
	To charge amortization expense on uranium mine to cost of goods sold.		

A = L + OE
+424,000
−424,000

Cash flows: no effect

A = L + OE
−371,000
+371,000

Cash flows: no effect

Note that the first entry to record the inventory and accumulated amortization is the same whether the uranium extracted is sold or not. The only difference occurs in the second entry when the resource extracted does not equal the resource sold. In the situation described above, Rabbit Lake Company would report $371,000 as the cost of the resource sold on its income statement and $53,000 ($424,000 − $371,000) as inventory in the current assets section of its balance sheet.

Another complexity in accounting for natural resources can occur when property, plant, and equipment are acquired for use in the development and production of the natural resource. If these assets are not expected to have any productive use after the natural resource is fully extracted, their estimated useful lives are limited to the years of expected productive capacity of the natural resource.

BEFORE YOU GO ON . . .

► Review It

1. How is amortization expense calculated for natural resources?
2. Explain how amortization expense can be both an asset (inventory) and an expense (cost of goods sold).

► Do It

Calculate amortization expense for the High Timber Company's first year of operations. Assume that High Timber invests $14 million in a tract of timber land. It is estimated to have 10 million cunits (1 cunit = 100 cubic feet) of timber and a $500,000 residual value. In the first year, 40,000 cunits of timber are cut, of which 30,000 cunits are sold.

Action Plan

- Determine the amortizable cost in total and per unit.
- Allocate the amortization between expense (units sold) and inventory (units on hand).

Solution

Under the units-of-activity method, an amortizable cost per unit is determined by dividing total cost minus residual value by the total estimated units. The calculation is as follows:

($14,000,000 − $500,000) ÷ 10,000,000 cunits = $1.35 amortizable cost per cunit

The cost per unit is then multiplied by the number of units cut and sold, to determine the amortization expense. Amortization expense for High Timber is $40,500 ($1.35 × 30,000) in the first year. The cost related to the remaining 10,000 cunits that have been cut, but not yet sold, will be allocated to inventory in the amount of $13,500 ($1.35 × 10,000).

Related exercise material: BE9–14 and E9–10.

Intangible Assets

study objective 7

Contrast the accounting for intangible assets with the accounting for tangible assets.

Both tangible and intangible long-lived assets benefit future periods and are used to produce products or provide services over these periods. Intangible assets are different from tangible assets because intangible assets do not have physical existence. Intangible assets are rights, privileges, and competitive advantages that result from the ownership of long-lived assets that do not possess physical substance.

Evidence that an intangible exists is provided by contracts, licences, and other documents. Intangibles may arise from:

1. Government grants such as patents, copyrights, and trademarks
2. The acquisition of another business in which the purchase price includes a payment for the company's favourable goodwill
3. Private monopolistic arrangements arising from contractual agreements such as franchises and leases

Some widely known intangibles are Alexander Graham Bell's patent on the telephone, the franchises of Tim Hortons, and the CBC trademark of the Canadian Broadcasting Corporation.

Similar to tangible assets, **intangible assets are recorded at cost**, which includes all costs of acquisition and other costs necessary to make the intangible asset ready for its intended use—including legal fees and similar charges.

There are several differences between accounting for intangible assets and accounting for other long-lived assets. Only certain types of intangible assets are amortized. To distinguish between those intangibles that are amortizable and those that are not, we categorize intangible assets as having either a limited life or an indefinite life.

If an intangible asset has a **limited life**, its amortizable cost (cost less residual value) should be allocated over the shorter of the (1) estimated useful life and (2) legal life. Normally, the useful life of an intangible asset is the shorter period, so it is the one used as the amortization period. Intangible assets are typically amortized on a straight-line basis. To record amortization, Amortization Expense is increased (debited) and the specific intangible asset account is decreased (credited). Unlike tangible assets, a contra account (i.e., Accumulated Amortization) is seldom used. Because most intangible assets cannot be replaced, it is not relevant for users to know the original cost and the percentage the intangible asset has been amortized, as it is for tangible assets.

If an intangible has an **indefinite life**, it is not amortized. However, its cost is reviewed and tested for an impairment loss annually, or more often depending on circumstances. Recall from earlier in this chapter that an impairment occurs if the asset's market value permanently falls below its book value. If any impairment is evident, the asset must be written down to its market value and an impairment loss must be recorded. If no impairment has occurred, the asset remains at its current value until the following year, when it is evaluated again.

At disposal, just as with tangible assets, the book value of the intangible asset is eliminated, and a gain or loss, if any, is recorded.

Types of Intangible Assets

As mentioned in the previous section, intangible assets are divided into two categories—those with limited lives and those with indefinite lives—in order to determine whether or not the intangible asset should be amortized.

Intangible Assets with Limited Lives

Examples of intangible assets with limited lives include patents and copyrights. We also include research and development costs in this section because these costs often lead to the creation of patents and copyrights.

Patents. A patent is an exclusive right issued by the Canadian Intellectual Property Office of Industry Canada that enables the recipient to manufacture, sell, or otherwise control an invention for a period of 20 years from the date of the application. A patent cannot be renewed. But the legal life of a patent may be extended if the recipient obtains new patents for improvements or other changes in the basic design.

The initial cost of a patent is the cash or cash equivalent price paid to acquire it. The saying "A patent is only as good as the money you're prepared to spend defending it" is very true. Many patents are subject to some type of litigation. An example is the $25-million patent infringement suit won by Nortel Networks against Ciena Corp. in protecting its fibre-optics patents. Legal costs to successfully defend the patent in an infringement suit are considered necessary to prove the patent's validity. They are added to the patent account and amortized over the remaining life of the patent.

The cost of a patent should be amortized over its 20-year legal life or its useful life, whichever is shorter. In determining useful life, obsolescence, demand, competition, and other economic factors should be considered. These may cause a patent to become economically ineffective before the end of its legal life.

Copyrights. Copyrights granted by the Canadian Intellectual Property Office give the owner an exclusive right to reproduce and sell an artistic or published work. Copyrights extend for the life of the creator plus 50 years. Generally, the useful life of a copyright is significantly shorter than its legal life.

The cost of a copyright consists of the **cost of acquiring and defending it**. The cost may only be the fee paid to register the copyright. Or, it may amount to a great deal more if a copyright infringement suit is involved.

ACCOUNTING IN ACTION ▶ @–Business Insight

Although the record industry won a copyright infringement case against Napster—an on-line music sharing network—the struggle to enforce copyright laws in the digital age continues to be an uphill battle. A recent survey found that 67 percent of those who download music from the Internet simply don't care whether the files are copyrighted or not. This figure is striking, given the flood of media coverage and legal cases aimed at educating the public about the threat file-sharing poses to the intellectual property industries.

Source: "Music Downloaders Remain Indifferent to Copyright," *Internet Magazine,* August 1, 2003.

Research and Development Costs. Research and development costs are not intangible assets by themselves. But because they may lead to patents and copyrights, we discuss them in this section. Many companies spend large sums of money on research and development (R&D). For example, in a recent year, Nortel Networks spent nearly $5 billion on R&D.

Research and development costs present two accounting problems: (1) It is sometimes difficult to determine the costs for specific projects. (2) It is also hard to know the extent and timing of future benefits. As a result, accounting distinguishes between research costs and development costs.

Research is planned investigation that is done to gain new knowledge and understanding. **All research costs should be expensed when incurred.**

Development is the use of research findings and knowledge for a plan or design. **Development costs with reasonably certain future benefits can be capitalized.** Management must intend to produce and market the product or process, a future market must be defined, and adequate resources must exist to complete the project. Otherwise, development costs must also be expensed.

To illustrate, assume that Laser Scanner Company spent $3 million on research and $2 million on development. These costs resulted in the development of two highly successful patents. The $3 million of research costs are expensed. The development costs of $2 million are capitalized and included in the cost of the patent, since the development was successful.

Intangible Assets with Indefinite Lives

Examples of intangible assets with indefinite lives include trademarks and trade names, franchises and licences, and goodwill. These intangible assets do not always fit perfectly in each category. Sometimes trademarks, trade names, franchises, or licences do have limited lives. In such cases, they would be amortized over their useful lives. It is more usual, however, for these intangible assets, along with goodwill, to have indefinite lives.

Trademarks and Trade Names. A trademark or trade name is a word, phrase, jingle, or symbol that identifies a particular enterprise or product. Trade names like President's Choice, KFC, Nike, Big Mac, the Blue Jays, and TSN create immediate product identification. They also enhance the sale of the product. The creator may obtain exclusive legal right to the trademark or trade name by registering it with the Canadian Intellectual Property Office. This registration provides continuous protection. It may be renewed every 15 years, as long as the trademark or trade name is in use.

In most cases, companies continuously renew their trademarks or trade names. In such cases, as long as the trademark or trade name continues to be marketable, it will have an indefinite useful life. Intangible assets with indefinite useful lives are not amortized. Instead, their values are tested annually for impairment, as explained earlier in this chapter.

If the trademark or trade name is purchased, its cost is the purchase price. If the trademark or trade name is developed internally rather than purchased, the cost includes legal fees, registration fees, design costs, successful legal defence costs, and other expenditures directly related to securing it.

Franchises and Licences. When you drive down the street in your Protegé purchased from a Mazda dealer, fill up your gas tank at the corner Petro-Canada station, buy coffee from Tim Hortons, eat lunch at Wendy's, live in a home purchased through a Royal LePage real estate broker, or vacation at a Delta Hotel, you are dealing with franchises. The Forzani Group also uses franchises—Sports Experts, Intersport, Atmosphere, and RnR—to sell its products.

A franchise is a contractual arrangement between a franchisor and a franchisee. The franchisor gives the franchisee permission to sell certain products, offer specific services, or use certain trademarks or trade names.

Another type of franchise granted by a government body permits the company to use public property in performing its services. Examples are the use of city streets for a bus line or taxi service, the use of public land for telephone and electric lines, and the use of airwaves for radio or TV broadcasting. Such operating rights are called licences.

When costs can be identified with the acquisition of the franchise or licence, an intangible asset should be recognized. Franchises and licences may be granted for a period of time: limited or indefinite. The cost of a limited-life franchise or licence should be amortized over its useful life. If the life is indefinite, the cost is not amortized. It should, however, be tested annually for impairment and written down, if required.

Annual payments, proportionate with sales, are sometimes required under a franchise agreement. These are called royalties and are recorded as operating expenses in the period in which they are incurred.

Goodwill. Usually, the largest intangible asset that appears on a company's balance sheet is goodwill. Goodwill is the value of favourable attributes that relate to a business enterprise. These include exceptional management, a desirable location, good customer relations, skilled employees, high-quality products, fair pricing policies, and harmonious relations with labour unions. Unlike property, plant, and equipment and natural resources, which can be sold individually in the marketplace, goodwill cannot be sold individually as it is part of the business as a whole.

If goodwill can be identified only with the business as a whole, how can it be determined? One could try to put a dollar value on the factors above (exceptional management, a desirable location, and so on), but the results would be subjective. Subjective valuations would not contribute to the reliability of financial statements. Therefore, **goodwill is recorded only when there is a purchase of an entire business**.

In recording the purchase of a business, goodwill is the excess of cost over the fair market value of the net assets (assets less liabilities) acquired. The net assets are recorded (debited) at their fair market values. Cash is credited for the purchase price and goodwill is debited for the difference. Because goodwill has an indefinite life, just as the company has an indefinite life, it is not amortized. Since goodwill is measured using the market value of a company—a subjective valuation which can easily change—it must be tested regularly for impairment.

ACCOUNTING IN ACTION ▶ Business Insight

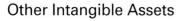

AOL Time Warner Inc. wrote down its intangible assets a staggering US$54 billion in the first quarter of 2002. AOL blamed the introduction of a new accounting standard requiring intangible assets with indefinite lives, such as goodwill, to be tested annually for impairment, rather than amortized. This write-off is the largest asset impairment loss recorded in corporate history. However, it is not expected to be the last. Most companies paid high prices for acquisitions during the high-tech boom. The market value of these acquisitions—many of which were overvalued—has since fallen with the bear market.

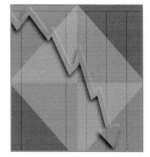

Other Intangible Assets

Other intangible assets sometimes found in corporate balance sheets include items such as customer lists, noncompetition agreements, sports contracts, startup costs, and rearrangement costs. As with other examples of intangibles that we have discussed, these assets are amortized over the shorter of their useful lives or legal lives. In reality, these types of costs usually have a very short useful life over which they provide benefit to the company. Some companies use the term "Deferred Charges" to classify these items. Others use the term "Other Assets". The trend has been toward listing these items separately, as neither term—Deferred Charges or Other Assets—has much value as information.

As noted throughout this section on intangible assets, amortizable intangible assets have varying useful lives and legal lives. These assets are amortized over the shorter of the two. Similar to tangible assets, intangible assets are tested for impairment if circumstances change and net book value declines below fair market value.

Unamortizable intangible assets have indefinite useful lives and are not amortized. Instead, their values are tested annually for impairment (or more often, if required). Illustration 9-16 summarizes the varying lives for intangible assets.

Illustration 9-16 ▶

Summary of intangible assets and amortization requirements

Intangible Asset	Legal Life	Amortization Period
Amortized		
Patents	20 years	Shorter of EUL* or legal life
Copyrights	Life of creator plus 50 years	Shorter of EUL or legal life
Franchises/Licences	Contract term	Shorter of EUL or contract term
Unamortized		
Trademarks/Trade names	15 years, renewable	Not amortized
Franchises/Licences	Indefinite	Not amortized
Goodwill	Indefinite	Not amortized
Other		
Research		Recorded as Research Expense
Development		Capitalized (if criteria met) as specific intangible asset

*EUL—Estimated Useful Life

BEFORE YOU GO ON . . .

▶Review It

1. What are the main differences between accounting for intangible and tangible assets?
2. Identify the major types of intangibles and the proper accounting for them.
3. Give some examples of intangible assets in your everyday surroundings.
4. Distinguish between the amortization policy for intangible assets with limited lives and the policy for those with indefinite lives.

▶Do It

The Dummies 'R' Us Company purchased a copyright to a new book series for $15,000 cash on August 1, 2004. The books are expected to have a saleable life of three years. One year later, the company spends an additional $6,000 cash to successfully defend this copyright in court. The company's year end is July 31. Journalize the (1) purchase of the copyright on August 1, 2004; (2) year-end amortization at July 31, 2005; (3) legal costs incurred on August 1, 2005; and (4) year-end amortization at July 31, 2006.

Action Plan

- Amortize intangible assets with limited lives over the shorter of their useful life and legal life (the legal life of a copyright is the life of the author plus 50 years).
- Treat costs to successfully defend an intangible asset as a capital expenditure because they benefit future periods.
- Revise amortization for additions to the cost of the asset, using the net book value at the time of the addition and the remaining useful life.

Solution

(1)

Aug. 1, 2004	Copyright	15,000	
	Cash		15,000
	To record purchase of copyright.		

(2)

July 31, 2005	Amortization Expense ($15,000 ÷ 3)	5,000	
	Copyright		5,000
	To record amortization expense.		

(3)

Aug. 1, 2005	Copyright	6,000	
	Cash		6,000
	To record costs incurred to defend copyright.		

(4)

July 31, 2006	Amortization Expense	8,000[1]	
	Copyright		8,000
	To record revised amortization expense.		

[1] $15,000 − $5,000 + $6,000 = $16,000 net book value ÷ 2 years remaining = $8,000

Related exercise material: BE9–15, E9–11 and E9–12.

Statement Presentation and Analysis

Presentation

Property, plant, and equipment and natural resources are often combined and reported in the balance sheet as "property, plant, and equipment," or "capital assets." Intangible assets are normally listed separately, following property, plant, and equipment. Goodwill must be disclosed separately. Other intangibles can be grouped under the caption "intangible assets" for reporting purposes if desired.

study objective 8

Illustrate how long-lived assets are reported and analysed.

For assets that are amortized, the balances and accumulated amortization should be disclosed in the balance sheet or notes. In addition, the amortization methods used should be described. The amount of amortization expense for the period should also be disclosed. For assets that are not amortized, the book value of each major type of asset should be disclosed in the balance sheet or notes. Impairment losses, if any, should be shown on a separate line on the income statement, with the details disclosed in a note.

The following is an excerpt from Research In Motion's balance sheet.

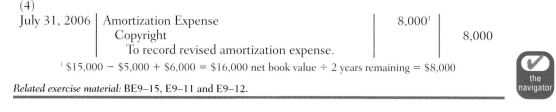

RESEARCH IN MOTION LIMITED
Balance Sheet (partial)
March 1, 2003
(in thousands of U.S. dollars)

Assets	
Capital assets (note 5)	$162,575
Intangible assets (note 6)	51,479
Goodwill (note 7)	30,588

Each category of long-lived assets is further detailed in the notes to the financial statements. For example, note 5 discloses the cost, accumulated amortization, and net book value of Research In Motion's capital assets, which include land; buildings and leaseholds; information technology; and furniture, fixtures, tooling, and equipment. Note 6 discloses the cost, accumulated amortization, and net book value of the company's intangible assets, which include acquired technology, licences, and patents. Note 7 describes the four companies Research In Motion acquired that resulted in the increase in goodwill.

Note 1, the summary of significant accounting policies, further discloses the amortization methods and rates used for capital and intangible assets. This note also states that long-lived assets were tested for impairment, and no impairment losses were found.

Analysis

Typically, long-lived assets are a substantial portion of a company's total assets. Asset turnover and return on assets are two commonly used ratios to assess the profitability of total assets. The asset turnover ratio, determined by dividing net sales by average total assets, shows how efficiently a company uses its assets to generate sales revenue.

The asset turnover ratio for The Forzani Group is calculated in Illustration 9-17:

Illustration 9-17 ▶

Asset turnover

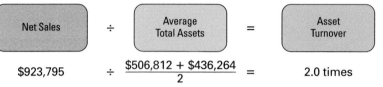

$$\$923,795 \quad \div \quad \frac{\$506,812 + \$436,264}{2} \quad = \quad 2.0 \text{ times}$$

The asset turnover ratio shows the dollars of sales produced for each dollar invested in assets. Each dollar invested in assets produced $2 in sales for Forzani. If a company is using its assets efficiently, each dollar of assets will create a high amount of sales. This ratio varies greatly among different industries—from those that are asset-intensive (e.g., utility companies) to those that are not (e.g., service companies).

The return on assets, calculated by dividing net income by average total assets, shows the profitability of assets used in the earnings process. Illustration 9-18 shows the return on assets for Forzani.

Illustration 9-18 ▶

Return on assets

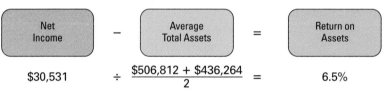

$$\$30,531 \quad \div \quad \frac{\$506,812 + \$436,264}{2} \quad = \quad 6.5\%$$

The asset turnover ratio shows the amount of sales generated by each dollar invested in assets. The return on assets ratio focuses instead on net income, showing the amount of net income generated by each dollar invested in assets. Forzani's return on assets was 6.5%. A high return on assets indicates a profitable company.

BEFORE YOU GO ON . . .

▶**Review It**

1. How are long-lived assets reported on the financial statements?
2. What information related to long-lived assets is disclosed in the notes to the financial statements?
3. What is the purpose of the asset turnover and return on assets ratios?

Related exercise material: BE9–16, BE9–17, BE9–18, E9–13, and E9–14.

Demonstration Problem 1

Additional
Demonstration
Problems

DuPage Company purchases a factory machine at a cost of $18,000 on January 1, 2005. The machine is expected to have a residual value of $2,000 at the end of its four-year useful life.

During its useful life, the machine is expected to be used for 16,000 hours. Actual annual use was as follows: in 2005, 4,500 hours; in 2006, 4,000 hours; in 2007, 3,500 hours; and in 2008, 4,000 hours.

Instructions

Prepare amortization schedules for the following methods: (a) straight-line, (b) units-of-activity, and (c) declining-balance using double the straight-line rate.

Solution to Demonstration Problem 1

(a)   **Straight-Line Method**

Year	Amortizable Cost	×	Amortization Rate	=	Amortization Expense	Accumulated Amortization	Net Book Value
						End of Year	
							$18,000
2005	$16,000[1]		25%[2]		$4,000	$ 4,000	14,000
2006	16,000		25%		4,000	8,000	10,000
2007	16,000		25%		4,000	12,000	6,000
2008	16,000		25%		4,000	16,000	2,000

[1] $18,000 − $2,000 = $16,000
[2] 100% ÷ 4 years = 25%

(b)   **Units-of-Activity Method**

Year	Units of Activity	×	Cost per Unit	=	Amortization Expense	Accumulated Amortization	Net Book Value
						End of Year	
							$18,000
2005	4,500		$1[1]		$4,500	$ 4,500	13,500
2006	4,000		1		4,000	8,500	9,500
2007	3,500		1		3,500	12,000	6,000
2008	4,000		1		4,000	16,000	2,000

[1] $18,000 − $2,000 = $16,000 amortizable cost ÷ 16,000 total units = $1/unit

(c)   **Declining-Balance Method**

Year	Net Book Value Beginning of Year	×	Amortization Rate (25%×2)	=	Amortization Expense	Accumulated Amortization	Net Book Value
						End of Year	
							$18,000
2005	$18,000		50%		$9,000	$ 9,000	9,000
2006	9,000		50%		4,500	13,500	4,500
2007	4,500		50%		2,250	15,750	2,250
2008	2,250		50%		250[1]	16,000	2,000

[1] Adjusted to $250 because ending book value should not be less than expected residual value.

Action Plan

- Deduct the residual value in the straight-line and units-of-activity methods, but not in the declining-balance method.
- In the declining-balance method, the amortization rate is applied to the net book value (cost − accumulated amortization).
- Amortization should never reduce the net book value of the asset below its expected residual value.

Demonstration Problem 2

On January 1, 2002, Skyline Limousine Co. purchased a speciality limo for $78,000. The vehicle is being amortized by the straight-line method using a four-year service life and a $4,000 residual value. The company's fiscal year ends on December 31.

Instructions

Prepare the journal entry or entries to record the disposal of the limo, assuming that it is:
(a) retired on January 1, 2006.
(b) sold for $15,000 on July 1, 2005.
(c) traded in on a new limousine on January 1, 2005, for a trade-in allowance of $25,000 and cash of $52,000. The fair market value of the old vehicle was $20,000.

Action Plan

- Update the amortization to the date of the disposal for any partial period.
- Determine the book value of the asset at the time of disposal.
- Calculate any gain or loss by comparing proceeds to book value.
- Remove the book value of the asset from the records. Do this by debiting accumulated amortization (for the total amortization to the date of disposal) and crediting the asset account for the cost of the asset. Record proceeds and any gain or loss.
- Ignore trade-in allowances.
- Record a new asset in an exchange situation at the fair market value of the asset given up plus the cash paid.

the navigator ✔

Solution to Demonstration Problem 2

$$\frac{\$78,000 - \$4,000}{4 \text{ years}} = \$18,500 \text{ annual amortization expense}$$

(a)

Jan. 1, 2006	Accumulated Amortization ($18,500 × 4 years)	74,000	
	Loss on Disposal	4,000	
	Limo		78,000
	To record retirement of limo.		

(b)

July 1, 2005	Amortization Expense ($18,500 × $\frac{6}{12}$)	9,250	
	Accumulated Amortization		9,250
	To record amortization for 6 months.		
	Cash	15,000	
	Accumulated Amortization ($18,500 × 3.5 years)	64,750	
	Gain on Disposal		1,750
	Limo		78,000
	To record sale of limo.		

(c)

Jan. 1, 2005	Limo (new) ($20,000 + $52,000)	72,000	
	Accumulated Amortization ($18,500 × 3 years)	55,500	
	Loss on Disposal [$20,000 − ($78,000 − $55,500)]	2,500	
	Limo (old)		78,000
	Cash		52,000
	To record exchange of limousines, plus cash.		

Summary of Study Objectives

1. *Demonstrate how the cost principle applies to property, plant, and equipment.* The cost of property, plant, and equipment includes all costs necessary to acquire the asset and make it ready for its intended use. Cost is measured by the cash or cash equivalent price paid. In a basket purchase situation, cost is allocated to each individual asset using relative fair market values.

2. *Explain the concept of, and be able to calculate, amortization.* Amortization is the allocation of the cost of a long-lived asset to expense over its useful (service) life in a rational and systematic manner. Amortization is not a process of valuation. Nor is it a process that results in an accumulation of cash.

There are three commonly used amortization methods:

Method	Effect on Annual Amortization	Calculation
Straight-line	Constant amount	(cost − residual value) ÷ estimated useful life (in years)
Declining-balance	Decreasing amount	net book value at beginning of year × straight-line amortization rate × declining-balance multiplier
Units-of-activity	Varying amount	(cost − residual value) ÷ total estimated useful life (in units of activity) × actual activity during year

3. *Describe and demonstrate the procedure for revising periodic amortization.* Revisions of periodic amortization are made in present and future periods, not retroactively. The new annual amortization is found by dividing the amortizable cost (net book value less the revised residual value) at the time of the revision by the remaining useful life.

4. *Distinguish between operating and capital expenditures, and prepare the entries for these expenditures.* Operating expenditures are incurred to maintain the operating efficiency and expected productive life of the asset. These costs are debited to Repair Expense as incurred. Capital costs increase the operating efficiency, productive capacity, or expected useful life of the asset. These expenditures are debited to the property, plant, or equipment account affected. They are subsequently amortized over an appropriate period of time, usually the remaining life of the asset.

5. *Explain and demonstrate how to account for the disposal of property, plant, and equipment.* The accounting for the disposal of a piece of property, plant, or equipment through retirement or sale is as follows:
(a) Update any unrecorded amortization.
(b) Calculate the net book value.
(c) Calculate any gain (proceeds less net book value) or loss (net book value less proceeds) on disposal.

(d) Eliminate the asset and accumulated amortization accounts at the date of disposal. Record the proceeds received and the gain or loss (if any).

In accounting for exchanges of similar assets, the steps are similar except that the proceeds are equal to the fair market value of the asset given up. The new asset received in the exchange is recorded at the total of the fair market value of the asset given up plus any cash paid.

6. *Calculate the periodic amortization of natural resources.* Natural resources generally use the units-of-activity method of amortization. Amortizable cost (cost less residual value) is calculated on a per unit basis by dividing the total amortizable cost by the number of units estimated to be in the resource. The amortizable cost per unit is multiplied by the number of units extracted and sold to determine the amortization expense. The cost of any resource extracted but not sold is recorded as inventory.

7. *Contrast the accounting for intangible assets with the accounting for tangible assets.* The accounting for intangible assets and the accounting for tangible assets are much the same. The straight-line method is used for amortizing intangible assets with limited useful lives. Intangible assets are normally amortized over the shorter of their useful life or their legal life. The accumulated amortization is usually credited directly to the relevant intangible asset account. When an intangible asset has an indefinite life, it is not amortized but is tested annually for impairment.

8. *Illustrate how long-lived assets are reported and analysed.* It is common for property, plant, and equipment, and natural resources to be combined under the heading Property, Plant, and Equipment. Intangibles are shown separately under the heading Intangible Assets or are listed separately. The balances of the major classes of assets and accumulated amortization (if the asset is amortizable) should be disclosed either within the balance sheet or in the notes. The amortization methods used should be described. The amount of amortization expense for the period should be disclosed.

The asset turnover ratio (net sales ÷ average total assets) is one measure used by companies to show how efficiently assets are used to generate sales revenue. A second ratio, return on assets (net income ÷ average total assets), calculates how profitably assets are used to generate net income.

Glossary

 Key Term Matching Activity

Additions and improvements Costs incurred to increase the operating efficiency, productive capacity, or expected useful life of property, plant, or equipment. (p. 439)

Amortizable cost The cost of a long-lived asset less its residual value. (p. 432)

Asset turnover A measure of how efficiently a company uses its total assets to generate sales. It is calculated by dividing net sales by average total assets. (p. 456)

Basket purchase The acquisition of a group of assets for a total price. Individual asset costs are determined by allocating relative fair market values. (p. 429)

Capital cost allowance (CCA) The concept used in the *Income Tax Act* to amortize long-lived assets for income tax purposes. Most amortizable assets use the declining-balance method with maximum rates specified for each class of assets. (p. 437)

Capital expenditures Expenditures that increase the company's investment in productive facilities. (p. 439)

Cash equivalent price An amount equal to the fair market value of the asset given up. If this is not determinable, the fair market value of the asset received is used. (p. 427)

Copyright An exclusive right granted by the federal government allowing the owner to reproduce and sell an artistic or published work. (p. 451)

Declining-balance method An amortization method that applies a constant rate (the straight-line rate, which is 100% divided by the useful life) to the declining net book value of the asset. This method produces a decreasing annual amortization expense over the useful life of the asset. (p. 434)

Franchise A contractual arrangement under which the franchisor grants the franchisee the right to sell certain products, offer specific services, or use certain trademarks or trade names, usually within a designated geographical area. (p. 452)

Goodwill The amount paid for a business in excess of the net identifiable assets. (p. 453)

Impairment loss An impairment loss results when the fair market value of an asset declines below its net book value. (p. 427)

Intangible assets Rights, privileges, and competitive advantages that result from the ownership of long-lived assets that do not possess physical substance. (p. 450)

Land improvements Structural additions to land with limited useful lives, such as paving, fencing, and lighting. (p. 428)

Licences Operating rights to use property. (p. 452)

Monetary exchange of assets An exchange of similar assets, including a significant monetary consideration (more than 10% of the total consideration), or an exchange of dissimilar assets. (p. 444)

Natural resources Long-lived assets that consist of standing timber and underground deposits of oil, gas, and minerals. Also called wasting assets. (p. 447)

Nonmonetary exchange of assets An exchange of similar assets that includes little monetary consideration (less than 10% of the total consideration), or none at all. (p. 444).

Operating expenditures Expenditures that are immediately charged against revenues as expenses. (p. 439)

Ordinary repairs Expenditures to maintain the operating efficiency and productive life of the unit. (p. 439)

Patent An exclusive right issued by the federal government that enables the recipient to manufacture, sell, or otherwise control an invention for a period of 20 years from the date of the application. (p. 451)

Property, plant, and equipment Tangible long-lived assets, such as land, land improvements, buildings, and equipment, that are used in the operation of the business and are not intended for sale to customers. (p. 427)

Research and development costs Expenditures that may lead to patents, copyrights, new processes, and new products. (p. 451)

Residual value An estimate of the asset's value at the end of its useful life. (p. 431)

Return on assets An overall measure of the profitability of total assets. It is calculated by dividing net income by average total assets. (p. 456)

Royalties Recurring amounts owed in payment for services provided (e.g., advertising, purchasing). These amounts are usually calculated as a percentage of sales.

They are found in intercompany relationships such as franchises. (p. 452)

Straight-line method An amortization method in which the amortizable cost of an asset is divided by the estimated useful life. This method produces the same periodic amortization for each year of the asset's useful life. (p. 432)

Tangible assets Long-lived resources that have physical substance, are used in the operations of the business, and are not intended for sale to customers. Tangible assets include property, plant, and equipment and natural resources. (p. 426)

Trade-in allowance A price reduction offered by the seller when a used asset is exchanged for a new asset as part of the deal. (p. 444)

Trademark (trade name) A word, phrase, jingle, or symbol that distinguishes or identifies a particular enterprise or product. (p. 452)

Units-of-activity method An amortization method in which useful life is expressed in terms of the total estimated units of production or use expected from the asset. Amortization expense is calculated by multiplying the amortizable cost per unit (cost less residual value divided by total estimated activity) by the actual activity that occurs during the year. (p. 435)

Useful life An estimate of the expected productive life of an asset. It is also called the service life. (p. 431)

Self-Study Questions

Chapter 9 Self-Test

Answers are at the end of the chapter.

(SO 1) AP 1. Corrieten Company purchased equipment, incurring the following costs:

Cash price	$24,000
Insurance during transit	200
Installation and testing	400
Total cost	$24,600

What amount should be recorded as the cost of the equipment?
(a) $24,000   (c) $24,600
(b) $24,200   (d) None of the above

(SO 1) AP 2. Asura Company purchased land, a building, and equipment for a package price of $200,000. The fair market value of the land at the time of acquisition was $75,000. The fair market value of the building was $80,000. The fair market value of the equipment was $50,000. What costs should be debited to the accounts Land, Building, and Equipment, respectively?
(a) $66,667; $66,667; and $66,666
(b) $73,171; $78,049; and $48,780
(c) $75,000; 80,000; and $50,000
(d) $200,000

3. Cuso Company purchased equipment on January 1,   (SO 2) AP
2004, at a total cost of $40,000. The equipment has an estimated residual value of $10,000 and an estimated useful life of five years. The amount of accumulated amortization at December 31, 2006, the end of the second year of the asset's life, if the straight-line method of amortization is used, is:
(a) $6,000.   (c) $18,000.
(b) $12,000.   (d) $24,000.

4. Kant Enterprises purchases a truck for $32,000 on   (SO 2) AP
July 1, 2005. The truck has an estimated residual value of $2,000, and an estimated useful life of five years, or a total mileage of 300,000 kilometres. If 50,000 kilometres are driven in 2005, what amount of amortization expense would Kant record at December 31, 2005, assuming it uses the units-of-activity method?
(a) $2,500   (c) $5,000
(b) $3,000   (d) $5,333

5. Refer to the data provided for Kant Enterprises in   (SO 2) AP
question 4. If Kant uses the double declining-balance method of amortization, what amount of amortization expense would it record at December 31, 2005?

(a) $6,000   (c) $12,000

(b) $6,400   (d) $12,800

(SO 3) K   6. When there is a change in estimated amortization:
   (a) previous amortization should be corrected.
   (b) current and future years' amortization should be revised.
   (c) only future years' amortization should be revised.
   (d) None of the above

(SO 4) K   7. Additions are:
   (a) capital expenditures.
   (b) debited to a repair expense account.
   (c) debited to an inventory account.
   (d) operating expenditures.

(SO 5) K   8. Oviatt Company sold equipment for $10,000. At that time, the equipment had a cost of $45,000 and accumulated amortization of $30,000. At disposal, Oviatt should record:
   (a) a $5,000 loss on disposal.
   (b) a $5,000 gain on disposal.
   (c) a $15,000 loss on disposal.
   (d) a $15,000 gain on disposal.

(SO 5) AP   9. The St. Laurent Company exchanged an old machine with a book value of $39,000 and a fair market value of $35,000 for a similar new machine. The new machine had a list price of $47,500. St. Laurent was offered a trade-in allowance of $37,500, and paid $10,000 cash in the exchange. At what amount should the new machine be recorded on St. Laurent's books?

(a) $35,000   (c) $47,500

(b) $45,000   (d) $49,000

(SO 6) AP   10. The Shady Tree Farm Company purchased a Christmas tree farm on April 1, 2004 for $500,000 with an estimated 100,000 harvestable Christmas trees. The land is expected to have an estimated residual value of $50,000. During the first year of operations, ended January 31, 2005, the company cut and sold 10,000 trees. Amortization expense for the year ended January 31 is:
   (a) $37,500.   (c) $45,000.
   (b) $40,500.   (d) $50,000.

(SO 7) AP   11. Pierce Company had $150,000 of development costs in its laboratory related to a patent granted on January 2, 2005. On July 31, 2005, Pierce paid $35,000 for legal fees in a successful defence of the patent. The total amount debited to Patents through July 31, 2005, should be:
   (a) $35,000.   (c) $185,000.
   (b) $150,000.   (d) None of the above

(SO 8) AP   12. WestJet Airlines Ltd. reported net sales of $680 million, net income of $52 million, and average total assets of $588 million in 2002. What are WestJet's return on assets and asset turnover?
   (a) 1.2% and 8.8 times   (c) 7.6% and 8.8 times
   (b) 8.8% and 1.2 times   (d) 8.8% and 9.9%

the navigator

Questions

(SO 1) C   1. Susan Leung is uncertain about the applicability of the cost principle to long-lived assets. Explain the principle to Susan.

(SO 1) C   2. How is cost for a piece of equipment measured in (a) a cash transaction, and (b) a noncash transaction?

(SO 1) C   3. Market values of property, plant, and equipment are more relevant than historical cost for decisions made by users, such as creditors, investors, and managers. Why has the cost principle survived despite its seeming lack of usefulness?

(SO 1) C   4. Jacques asks why it is necessary to allocate the total cost to individual assets in a basket purchase situation. For example, if we purchase land and a building for $250,000, why can't we just debit an account called Land and Building for $250,000?

(SO 2) C   5. What is the purpose of amortization? How is amortization related to the change in an asset's market value?

(SO 2) K   6. Cecile is studying for the next accounting exam. She asks for your help on two questions: (a) What is residual value? (b) Is residual value used in determining amortizable cost under all amortization methods? Answer each question for her.

(SO 2) C   7. Contrast the straight-line, declining-balance, and units-of-activity methods in terms of (a) useful life, and (b) the pattern of periodic amortization over useful life.

(SO 2) C   8. Contrast the effects of the three amortization methods on net book value, amortization expense, and net income (1) in the early years of an asset's life, and (2) over the total life of the asset.

(SO 3) C   9. In the third year of an asset's four-year useful life, the company decides that the asset will have a six-year service life. How should the revision of amortization be recorded? Why?

(SO 4) C   10. Distinguish between operating expenditures and capital expenditures during an asset's useful life and describe the accounting treatment of each.

(SO 5) K   11. How is a gain or loss on the sale of property, plant, or equipment calculated?

(SO 5) C   12. Ewing Company owns a machine that is fully amortized but is still being used. How should Ewing account for this asset and report it in the financial statements?

(SO 6) C 13. Explain how annual amortization is calculated for natural resources. Why is the amortization of natural resources initially recorded as a current asset under inventory rather than as an expense?

(SO 7) C 14. What are the characteristics of an intangible asset?

(SO 7) C 15. Describe the differences in accounting for an intangible asset with a limited life versus one with an indefinite life.

(SO 7) C 16. Heflin Company hires an accounting student who says that intangible assets should always be amortized over their legal lives. Is the student correct? Explain.

(SO 7) C 17. Goodwill is related to the favourable attributes of a business enterprise. What types of attributes could result in goodwill?

(SO 7) C 18. Bob Leno, a business student, is working on a case problem for one of his classes. In this case problem, the company needs to raise cash to market a new product it has developed. Saul Cain, an engineering student, takes one look at the company's balance sheet and says, "This company has an awful lot of goodwill. Why don't you recommend that they sell some of it to raise cash?" How should Bob respond to Saul's suggestion?

(SO 7) C 19. Research and development costs often provide companies with benefits that last a number of years. For example, these costs can lead to the development of a patent that will increase the company's income for many years. However, generally accepted accounting principles require that most of these costs be recorded as expenses when incurred. Why?

(SO 8) K 20. What information related to long-lived assets should be disclosed in the notes to the financial statements?

(SO 8) C 21. What information do the asset turnover and return on assets ratios show about a company?

Brief Exercises

Determine cost of land.
(SO 1) AP

BE9–1 The following costs were incurred by Shumway Company in purchasing land: cash price, $50,000; removal of old building, $5,000; legal fees, $2,500; clearing and grading, $3,500; installation of fence, $3,000. What is the cost of the land?

Determine cost of truck.
(SO 1) AP

BE9–2 Basler Company incurs the following costs in purchasing a truck: cash price, $23,000; painting and lettering, $400; motor vehicle licence, $100; and one-year accident insurance policy, $2,000. What is the cost of the truck?

Record basket purchase.
(SO 1) AP

BE9–3 Olympic Company purchased land, land improvements, and a building on January 1, 2005, for $300,000. The company paid $80,000 cash and signed a mortgage note payable for the remainder. Management's best estimate of the value of the land was $100,000, of the land improvements, $30,000, and of the building, $200,000. Prepare the journal entry to record the acquisition.

Calculate straight-line amortization.
(SO 2) AP

BE9–4 On January 2, 2005, Mabasa Company acquires a delivery truck at a cost of $42,000. The truck is expected to have a residual value of $2,000 at the end of its four-year useful life. Calculate annual amortization expense each year using the straight-line method. Mabasa has a December 31 fiscal year end.

Calculate declining-balance amortization.
(SO 2) AP

BE9–5 Amortization information for Mabasa Company is given in BE9–4. Assuming the declining-balance amortization rate is double the straight-line rate, calculate the annual amortization expense for each year under the declining-balance method.

Calculate amortization using the units-of-activity method.
(SO 2) AP

BE9–6 Speedy Taxi Service uses the units-of-activity method in calculating amortization on its taxicabs. Each cab is expected to be driven 325,000 kilometres. Taxi no. 10 cost $33,000 and is expected to have a residual value of $500. Taxi no. 10 is driven 125,000 kilometres in year 1, 105,000 kilometres in year 2, and 95,000 kilometres in year 3. Calculate the amortization expense for each year.

Calculate partial-year amortization.
(SO 2) AP

BE9–7 Amortization information for Mabasa Company is given in BE9–4. Assuming the delivery truck was purchased on April 9, 2005, calculate the amortization for each year of the asset's life if the company uses straight-line amortization and has a policy to prorate amortization to the nearest month.

Calculate partial-year amortization.
(SO 2) AP

BE9–8 Amortization information for Mabasa Company is given in BE9–4. Assuming the delivery truck was purchased on April 9, 2005 calculate the amortization for each year of the asset's life if the company uses double declining-balance amortization and has a policy to prorate amortization to the nearest month.

BE9–9 On January 2, 2002, Asler Company purchased equipment for $32,000. At the time the equipment was estimated to have a useful life of five years and a residual value of $2,000. On December 31, 2005, prior to recording the year's amortization, the company concludes that the equipment will have a total useful life of four years and a residual value of $1,000. The company uses straight-line amortization and has a December 31 fiscal year end. Calculate the 2005 amortization expense.

Calculate revised amortization
(SO 3) AP

BE9–10 Indicate whether each of the following items is an operating expenditure (O) or a capital expenditure (C) in the space provided.

(a) ____ Repaired building roof, $500
(b) ____ Replaced building roof, $7,500
(c) ____ Purchased building, $80,000
(d) ____ Purchased supplies, $350
(e) ____ Purchased truck, $35,000
(f) ____ Purchased oil and gas for truck, $75
(g) ____ Replaced tires on truck, $500
(h) ____ Rebuilt engine on truck, $5,000
(i) ____ Added a new wing to building, $250,000
(j) ____ Painted interior of building, $1,500

Identify operating or capital expenditures.
(SO 4) K

BE9–11 Ruiz Company retires its delivery equipment, which cost $41,000. No residual value is received. Prepare journal entries to record the transaction if (a) accumulated amortization is also $41,000 on this delivery equipment, and (b) the accumulated amortization is $38,000 instead of $41,000.

Record disposal by retirement.
(SO 5) AP

BE9–12 Wiley Company sells office equipment on September 30, 2005, for $21,000 cash. The office equipment originally cost $72,000 and, as at December 31, 2004, had accumulated amortization of $42,000. Annual amortization is $14,000. Prepare the journal entries to (a) update amortization to September 30, 2005, (b) record the sale of the equipment, and (c) record the sale of equipment if Wiley Company received $15,000 cash for it.

Record disposal by sale.
(SO 5) AP

BE9–13 Subramanian Company has machinery with an original cost of $65,000 and, as at December 31, 2004, accumulated amortization of $48,000. On January 7, 2005, Subramanian exchanges the machinery, plus $62,000 cash, for new machinery. The old machinery has a fair market value of $14,000. The new machinery has a list price of $80,000, but the dealer gave Subramanian an $18,000 trade-in allowance on the old machinery. Record the January 7, 2005, journal entry for the machinery exchange.

Record exchange of machinery.
(SO 5) AP

BE9–14 Cuono Mining Co. purchased a mine for $7 million that is estimated to have 28 million tonnes of ore and a residual value of $500,000. In the first year, 6 million tonnes of ore are extracted and 5 million tonnes are sold.

(a) Prepare the journal entry to record the amortization and the cost of the ore sold for the first year ended August 31, 2005.
(b) Show how this mine and the ore on hand are reported on the balance sheet at the end of the first year.

Record amortization and show balance sheet presentation for natural resources.
(SO 6) AP

BE9–15 Surkis Company purchases a patent for $180,000 cash on January 2, 2005. Its legal life is 20 years and its estimated useful life is 10 years.

(a) Prepare the journal entry to record the purchase of the patent on January 2, 2005.
(b) Prepare the journal entry to record the amortization expense for the first year ended December 31, 2005.
(c) Show how this patent is reported on the balance sheet at the end of the first year.

Record acquisition and amortization, and show balance sheet presentation for patent.
(SO 7) AP

BE9–16 Indicate whether each of the following assets is property, plant, and equipment (PPE), a natural resource (NR), or an intangible asset (I). If the asset doesn't fit any of these categories, insert NA (not applicable) in the space provided.

(a) ____ Patent
(b) ____ Land
(c) ____ Building
(d) ____ Cash
(e) ____ Licence right
(f) ____ Machinery
(g) ____ Inventory
(h) ____ Timber tract
(i) ____ Cut and processed timber
(j) ____ Trademark
(k) ____ Franchise
(l) ____ Investment in common shares
(m) ____ Oil well
(n) ____ Coal mine
(o) ____ Natural gas deposit
(p) ____ Goodwill

Classify long-lived assets.
(SO 8) K

Prepare partial balance sheet.
(SO 8) AP

BE9–17 Canadian Tire Corporation, Limited reports the following selected information about long-lived assets at December 28, 2002 (in millions):

Accounts	Amounts
Accumulated amortization—assets under capital lease	$ 7.2
Accumulated amortization—buildings	558.8
Accumulated amortization—computer software	116.9
Accumulated amortization—fixtures and equipment	270.5
Accumulated amortization—leasehold improvements	57.2
Assets under capital lease	23.5
Buildings	1,806.3
Computer software	172.4
Fixtures and equipment	392.9
Goodwill	32.8
Land	613.9
Leasehold improvements	179.2

Included in land and buildings are property held for disposal at a cost of $87.5 and accumulated amortization of $37.3. Prepare a partial balance sheet for Canadian Tire.

Calculate ratios.
(SO 8) AP

BE9–18 Hudson's Bay Company reports the following in its 2003 financial statements (in millions):

Net sales, $7,383.8   Total assets, January 31, 2003, $4,275.7
Net earnings, $111.5   Total assets, January 31, 2002, $4,534.2

Calculate Hudson's Bay's return on assets and asset turnover for 2003.

Exercises

Comment on and classify expenditures.
(SO 1) AP

E9–1 The following expenditures related to assets were made by Kosinski Company during the first two months of 2005:

1. Paid $250 to have the company name and advertising slogan painted on a new delivery truck.
2. Paid a $75 motor vehicle licence fee for the new truck.
3. Paid $17,500 for paving the parking lots and driveways on a new plant site.
4. Paid $4,000 in legal fees on a purchase of land.
5. Paid $8,000 for the installation of new factory machinery.
6. Paid $900 for a one-year accident insurance policy on the new delivery truck.
7. Paid $200 for insurance to cover potential damage to the new factory machinery while it was in transit.

Instructions

(a) Explain the application of the cost principle in determining the acquisition cost of property, plant, and equipment.
(b) List the numbers of the foregoing transactions, and opposite each number indicate the account title to which the expenditure should be debited.

Determine cost of land.
(SO 1) AP

E9–2 Orbis Company acquired land for which it paid $100,000 cash. It planned to construct a small office building. An old warehouse on the property was torn down at a cost of $6,600. The residual materials were sold for $1,700. Additional costs before construction began included a $1,300 legal fee for work concerning the land purchase, a $7,800 architect's fee, and $14,000 to put in driveways and a parking lot.

Instructions

(a) Determine the amount to be reported as the cost of the land.
(b) For each cost not used in part (a), indicate the account to be debited.

Record basket purchase and calculate amortization.
(SO 1, 2) AP

E9–3 Hohenberger Farms purchased real estate for $675,000. It paid $75,000 cash and incurred a mortgage payable for $600,000. Legal fees of $12,000 were paid in cash. The real estate included land appraised at $500,000, buildings appraised at $180,000, and fences and other land improvements appraised at $40,000. The buildings have an estimated useful life of 40 years with a $20,000 residual value. Land improvements have an estimated 10-year useful life with no residual value.

Instructions

(a) Calculate the cost that should be allocated to each asset purchased.
(b) Prepare the journal entry to record the purchase of the real estate.
(c) Calculate the annual amortization expense for the buildings and land improvements assuming Hohenberger Farms uses straight-line amortization.

E9–4 Interprovincial Bus Lines purchases a bus on January 2, 2004, at a cost of $149,000. Over its four-year useful life, the bus is expected to be driven 300,000 kilometres and to have a residual value of $29,000. The company has a December 31 fiscal year end.

Calculate amortization using three methods; comment on choice of method.
(SO 2) AP

Interactive Homework

Instructions

(a) Prepare an amortization schedule for the life of the bus under each of the following methods: (1) straight-line, (2) declining-balance using double the straight-line rate, and (3) units-of-activity. Assume the actual distance driven was: 78,000 kilometres in 2004; 76,000 kilometres in 2005; 72,000 kilometres in 2006; and 74,000 kilometres in 2007.
(b) Which amortization method should the company use? Why?

E9–5 Stojko Company purchased a new machine on April 6, 2004, at a cost of $90,000. The company estimated that the machine will have a residual value of $12,000. The machine is expected to be used for 10,000 working hours during its five-year life. Stojko Company uses a calendar year end. Stojko prorates amortization to the nearest month.

Calculate amortization using three methods, and answer questions about impact of each method.
(SO 2) AP

Instructions

(a) Prepare an amortization schedule for the life of the asset under each of the following methods: (1) straight-line, (2) declining-balance using double the straight-line rate, and (3) units-of-activity. Assume the actual machine usage was 1,300 hours in 2004; 1,800 hours in 2005; 2,100 hours in 2006; 2,000 hours in 2007; 2,300 hours in 2008; and 500 hours in 2009.
(b) Which method results in the highest income for the first two years? Over the life of the asset?
(c) Which method results in the highest cash flow for the first two years? Over the life of the asset?

E9–6 Lindy Weink, the new comptroller of Lafrenière Company, has reviewed the expected useful lives and residual values of selected amortizable assets at the beginning of 2005. Her findings are as follows:

Calculate and record revised amortization.
(SO 3) AP

Type of Asset	Date Acquired	Cost	Total Useful Life in Years		Residual Value	
			Current	Proposed	Current	Proposed
Building	Jan. 1, 1995	$800,000	20	25	$40,000	$62,000
Equipment	July 1, 2002	120,000	5	4	5,000	3,600

After discussion, management agrees to accept Lindy's proposed changes. All assets are amortized by the straight-line method. Lafrenière Company uses a calendar year in preparing annual financial statements.

Instructions

(a) Calculate the net book value of each asset on January 1, 2005.
(b) Calculate the revised annual amortization on each asset.
(c) Prepare the entry (or entries) to record amortization in 2005.

E9–7 Mactaquac Company purchased a piece of high-tech equipment on July 1, 2003, for $25,000 cash. The equipment was expected to last four years and has a residual value of $2,000. Mactaquac uses the straight-line method of amortization. The company's fiscal year end is June 30.

Record asset addition and amortization.
(SO 2, 3, 4) AP

On July 1, 2004, Mactaquac purchased and installed a new part for the equipment that is expected to substantially improve its productivity. Mactaquac paid $5,000 cash for the part. It paid an additional $500 for the installation and testing of this part. The equipment is expected to last six years in total now and has a revised residual value of $5,000.

Instructions

(a) Prepare the journal entry to record the purchase of the equipment on July 1, 2003.
(b) Prepare the journal entry to record the amortization of the equipment on June 30, 2004.
(c) Prepare the journal entry to record the purchase of the part, and its installation and testing, on July 1, 2004.
(d) Prepare the journal entry to record the amortization of the equipment on June 30, 2005.

Record disposal of property, plant, and equipment.
(SO 5) AP

Interactive Homework

E9–8   Presented below are selected transactions of Beck Company for 2005. Beck Company uses straight-line amortization.

Mar.   1   Retired a piece of machinery that was purchased on January 1, 1996. The machinery cost $62,000 on that date. It had a useful life of 10 years with no residual value.

June 30   Sold a computer that was purchased on January 1, 2003. The computer cost $5,475. It had a useful life of three years with no residual value. The computer was sold for $500.

Dec. 31   Traded in an old delivery truck for a new delivery truck receiving a $10,000 trade-in allowance and paying $33,000 in cash. The old delivery truck was purchased January 3, 2001, at a cost of $30,000. It was amortized based on a six-year useful life with a $3,000 residual value. The old delivery truck had a fair market value of $8,500 on December 31, 2005.

Instructions

Journalize all entries required on the above dates. For assets disposed of, include entries to update amortization for partial periods, where applicable.

Determine effect of amortization method over life of asset.
(SO 2, 5) AN

E9–9   The Rahim Corporation purchased a computer for $12,000. The company planned to keep it for four years, after which it hoped to sell it for $2,000.

Instructions

(a) Calculate the amortization expense for each of the four years under (1) the straight-line method and (2) the double declining-balance method.
(b) Assume Rahim sold the computer for $1,750 at the end of the third year. Calculate the loss on disposal under each amortization method.
(c) Determine the impact of each method on net income (total amortization expense plus loss on disposal) from use of the computer over the three-year period.

Record amortization for natural resources.
(SO 6) AP

Interactive Homework

E9–10   On July 1, 2005, Phillips Inc. invests $520,000 in a mine estimated to have 800,000 tonnes of ore. The company estimates that, at the end of production at the mine, the property will be sold for $90,000. During the last six months of 2005, 100,000 tonnes of ore are mined but only 75,000 tonnes are sold.

Instructions

(a) Prepare the journal entries to record the 2005 amortization and the cost of the ore sold.
(b) How will the mine and the ore on hand be reported on the December 31, 2005, balance sheet?

Apply accounting concepts.
(SO 1, 2, 7) AN

E9–11   The following situations are independent of one another:

1. An accounting co-op student can't understand why the company is only amortizing its buildings and equipment, but not its land. The student prepared journal entries to amortize all of the company's property, plant, and equipment for the current year end.

2. The same co-op student also thinks the company's amortization policy on its intangible assets is wrong. The company is currently amortizing its patents but not its goodwill. The student fixed that for the current year end by adding goodwill to her adjusting entry for amortization. She told a fellow student that she felt she had improved the consistency of the company's accounting policies by making these changes.

3. The same company has a building still in use that has a zero book value but a substantial market value. The co-op student felt that this practice didn't benefit the company's users—especially the bank—and wrote the building up to its market value. After all, she reasoned, you can write down assets if market values are lower. She feels that writing them up if market value is higher is yet another example of the improved consistency that her employment has brought to the company's accounting practices.

Instructions

Explain whether or not the accounting treatment in each of the above situations is in accordance with generally accepted accounting principles. Explain what accounting principle or assumption, if any, has been violated and what the appropriate accounting treatment should be.

E9–12 Doucette Company, established in 2005, has the following transactions related to intangible assets:

Jan. 2 Purchased a patent with an estimated useful life of five years and a legal life of 20 years for $450,000.
Apr. 1 Purchased goodwill (indefinite life) for $360,000.
July 1 A 10-year franchise which expires on July 1, 2015, is purchased for $250,000.
Sept. 1 Research costs of $185,000 are incurred.
       30 Development costs of $50,000 are incurred. (No marketable products have been identified yet.)

Record acquisition and amortization of intangible assets.
(SO 2, 7) AP

Interactive Homework

Instructions

(a) Prepare the necessary entries to record these intangibles. All costs incurred were for cash.
(b) Make the entries as at December 31, 2005, recording any necessary amortization. There was no impairment of goodwill.

E9–13 BCE Inc. reported the following selected information as at December 31, 2002 (in millions):

Classify long-lived assets.
(SO 8) AP

Accounts	Amounts
Accumulated amortization—buildings	$ 1,307
Accumulated amortization—finite-life intangible assets	1,335
Accumulated amortization—machinery and equipment	3,253
Accumulated amortization—other property, plant, and equipment	139
Accumulated amortization—telecommunications assets	21,848
Amortization expense	3,146
Buildings	2,585
Cash and cash equivalents	306
Common shares	16,520
Finite-life intangible assets	3,021
Goodwill	10,103
Impairment charge	770
Indefinite-life intangible asset	900
Land	99
Machinery and equipment	6,144
Other long-term assets	4,355
Other property, plant, and equipment	357
Plant under construction	1,743
Telecommunications assets	34,573

Instructions

(a) Identify in which financial statement (balance sheet or income statement) and which section (e.g., current assets) each of the above items should be reported.
(b) Prepare the tangible and intangible assets sections of the balance sheet as at December 31, 2002.

E9–14 Sleeman Breweries Ltd. reported the following information for the fiscal years ended December 28, 2002, and December 29, 2001 (in thousands):

Calculate asset turnover and return on assets.
(SO 8) AN

	2002	2001
Net revenues	$157,053	$141,615
Net income	12,321	9,765
Total assets, end of year	220,081	197,642
Total assets, beginning of year	197,642	182,179

Instructions

(a) Calculate Sleeman's asset turnover and return on assets for the two years.
(b) Comment on what the ratios reveal about Sleeman Breweries Ltd.'s effectiveness in using its assets to generate revenues and produce net income.

Problems: Set A

Determine acquisition costs of land and building.
(SO 1) AP

P9–1A Kadlec Company was established on January 1. During the first year of operations, the following property, plant, and equipment expenditures and receipts were recorded:

Expenditures

1. Cost of real estate purchased as a plant site (land fair market value $180,000 and building fair market value $30,000)	$ 220,000
2. Legal fees on real estate purchase	4,000
3. Property tax on land paid for the current year	15,000
4. Cost of demolishing building to make land suitable for construction of new building	21,000
5. Excavation costs for new building	20,000
6. Cost of filling and grading the land	7,000
7. Architect's fees for building plans	30,000
8. Full payment to building contractor	650,000
9. Cost of fences around the property	6,000
10. Paving of the parking lots and driveways	34,000
	$1,007,000

Receipts

11. Proceeds for residual materials of demolished building	$ 10,500

Instructions

Analyse the above transactions using the following column headings. Insert the number of each transaction in the Item column. Insert the amounts in the appropriate columns. For amounts entered in the Other Accounts column, indicate the account titles.

Item   Land   Land Improvements   Building   Other Accounts (specify title)

Calculate and discuss amortization under different methods for partial periods.
(SO 2) AP

P9–2A In recent years, Flakeboard Company purchased three machines. Various amortization methods were selected. Information concerning the machines is summarized below:

Machine	Acquired	Cost	Residual Value	Useful Life in Years	Amortization Method
1	Mar. 25, 2002	$96,000	$4,000	10	Straight-line
2	May 7, 2003	60,000	8,000	8	Declining-balance
3	Nov. 15, 2004	72,000	6,000	6	Units-of-activity

For the declining-balance method, the company uses double the straight-line rate. For the units-of-activity method, total machine hours are expected to be 24,000. Actual hours of use in the first two years were 1,100 in 2004 and 4,550 in 2005.

Instructions

(a) If Flakeboard has a policy of recording amortization to the nearest month, calculate the amount of accumulated amortization on each machine at December 31, 2005. Round your answers to the nearest dollar.

(b) If Flakeboard has a policy of recording a half year's amortization in the year of acquisition and disposal, calculate the amount of accumulated amortization on each machine at December 31, 2005. Round your answers to the nearest dollar.

(c) Should Flakeboard consider recording amortization to the nearest day? Why or why not?

(d) How will Flakeboard's choice of how to prorate annual amortization in the period of acquisition affect machine 3? Explain.

Calculate amortization under different methods, and consider effects.
(SO 2) AN

P9–3A White-line Company purchased a machine on account on September 3, 2003, at an invoice price of $85,000. On September 4, 2003, it paid $5,400 for delivery of the machine. A one-year, $975 insurance policy on the machine was purchased on September 6, 2003. On September 20, 2003, White-line paid $2,500 for installation and testing of the machine. The machine was ready for use on September 25, 2003.

White-line estimates the useful life of the machine will be four years, with a residual value of $6,000 at the end of that period. White-line also estimates that, in terms of activity, the useful life of the machine will be 25,000 units. White-line has a December 31 fiscal year end and records amortization to the nearest month.

Instructions

(a) Determine the cost of the machine.
(b) Calculate the amount of amortization expense that White-line should record during each fiscal year of the asset's life under the following assumptions:
    1. White-line uses the straight-line method of amortization.
    2. White-line uses the declining-balance method at double the straight-line rate.
    3. White-line uses the units-of-activity method. Assume actual usage is as follows: 1,500 units in 2003; 7,000 units in 2004; 6,500 units in 2005; 5,500 units in 2006; and 4,500 units in 2007.
(c) Which amortization method reports the highest amount of amortization expense in 2003? In 2006? Over the life of the asset?
(d) Which method would result in the highest net income in 2003? In 2006? Over the life of the asset?
(e) Which method would result in the highest cash flow in 2003? In 2006? Over the life of the asset?

P9–4A At the beginning of 2002, Bérubé Company acquired equipment costing $60,000. It was estimated that this equipment would have a useful life of five years and a residual value of $4,500. The straight-line method of amortization was considered the most appropriate to use with this type of equipment, and amortization is to be recorded at the end of each calendar year.

Calculate revisions to amortization expense. (SO 3) AP

At the beginning of 2004 (the third year of the equipment's life), the company's engineers reconsidered their expectations. They estimated that the equipment's useful life would probably be six years (in total) instead of five years. The estimated residual value was not changed.

Three years later, at the beginning of 2007, the estimated residual value was reduced to $2,500.

Instructions

(a) Prepare an amortization schedule for the equipment, including the revisions to estimated useful life and residual value.
(b) If the company had not revised the residual value, what would the net book value of the equipment have been at the end of its useful life?

P9–5A The transactions below are expenditures related to property, plant, and equipment.

Account for operating and capital expenditures. (SO 4) AP

  1. Operator controls on equipment were replaced for $7,000, because the control devices that came with it were not adequate.
  2. A total of $4,600 was spent for decorative landscaping (planting flowers and shrubs, etc.).
  3. A new air-conditioning system for the factory offices was bought for $36,000.
  4. Windows broken in a labour dispute (not covered by insurance) were replaced for $2,400.
  5. A fee of $1,500 was paid to have new machinery adjusted and tested before it was used.
  6. Machinery damaged by a forklift truck was repaired for $5,000.
  7. The transmission in a delivery vehicle was repaired for $1,600.

Instructions

For each of the transactions listed above, indicate the title of the account that you think should be debited in recording the transaction. Briefly explain your reasoning.

P9–6A Cuylits Company owned processing equipment that had a cost of $125,000. It had an expected useful life of five years and an expected residual value of $10,000. Amortization was recorded each December 31. The straight-line method of amortization is used and amortization is calculated to the nearest month.

Record operating and capital expenditures. Calculate revision to amortization expense. (SO 2, 3, 4) AP

During its third year of service, the following cash expenditures were made on this equipment:

Feb.   7 Lubricated and adjusted the equipment to maintain optimum performance, $1,000.
Mar. 19 Replaced a number of belts, hoses, etc., which were showing signs of wear, $2,500.
July   7 Completed an overhaul of the equipment at a cost of $15,000. The work included the installation of new computer controls to replace the original controls, which were technologically obsolete. As a result of this work, the estimated useful life of the equipment was increased to seven years. The estimated residual value was increased to $12,000.

Instructions

(a) Prepare journal entries to record each of the above transactions.
(b) Calculate the amortization expense that should be recorded for this equipment in (1) the second year of its life, (2) the third year of its life (the year in which the above transactions took place), and (3) the fourth year of its life.
(c) What will accumulated amortization equal at the end of the asset's estimated useful life?

Calculate amortization using two methods. Calculate gain or loss on disposal and total expense over life of asset.
(SO 2, 5) AN

P9–7A Forristal Farmers purchased a piece of equipment at the beginning of its fiscal year at a cost of $31,000. The equipment has an estimated useful life of four years with an estimated residual value at the end of the four years of $1,000. The president is debating the merits of using the single declining-balance method of amortization as opposed to the straight-line method of amortization. The president feels that the straight-line method will have a more favourable impact on the income statement.

Instructions

(a) Prepare a schedule comparing the amortization expense and net book values for each of the four years, and in total for the four years, under (1) the straight-line method, and (2) the declining-balance method, using one times the straight-line rate.
(b) Assume that the equipment is sold at the end of year 3 for $10,000.
   1. Calculate the gain or loss on the sale of the equipment, under (a) the straight-line method, and (b) the declining-balance method.
   2. Prepare a schedule to show the overall impact of the total amortization expense combined with the gain or loss on sale for the three-year period under each method of amortization (consider the total effect on net income over the three-year period). Comment on your results.

Record disposal of equipment under various alternatives.
(SO 2, 5) AP

P9–8A Express Co. has delivery equipment that cost $65,000 when it was purchased on July 1, 2002. The delivery equipment has a useful life of five years, with an expected residual value of $5,000. The equipment is disposed of on September 25, 2005. Express Co. uses the straight-line method of amortization.

Instructions

(a) Prepare a journal entry to update amortization in 2005 to the date of disposal. Assume Express Co. has a December 31 fiscal year end and calculates amortization for partial periods to the nearest month.
(b) Record the disposal under the following assumptions:
   1. It was scrapped as having no value.
   2. It was sold for $30,000.
   3. It was sold for $19,000.
   4. It was traded for new delivery equipment with a list price of $87,000. Express was given a trade-in allowance of $28,000 on the old delivery equipment and paid the balance in cash. Express determined the fair market value of the old equipment to be $22,000 at the date of the exchange.

Record property, plant, and equipment transactions; prepare partial balance sheet.
(SO 1, 2, 3, 4, 5, 8) AP

P9–9A Ledesma Investments has a June 30 fiscal year end. It uses straight-line amortization and has a policy of recording amortization for partial periods to the nearest month. The following transactions involved property, plant and equipment:

July   3, 2001   Purchased assets from a recently bankrupt business for $745,000. Paid $100,000 of the purchase price in cash and issued a mortgage payable for the balance. An appraisal provided the following information on the fair market values of the property: land, $495,000; building, $360,000; and machinery, $45,000.

June 30, 2002   Recorded amortization on the amortizable assets. The building has an estimated useful life of 40 years and a $20,000 residual value. The machinery has an estimated useful life of eight years and a $4,250 residual value.

June 30, 2003   Recorded amortization on the amortizable assets.

Nov. 17, 2003   Paid $850 cash for minor repairs to the machinery.

June 30, 2004   Reviewed the estimated useful lives and residual values before making the year-end adjusting entries for amortization. As a result of the high usage of the machinery, decided that the total estimated useful life should be reduced to five years from the original eight years and that the residual value should be reduced to $3,500. There were no changes in estimates for the building. Recorded annual amortization.

Dec. 28, 2004 Purchased new machinery with a list price of $55,000. Traded in the machinery purchased in 2001 and received a $20,000 trade-in allowance, paying the balance in cash. An independent appraisal stated the fair market value of the old machinery was $15,000. The new machinery has a useful life of five years and a residual value of $5,000.

June 30, 2005 Recorded amortization on the amortizable assets.

Instructions

(a) Prepare journal entries to record the above transactions.

(b) Show how the property, plant, and equipment would appear on the June 30, 2005, balance sheet.

(c) What accounts and amounts will be included on the income statement for the year ended June 30, 2005, with respect to long-lived assets?

P9–10A Due to rapid turnover in the accounting department, a number of transactions involving intangible assets were improperly recorded by Riley Corporation in the year ended December 31, 2005:

1. Riley developed a new patented manufacturing process early in the year, incurring research and development costs of $120,000. Of this amount, 45% was considered to be development costs that could be capitalized. Riley recorded the entire $120,000 in the patents account and amortized it using a 15-year estimated useful life.

2. The company purchased a patent for $47,500. In early January, Riley capitalized $139,400 as the cost of the patent because that's how much Riley believed it was worth. Riley credited the account Gain on Patent Appreciation for the difference. Patent amortization expense of $6,970 was recorded, based on a 20-year legal life. The estimated useful life was 12 years.

3. On July 1, 2005, Riley purchased a small company and, as a result, acquired goodwill of $60,000. Riley recorded a half-year's amortization in 2005, $1,500. There was no impairment of goodwill and it is expected to benefit the company indefinitely.

4. At year end, the company made a $6,000 charitable donation which it debited to goodwill.

Instructions

Prepare all journal entries needed to correct any errors made during the year 2005.

P9–11A The intangible assets reported by Ip Company at December 31, 2004, are presented below:

Patent ($70,000 cost less $7,000 amortization)	$ 63,000
Copyright ($48,000 cost less $19,200 amortization)	28,800
Goodwill	210,000
	$301,800

The patent was acquired in January 2004 and has an estimated useful life of 10 years. The copyright was acquired in January 2001 and also has an estimated useful life of 10 years. The following cash transactions may have affected intangible assets during the year 2005:

Jan.   2 Paid $22,500 of legal costs to successfully defend the patent against infringement by another company.

June 30 Developed a new product, incurring $220,000 in research costs and $60,000 in development costs, which were paid in cash. A patent was granted for the product on July 1. Its expected useful life is equal to its legal life.

Sept. 1 Paid $110,000 to an Olympic gold medallist to appear in commercials advertising the company's products. The commercials will air in September and October.

Oct.   1 Acquired a copyright for $160,000 cash. The copyright has an expected useful life of five years.

Dec. 31 Determined the fair market value of the goodwill to be $150,000. Ip Company believes this drop in value to be a permanent impairment.

Prepare entries to correct errors made in recording and amortizing intangible assets.
(SO 7) AN

Record intangible asset transactions; prepare partial balance sheet.
(SO 7, 8) AP

Instructions

(a) Prepare journal entries to record the above transactions.
(b) Prepare journal entries to record the 2005 amortization expense for intangible assets. Round your answers to the nearest dollar.
(c) Prepare the intangible assets section of the balance sheet at December 31, 2005.

Record equipment and natural resource transactions; prepare partial balance sheet.
(SO 2, 6, 8) AP

P9–12A The Yount Mining Company has a December 31 fiscal year end. The following information related to the Gough Alexander mine is available:

1. Yount purchased the Gough Alexander mine on March 31, 2004, for $2.6 million cash. On the same day, modernization of the mine was completed at a cash cost of $260,000. It is estimated that this mine will yield 560,000 tonnes of ore. The estimated residual value of the mine is $200,000. Yount expects it will extract all the ore, and then close and sell the mine site in four years.
2. On April 6, 2004, Yount moved equipment to the Gough Alexander mine from another mine site. The equipment was originally purchased on September 29, 2002, at a cost of $500,000. The equipment was being amortized on a straight-line basis over an estimated useful life of eight years with a residual value of $20,000. Yount has a policy of recording amortization for partial periods to the nearest month. The estimated useful life and residual value of the equipment did not change after the relocation. The equipment will be moved to a new site when the Gough Alexander mine is closed.
3. During 2004, Yount extracted 120,000 tonnes of ore from the mine. It sold 100,000 tonnes.
4. During 2005, Yount extracted 110,000 tonnes of ore from the mine. By December 31, 2005, all of the ore that had been extracted was sold.

Instructions

(a) Prepare the 2004 and 2005 journal entries required for the above, including year-end adjustments.
(b) Show how the Gough Alexander mine will be reported on Yount's December 31, 2005, balance sheet.
(c) What is the net book value of the equipment on December 31, 2005?

Calculate ratios and comment.
(SO 8) AN

P9–13A Andruski Company and Brar Company, two companies of roughly the same size, both manufacture in-line skates. An investigation of their financial statements reveals the following information:

	Andruski Company	Brar Company
Net sales	$ 950,000	$1,300,000
Net income	245,000	310,000
Total assets, start of year	2,250,000	2,465,000
Total assets, end of year	2,800,000	3,295,000

Instructions

(a) For each company, calculate the asset turnover and return on assets ratios.
(b) Based on your results in part (a), comment on the relative effectiveness of the two companies at using their assets to generate sales and produce net income.

Problems: Set B

P9–1B Weisman Company was organized on January 1. During the first year of operations, the following expenditures were recorded by the accountant in a T account called Land and Building:

Record acquisition costs of land and building.
(SO 1) AP

Land and Building	
280,000 (1)	
7,200 (2)	
3,800 (3)	
5,800 (4)	
10,000 (5)	
3,500 (6)	
Bal. 310,300	

Explanations of the T account amounts follow:

1. Cost of real estate purchased as a package, $280,000 (fair market value of land, $200,000; fair market value of building, $100,000; fair market value of driveway and parking lot, $25,000)
2. Installation cost of fences around property
3. Legal fees on real estate purchase in (1) above
4. Property taxes on land and building for current year
5. Landscaping costs
6. Interior and exterior painting

Instructions

Prepare any entries necessary to correct the recording of the above transactions. Round your answers to the nearest dollar.

P9–2B In recent years, Tarcher Company purchased three machines. Various amortization methods were selected. Information concerning the machines is summarized below:

Calculate and discuss amortization under different methods for partial periods.
(SO 2) AP

Machine	Acquired	Cost	Residual Value	Useful Life in Years	Amortization Method
1	Feb. 21, 2001	$48,940	$4,000	7	Straight-line
2	Jun. 11, 2003	84,000	4,500	10	Declining-balance
3	Sep. 20, 2004	78,800	3,500	5	Units-of-activity

For the declining-balance method, the company uses double the straight-line rate. For the units-of-activity method, total machine hours are expected to be 30,000. Actual hours in the first two years were 1,500 in 2004 and 7,200 in 2005.

Instructions

(a) If Tarcher has a policy of recording amortization to the nearest month, calculate the amount of accumulated amortization on each machine at December 31, 2005. Round your answers to the nearest dollar.

(b) If Tarcher has a policy of recording a half year's amortization in the year of acquisition and disposal, calculate the amount of accumulated amortization on each machine at December 31, 2005. Round your answers to the nearest dollar.

(c) Which policy should Tarcher follow—recording amortization to the nearest month in the year of acquisition or recording a half year's amortization in the year of acquisition? Why or why not?

(d) How will Tarcher's choice of how to record amortization in the year of acquisition affect machine 3? Explain.

P9–3B Mazlish Company purchased a machine on account on April 6, 2003, at an invoice price of $180,000. On April 7, 2003, it paid $900 for delivery of the machine. A one-year, $2,275 insurance policy on the machine was purchased on April 9, 2003. On April 22, 2003, Mazlish paid $3,300 for installation and testing of the machine. The machine was ready for use on April 27, 2003.

Calculate amortization under different methods, and consider effects.
(SO 2) AN

Mazlish estimates the useful life of the machine will be five years, with a residual value of $11,500 at the end of that period. Mazlish estimates that the useful life of the machine, in terms of activity, will be 55,000 units. Mazlish has a December 31 fiscal year end and records amortization to the nearest month.

Instructions

(a) Determine the cost of the machine.
(b) Calculate the amount of amortization expense that Mazlish should record during each fiscal year of the asset's life under the following assumptions:
    1. Mazlish uses the straight-line method of amortization.
    2. Mazlish uses the declining-balance method at double the straight-line rate.
    3. Mazlish uses the units-of-activity method. Assume actual usage is as follows: 8,500 units in 2003; 12,000 units in 2004; 11,500 units in 2005; 10,500 units in 2006; 9,500 units in 2007; and 3,000 units in 2008.
(c) Which amortization method reports the lowest amount of amortization expense in 2003? In 2006? Over the life of the asset?
(d) Which method would result in the lowest net income in 2003? In 2006? Over the life of the asset?
(e) Which method would result in the lowest cash flow in 2003? In 2006? Over the life of the asset?

Calculate revisions to amortization expense. (SO 3) AP

P9–4B On January 4, 2006, Harrington Company acquired equipment costing $65,000. It was estimated at that time that this equipment would have a useful life of eight years and a residual value of $3,000. The straight-line method of amortization is used by Harrington for its equipment. Its fiscal year end is December 31.

At the beginning of 2006 (the beginning of the third year of the equipment's life), the company's engineers reconsidered their expectations. They estimated that the equipment's useful life would more likely be five years in total, instead of the previously estimated eight. The estimated residual value was also reduced to $1,500.

Instructions

(a) What should the net book value of the equipment equal at the end of its useful life?
(b) Prepare an amortization schedule for the equipment, including the revisions to estimated useful life and residual value. Is the ending net book value equal to your prediction in (a) above?

Account for operating and capital expenditures. (SO 4) AP

P9–5B The transactions below are expenditures for a forklift:

1. Rebuilding of the diesel engine that has over 20,000 hours, $10,000
2. New tires, $6,000
3. New safety cab, $5,000
4. Replacement of a windshield (not covered by insurance), $1,200
5. Training the operator, $1,600
6. New paint job after the company changed its logo and colours, $2,000
7. Insurance policy, $1,110

Instructions

For each of the transactions listed above, indicate the title of the account that you think should be debited in recording the transaction. Briefly explain your reasoning.

Record operating and capital expenditures. Calculate revision to amortization expense. (SO 2, 3, 4) AP

P9–6B Copps Co. owns woodworking equipment that had a cost of $220,000. When new, it had an expected useful life of five years and an expected residual value of $20,000. Amortization is recorded each December 31. The straight-line method is used and amortization is calculated to the nearest month.

During its fourth year of service, the following expenditures were made for this equipment:

Jan. 18 Painted the equipment to make it look new, $1,500.
Mar. 5 Replaced a number of bearings and guides which were showing signs of wear, $2,400.
June 29 Completed an overhaul of the equipment at a cost of $33,000. The work included the installation of new optimizer controls to replace the original controls, which were obsolete. As a result of this work, the total estimated useful life of the equipment was expected to be increased by four years to a total of nine years. The estimated residual value was increased to $25,000.

Instructions

(a) Prepare journal entries to record each of the above transactions.
(b) Calculate the amortization expense that should be recorded for this equipment in (1) the third year of its life, (2) the fourth year of its life (the year in which the above transactions took place), and (3) the fifth year of its life.
(c) What will accumulated amortization equal at the end of the asset's estimated useful life?

P9–7B Rapid Transportation Ltd. purchased a new bus at a cost of $80,000. The bus has an estimated useful life of three years with an estimated residual value at the end of the three years of $8,000. Management is contemplating the merits of using the units-of-activity method of amortization, as opposed to the straight-line method which it currently uses.

Under the units-of-activity method, management estimates a total estimated useful life of 300,000 kilometres: 120,000 kilometres driven in year 1; 100,000 kilometres in year 2; and 80,000 kilometres in year 3.

Instructions

(a) Prepare a schedule comparing the amortization expense and the book values for each of the three years, and in total for the three years, under the straight-line method and the units-of-activity method.
(b) Assume that the bus is sold at the end of its second year for $25,000.
  1. Calculate the gain or loss on the sale of equipment, under (a) the straight-line method and (b) the units-of-activity method.
  2. Prepare a schedule to show the overall impact of the total amortization expense combined with the gain or loss on sale for the two-year period under each method of amortization (consider the total effect on net earnings over the two-year period). Comment on your results.

Calculate amortization using two methods. Calculate gain or loss on disposal and total expense over life of asset.
(SO 2, 5) AN

P9–8B Hemmingsen Co. has office furniture that cost $85,000 when purchased on March 19, 2001. At that time, it was expected to have a useful life of five years and a $1,000 residual value. Hemmingsen Co. uses the straight-line method of amortization and has a calendar year end. The office furniture is disposed of on July 2, 2005.

Record disposal of furniture under various alternatives.
(SO 2, 5) AP

Instructions

(a) Prepare a journal entry to update amortization in 2005 to at the date of disposal. Assume Hemmingsen Co. calculates amortization for partial periods to the nearest month.
(b) Record the disposal under the following assumptions:
  (1) It was scrapped as having no value.
  (2) It was sold for $16,000.
  (3) It was sold for $11,500.
  (4) It was traded for new office furniture with a catalogue price of $96,000. Hemmingsen was given a trade-in allowance of $15,000 on the old office furniture and paid the balance in cash. Hemmingsen determined the fair market value of the old office furniture to be $12,000 at the date of the exchange.

P9–9B Menda Investments has a September 30 fiscal year end. It uses straight-line amortization and has a policy of recording amortization for partial periods to the nearest month. The following transactions involved property, plant, and equipment:

Record property, plant, and equipment transactions; prepare partial balance sheet.
(SO 1, 2, 3, 4, 5, 8) AP

Oct. 6, 2001 Purchased assets from a recently bankrupt business for $550,000. Paid $100,000 of the purchase price in cash and issued a mortgage payable for the balance. An appraisal provided the following information on the fair market values of the property: land, $318,750; building, $256,250; and machinery, $50,000.

Sep. 30, 2002 Recorded amortization on the amortizable assets. The building has an estimated useful life of 40 years and a $15,000 residual value. The machinery has an estimated useful life of 10 years and a $5,000 residual value.

Sep. 30, 2003 Recorded amortization on the amortizable assets.

Dec. 16, 2003 Paid $900 cash for minor repairs to the machinery.

Sep. 30, 2004 Reviewed the estimated useful lives and residual values before making the year-end adjusting entries for amortization. As a result of the high usage of the machinery, decided that the total estimated useful life should be reduced to five years from the original 10 years and that the residual value should be reduced to $2,000. There were no changes in estimates for the building. Recorded annual amortization.

June 28, 2005 Purchased new machinery with a list price of $65,000. Traded in the machinery purchased in 2001 and received a $23,000 trade-in allowance, paying the balance in cash. An independent appraisal stated the fair market value of the old machinery was $18,000. The new machinery has an estimated useful life of five years and a residual value of $6,000.

Sep.   30, 2005 Recorded the amortization on the amortizable assets.

Instructions

(a) Prepare journal entries to record the above.
(b) Show how the property, plant, and equipment would appear on the September 30, 2005, balance sheet.
(c) What accounts and amounts will be included on the income statement for the year ended September 30, 2005, with respect to long-lived assets?

Prepare entries to correct errors made in recording and amortizing intangible assets.
(SO 7) AN

P9–10B Due to rapid turnover in the accounting department, a number of transactions that involved intangible assets were improperly recorded by the Hahn Company in the year ended August 31, 2005.

1. Hahn developed a newly shaped Z-cleat for running shoes. It had research costs of $60,000 and development costs of $35,000. It debited these costs to the patent account.
2. The company registered the patent for the Z-cleat. Legal fees and registration costs totalled $21,000. The company debited these costs to Legal Fees Expense.
3. The company fought a competitor successfully in court, defending its patent. It incurred $38,000 of legal fees. These were debited to Legal Fees Expense.
4. The company sold the rights to manufacture and distribute these cleats to Fleet Foot Inc. for an annual fee of $50,000. Hahn recorded the receipt of this fee as a credit to the patent account.
5. The company recorded amortization of the patent of $2,250 per year [($60,000 + $35,000 − $50,000) ÷ 20 years] over its legal life of 20 years. The expected economic life of the patent is five years.

Instructions

Prepare all journal entries needed to correct any errors made during 2005.

Record intangible asset transactions; prepare partial balance sheet.
(SO 7, 8) AP

P9–11B The intangible assets section of Ghani Corporation's balance sheet at December 31, 2004, is presented here:

Patent ($60,000 cost less $6,000 amortization)	$ 54,000
Copyright ($36,000 cost less $25,200 amortization)	10,800
Goodwill	125,000
Total	$189,800

The patent was acquired in January 2004 and has a useful life of 10 years. The copyright was acquired in January 2001 and also has a useful life of 10 years. The following cash transactions may have affected intangible assets during 2005:

Jan.   2   Paid $27,000 in legal costs to successfully defend the patent against infringement by another company.

Jan.–June Developed a new product, incurring $210,000 in research and $50,000 in development costs. A patent was granted for the product on July 1, and its useful life is equal to its legal life.

Sept. 1   Paid $60,000 to a popular hockey player to appear in commercials advertising the company's products. The commercials will air in September and October.

Oct.   1   Acquired a copyright for $180,000. The copyright has a useful life of 25 years.

Dec. 31   The company determined the fair market value of goodwill to be $85,000. This decline in value is believed to represent a permanent impairment.

Instructions

(a) Prepare journal entries to record the transactions.
(b) Prepare journal entries to record the 2005 amortization expense.
(c) Prepare the intangible assets section of the balance sheet at December 31, 2005.

P9–12B The Cypress Timber Company has a December 31 fiscal year end. The following information related to the Westerlund tract of timber land is available:

Record equipment and natural resource transactions; prepare partial balance sheet. (SO 2, 6, 8) AP

1. Cypress purchased a 50,000-hectare tract of timber land at Westerlund on June 7, 2004, for $50 million, paying $10 million cash and signing an 8% mortgage payable for the balance. Principal payments of $8 million and the annual interest is due each December 31 on the mortgage. It is estimated that this tract will yield 1 million tonnes of timber. The estimated residual value of the timber tract is $2 million. Cypress expects it will cut all the trees and then sell the Westerlund site in five years.
2. On June 26, 2004, Cypress purchased and installed weighing equipment at the Westerlund timber site for $200,000 cash. The weighing equipment will be amortized on a straight-line basis over an estimated useful life of seven years with a residual value of $20,000. Cypress has a policy of recording amortization for partial periods to the nearest month. The weighing equipment will be moved to a new site after the Westerlund site is harvested.
3. During 2004, Cypress cut 110,000 tonnes of timber and sold 100,000 tonnes.
4. During 2005, Cypress cut 230,000 tonnes of timber. By December 31, 2005, all of the timber that had been cut was sold.

Instructions

(a) Prepare 2004 and 2005 journal entries as required for the above including year-end adjustments.
(b) Show how property, plant, and equipment will be recorded on Cypress's December 31, 2005, balance sheet.

P9–13B St. Amand Company and St. Helene Company, two companies of roughly the same size, both manufacture sea kayaks. An investigation of their financial statements reveals the following information:

Calculate ratios and comment. (SO 8) AN

	St. Amand Company	St. Helene Company
Net sales	$4,375,000	$2,775,000
Net income	400,000	350,000
Total assets, start of year	3,780,000	2,540,000
Total assets, end of year	4,290,000	2,175,000

Instructions

(a) For each company, calculate the asset turnover and return on assets ratios.
(b) Based on your results in part (a), comment on the relative effectiveness of the two companies at using their assets to generate sales and produce net income.

Continuing Cookie Chronicle

(Note: This is a continuation of the Cookie Chronicle from Chapters 1 through 8.)

Part 1

Now that she is selling mixers and her customers can use credit cards to pay for them, Natalie is thinking of upgrading her website to include the online sale of mixers and payment by credit card. This would enable her to sell these mixers to a wider range of customers using the Internet.

Natalie contacts her brother who originally prepared the Internet site for her. He agrees to upgrade the site so it can handle credit card security issues as well as direct order entry. The estimated cost of the upgrade is $1,800. This cost would be incurred and paid for during the month of August, 2005, and the upgrade would be operational September 1, 2005. Recall that Natalie's website had an original cost of $600 and is being amortized using the straight-line method over 24 months, starting December 1, 2004, with zero residual value. Additional costs for website maintenance and insurance are estimated to be $1,200 per year.

If Natalie decides to upgrade the website, its useful life will not change and there will be no change in residual value.

Instructions

(a) Prepare the journal entry to record the upgrade.
(b) Calculate the monthly amortization expense before the upgrade and the accumulated amortization and net book value on August 31, 2005.
(c) Calculate the revised monthly amortization expense as of September 1, 2005.
(d) Calculate the accumulated amortization and net book value on December 31, 2005.
(e) Explain to Natalie the difference in accounting for the website upgrade costs and accounting for the costs incurred for website maintenance and insurance. In your explanation, comment on the generally accepted accounting principles that affect the accounting for these transactions.

Part 2

Natalie is also thinking of buying a van that will only be used for business. The cost of the van is estimated at $32,500. Natalie would spend an additional $2,500 to have the van painted. In addition, she wants the back seat of the van removed so that she will have lots of room to transport her mixer inventory as well as her baking supplies. The cost of taking out the back seat and installing shelving units is estimated at $1,500. She expects the van to last her about five years and to drive it for 200,000 kilometres. The annual cost of vehicle insurance will be $2,400. Natalie estimates that at the end of the five-year useful life the van will sell for $6,500. Assume that she will buy the van on August 15, 2005, and it will be ready for use on September 1, 2005.

Natalie is concerned about the impact of the van's cost on her income statement and balance sheet. She has come to you for advice on calculating the van's amortization.

Instructions

(a) Determine the cost of the van.
(b) Prepare three amortization tables: one for straight-line amortization (similar to the one in Illustration 9-7), one for double-declining balance amortization (Illustration 9-9), and one for units-of-activity amortization (Illustration 9-11). For units-of-activity, Natalie estimates she will drive the van as follows: 15,000 km in 2005; 45,000 km in 2006; 50,000 km in 2007; 45,000 km in 2008; 35,000 km in 2009; and 10,000 km in 2010. Recall that Cookie Creations has a December 31 fiscal year end.
(c) What impact will the three methods of amortization have on Natalie's balance sheet at December 31, 2005? What impact will the three methods have on Natalie's income statement in 2005?
(d) What impact will the three methods of amortization have on Natalie's income statement over the van's total five-year useful life?
(e) What impact will the three methods of amortization have on her cash flow over the van's total five-year useful life?
(f) Which method of amortization would you recommend Natalie use?

Financial Reporting and Analysis

Practice Tools

Financial Reporting Problem

BYP9–1 Refer to the financial statements and the Notes to Consolidated Statements for **The Forzani Group Ltd.** which are reproduced in Appendix A.

Instructions

(a) Identify the following amounts for the company's capital assets at February 2, 2003: (1) cost, (2) accumulated amortization, and (3) net book value.

(b) What was the amount of capital assets purchased during the 2003 fiscal year? What was the amount received from the disposal of capital assets in 2003? (*Hint:* Look at the statement of cash flows to determine these amounts.)

(c) What methods of amortization are used by Forzani for financial reporting purposes?

(d) What expected useful life was used for calculating the amortization on the "furniture, fixtures, equipment, and automotive" grouping of capital assets?

(e) What types of intangible assets does Forzani have? Did the company report any impairment losses in 2003?

Interpreting Financial Statements

BYP9–2 **Maple Leaf Foods** is Canada's largest food processor. The company also has operations in the U.S., Asia, and Europe.

Several years ago, labour disputes occurred at three of Maple Leaf's meat products plants, one of which was a fresh pork facility. Prior to the labour dispute, the fresh pork facility in Burlington, Ontario, processed about 32,000 hogs per week on a single shift. After the dispute was over, the facility processed only about 18,000 hogs per week at first. The hog supply was gradually increased over the rest of the year until 44,000 hogs per week were processed on each shift.

This dispute had a negative impact on Maple Leaf's financial results. Maple Leaf paid $37 million of labour dispute costs and payments to employees when the strike at the Burlington fresh pork facility was settled.

Subsequently, Maple Leaf invested $40 million to add a second shift capacity to the facility. After its completion, Maple Leaf was able to process 85,000 hogs per week on a double shift.

Instructions

(a) Identify and discuss the advantages and disadvantages of each amortization method for Maple Leaf Foods' pork facilities. Which method would you recommend that Maple Leaf use to amortize the Burlington plant and equipment? Explain why you chose the method you did.

(b) How should Maple Leaf account for the $37 million of labour dispute costs? Determine which financial statement this amount should be reported on and where it should appear in the statement.

(c) How should Maple Leaf account for the $40-million investment it made to create a world-class prepared meats facility? Discuss whether these costs should be treated as operating expenditures or capital expenditures.

Accounting on the Web

BYP9–3 This problem uses corporate financial statements to identify a company's long-lived assets and amortization methods. The profitability of assets is also calculated.

Instructions

Specific requirements of this Internet case are available on the Weygandt website.

Critical Thinking

Collaborative Learning Activity

BYP9–4 Lévesque Company and Fabre Company are two proprietorships that are similar in many respects. One difference is that Lévesque Company uses the straight-line method of amortization and Fabre Company uses the declining-balance method at the straight-line rate. On January 2, 2003, each company acquires the following amortizable assets:

Asset	Cost	Residual Value	Useful Life
Building	$320,000	$20,000	30 years
Equipment	110,000	10,000	5 years

Including the appropriate amortization expense, annual net income for the companies in the years 2003, 2004, and 2005, and total income for the three years were as follows:

	2003	2004	2005	Total
Lévesque Company	$84,000	$88,400	$90,000	$262,400
Fabre Company	68,000	76,000	85,000	229,000

At December 31, 2005, the balance sheets of the two companies are similar, but Fabre Company has fewer assets and less owner's equity than Lévesque Company.

Steven Yajchuk is interested in buying one of the companies, and he comes to you for advice.

Instructions

With the class divided into groups, answer the following:

(a) Determine the annual and total amortization recorded by each company during the three years. Round your answers to the nearest dollar.
(b) Assuming that Fabre Company also used the straight-line method of amortization instead of the declining-balance method as in (a), prepare comparative income data for the three years.
(c) Which company should Mr. Yajchuk buy? Why?

Communication Activity

BYP9–5 In 2002, a new accounting standard was implemented for intangible assets. Intangible assets, such as goodwill, must now be tested for impairment, rather than amortized. This means that if the value of a company's recorded goodwill exceeds its fair market value, the difference—called an impairment loss—is expensed against net income. Otherwise, the goodwill remains at its carrying, or book, value indefinitely. The Accounting Standards Board (ASB) said that accounting for goodwill was one of the most challenging issues it ever faced.

Instructions

Write a memo commenting on the advantages and disadvantages of this new accounting standard. Why do you think the ASB found this issue so challenging?

Ethics Case

BYP9–6 Finney Container Company has declining sales of its principal product, non-biodegradable plastic cartons. The president, Philip Shapiro, instructs his comptroller to lengthen the estimated asset lives in order to reduce the amortization expense and increase net income.

A processing line of automated plastic extruding equipment, purchased for $3 million in January 2003, was originally estimated to have a useful life of five years and a residual value of $200,000. Amortization has been recorded for two years on that basis. The president wants the equipment's estimated useful life changed to seven years (total), and continued use of the straight-line method. The comptroller is hesitant to make the change, believing it is unethical to increase net income in this manner. The president says, "Hey, the useful life is only an estimate. Besides, I've heard that our competition uses a seven-year estimated life on its production equipment."

Instructions
(a) Who are the stakeholders in this situation?
(b) Is the suggested change in asset life unethical, or simply a shrewd business practice by an astute president?
(c) What is the effect of the president's proposed change on net income in the year of the change?

Answers to Self-Study Questions
1. c   2. b   3. b   4. c   5. b   6. b   7. a   8. a   9. b   10. c   11. c   12. b

Answer to Forzani Review It Question 4
Forzani reports (in thousands) land, $638; buildings, $6,280; building on leased land, $3,159; furniture, fixtures, equipment, and automotive, $97,117; and leasehold improvements, $145,150.

concepts for review >>

Before studying this chapter, you should understand or, if necessary, review:

a. How to make adjusting entries for unearned revenue (Ch. 3, p. 107) and accrued expenses. (Ch. 3, pp. 110–111)

b. The importance of liquidity in evaluating the financial position of a company. (Ch. 4, pp. 173–175)

c. The principles of internal control. (Ch. 7, p. 331)

d. Accounting for notes receivable. (Ch. 8, pp. 398–400)

Does Size Matter?

EDMONTON, Alta.—Sometimes the word "big" just isn't enough. Consider the West Edmonton Mall, which is not only listed in the Guinness Book of World Records as the world's largest shopping centre, at 5.3 million square feet, but also boasts six other records. Those records include the world's largest parking lot (over 20,000 cars) and the world's largest indoor theme park (with its triple-loop "Mindbender" roller coaster).

In addition to the theme park, the indoor lake, the Fantasyland Hotel, and the NHL-sized arena (second home of the Edmonton Oilers), the mall, located in the west end of the City of Edmonton, has over 800 stores and services. Each of these businesses is a tenant, renting space from West Edmonton Mall Property Inc. This company is privately held and family owned.

West Edmonton Mall: www.westedmontonmall.com

Needless to say, for a place of this size, the bills are also, well, big. Paul Balchen, West Edmonton Mall comptroller, estimates that current liabilities usually total between $12 million and $14 million.

Still, it's "much like any other business," Mr. Balchen says, glancing at the mall's balance sheet for July 31, 2003. "We have accounts payable of at least $3 million, and sales taxes—GST only, of course, since this is Alberta—of about $600,000." The next line, accrued liabilities, is another $3 million. That includes a "million-dollar plus ($1,000,000+) power bill," explains Mr. Balchen, "which would be accrued for July but not due until August." Clearly, a mall that covers 48 city blocks uses a lot of air conditioning!

Then, of course, there is the accrued interest on the long-term obligation for the property itself, which amounts to just over $1 million a month. There's also in excess of $1 million in property and corporate income taxes.

The final line on this section of the balance sheet, says Mr. Balchen, is unearned revenue. "That's another million dollars or so," he explains. "Mostly payments from the tenant businesses for the following month, or things like advance payments from hockey leagues for use of the ice rink."

"Even though some of the figures appear large, we have the same accounts on our balance sheet as anyone," Mr. Balchen explains. Large or small, every business needs to keep careful track of its liabilities, pay them in a timely fashion, and plan for the future.

the navigator ✓

- Understand *Concepts for Review*
- Read *Feature Story*
- Scan *Study Objectives*
- Read *Chapter Preview*
- Read text and answer *Before You Go On*
- Work *Demonstration Problem*
- Review *Summary of Study Objectives*
- Answer *Self-Study Questions*
- Complete assignments

chapter 10
Current Liabilities

study objectives >>

After studying this chapter, you should be able to:

1. Explain a current liability and distinguish between the major types of current liabilities.
2. Explain the accounting, and prepare the journal entries, for definitely determinable liabilities.
3. Explain the accounting, and prepare the journal entries, for estimated liabilities.
4. Describe the accounting and disclosure requirements for contingent liabilities, and prepare the necessary journal entries.
5. Explain and illustrate the financial statement presentation of current liabilities.
6. Calculate the payroll for a pay period (Appendix 10A).

Whether it is a huge company such as the West Edmonton Mall, or a small company such as your local convenience store, every company has current liabilities. In Chapter 4, we defined liabilities as creditors' claims on total assets. These claims (debts) must be paid some time in the future by the transfer of assets or services. This future payment date is the reason for the two basic classifications of liabilities: (1) current liabilities and (2) long-term liabilities. We will explain current liabilities in this chapter. We will explain long-term liabilities in Chapter 15.

This chapter is organized as follows:

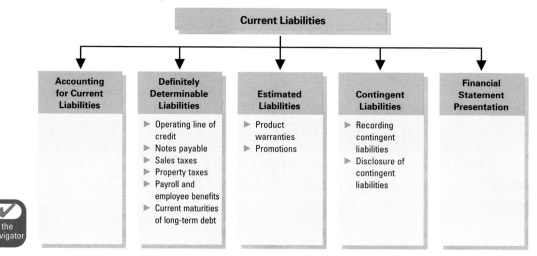

Accounting for Current Liabilities

study objective 1

Explain a current liability and distinguish between the major types of current liabilities.

As explained in Chapter 4, a current liability is a debt with two key features: (1) It is likely to be paid within one year. (2) It will be paid from existing current assets (e.g., cash) or through the creation of other current liabilities. Most companies pay current liabilities out of current assets, rather than by creating other liabilities (e.g., paying an account payable by issuing a note payable). Debts that do not meet both criteria are classified as long-term liabilities.

Liabilities may be described as **definitely determinable**, **estimated**, or **contingent**. With a definitely determinable liability, we know who we owe, when we owe, and how much we owe. There is no uncertainty about its existence, amount, or timing. Examples of definitely determinable current liabilities include operating lines of credit, notes payable, accounts payable, unearned revenues, and current maturities of long-term debt. This category also includes accrued liabilities such as sales taxes, property taxes, payroll and employee benefits, and interest payable.

For some other liabilities, we may know that we owe someone, but must estimate the amount or timing. In most cases, we can estimate these types of liabilities and match expenses with associated revenues in the appropriate period. Examples of estimated current liabilities include product warranties and promotions.

Contingent liabilities are potential liabilities that depend on a future event's confirming their existence, amount, or timing. A typical example of a contingent liability is a pending lawsuit.

We will discuss each type of current liability in the following sections.

Definitely Determinable Liabilities

A definitely determinable liability is one with a known amount, payee, and due date. Most current liabilities fall into this category. The entries for many of these liabilities have been explained in previous chapters, including the entries for accounts payable and unearned revenues. We will discuss the accounting for other types of current liabilities in this section, including operating lines of credit, notes payable, sales taxes payable, property taxes payable, payroll and employee benefits payable, and current maturities of long-term debt.

study objective 2

Explain the accounting, and prepare the journal entries, for definitely determinable liabilities.

Operating Line of Credit

Current assets (such as accounts receivable) do not always turn into cash at the exact time that current liabilities (such as accounts payable) must be paid. Consequently, most companies have an operating line of credit at their bank to help them manage temporary cash shortfalls. This means that the company has been pre-authorized by the bank to borrow money, up to a pre-set limit, when it is needed.

Ottawa-based In-Touch Survey Systems, for example, has a $500,000 operating line of credit with the National Bank. The company president, Peter Andrews, says, "The credit facility provides us with the financial flexibility to execute our business strategy." He also notes that very little of the operating line of credit has been used. "We only expect to use the money to manage very short-term cash requirements."

Security, called collateral, is usually required by the bank as protection in the event of a default on the loan. Collateral normally includes some, or all, of the company's current assets (e.g., accounts receivable or inventories), investments, or property, plant, and equipment.

Line of credit borrowings are normally on a short-term basis, repayable immediately upon request—that is, on demand—by the bank. In reality, repayment is seldom demanded without notice. A line of credit makes it very easy for a company to borrow money. It doesn't have to make a call or visit its bank to actually arrange the transaction. The bank simply covers any cheques written in excess of the bank account balance, up to the approved credit limit.

A number of companies show a negative, or overdrawn, cash balance at year end as a result of using their line of credit. This amount is usually termed bank indebtedness, bank overdraft, or bank advances. No special entry is required to record the overdrawn amount. The normal credits to cash will simply accumulate and be reported as a current liability with a suitable note disclosure. Interest is usually charged on the overdrawn amount at a floating rate, such as prime plus a specified percentage. The prime rate is the interest rate that banks charge their best customers. This rate is usually increased by a specified percentage that reflects the risk profile of the company.

Notes Payable

The line of credit described above is similar to a note payable. Notes payable are obligations in the form of written promissory notes. Notes payable are often used instead of accounts payable. This gives the lender proof of the obligation in case legal action is needed to collect the debt. Notes payable are also frequently issued to meet short-term financing needs.

Notes are issued for varying periods. Those due for payment within one year of the balance sheet date are classified as current liabilities. Most notes are interest-bearing, with interest due monthly or at maturity.

Helpful hint Notes payable are the opposite of notes receivable, and the accounting is similar.

To illustrate the accounting for notes payable, assume that the Caisse Populaire agrees to lend $100,000 on March 1, 2005, to Kok Co. through a $100,000, 6%, four-month note payable. Interest is payable at the maturity date of the note. Kok Co. will receive $100,000 cash and make the following journal entry:

A = L + OE
+100,000 +100,000

↑ Cash flows: +100,000

Mar. 1	Cash	100,000	
	Note Payable		100,000
	To record issue of 6%, 4-month note to		
	Caisse Populaire.		

Interest accrues over the life of the note, and must be recorded periodically. If Kok Co. prepares financial statements quarterly during a calendar year, an adjusting entry is required to recognize interest expense and interest payable of $500 ($100,000 $\times$ 6% $\times \frac{1}{12}$) at March 31. The adjusting entry is as follows:

A = L + OE
+500 -500

Cash flows: no effect

Mar. 31	Interest Expense	500	
	Interest Payable		500
	To accrue interest for one month on		
	Caisse Populaire note.		

Helpful hint The formula to calculate interest is as follows:
   face value of note
$\times$ annual interest rate
$\times$ time in terms of one year
= interest

In the March 31 interim financial statements, the current liabilities section of the balance sheet will show notes payable of $100,000 and interest payable of $500. In addition, interest expense of $500 will be reported in the income statement.

At maturity (July 1, 2005), Kok Co. must pay the face value of the note ($100,000) plus $2,000 interest ($100,000 $\times$ 6% $\times \frac{4}{12}$). But first, the interest must be brought up to date for the three previous months ($1,500 = $100,000 $\times$ 6% $\times \frac{3}{12}$), since interest was last recorded on March 31. The entries to record the accrual of interest and payment of the note and accrued interest follow:

A = L + OE
+1,500 -1,500

Cash flows: no effect

July 1	Interest Expense	1,500	
	Interest Payable		1,500
	To accrue interest for April, May, and June.		

A = L + OE
-102,000 -100,000
          -2,000

↓ Cash flows: -102,000

1	Note Payable	100,000	
	Interest Payable ($500 + $1,500)	2,000	
	Cash ($100,000 + $2,000)		102,000
	To record payment of Caisse Populaire note		
	and accrued interest.		

Sales Taxes

As a consumer, you are well aware that many of the products you buy at retail stores are subject to sales taxes. The taxes are expressed as a percentage of the sales price. As discussed in earlier chapters and in Appendix B, sales taxes usually take the form of the Goods and Services Tax (GST) and Provincial Sales Tax (PST). Federal GST is assessed at 7% across Canada. Provincial sales tax rates vary from 0% to 10% across Canada.

As Paul Balchen notes in our feature story about the West Edmonton Mall, the mall owes no provincial sales tax (Alberta has a 0% provincial sales tax rate) but does owe about $600,000 of GST. In Newfoundland and Labrador, Nova Scotia, and New Brunswick, the PST and GST have been combined into one 15% Harmonized Sales Tax (HST).

Whether GST, PST, or HST, the retailer collects the tax from the customer when the sale occurs. Periodically, the retailer remits (sends) the GST (or HST) collected to the Receiver General of Canada, the collection agent for the Canada Customs and Revenue Agency. PST collections are remitted to the provincial Minister of Finance or Treasurer, as the case may be. In the case of GST (or HST), collections may be offset against payments. In such cases, only the net amount owing (recoverable) must be paid (refunded).

The amount of the sale and the amount of the sales tax collected are usually rung up separately on the cash register. The cash register readings are then used to credit sales or services and the appropriate sales taxes payable accounts. For example, if the March 25 cash register reading for Comeau Company shows sales of $10,000, goods and services tax of $700 ($10,000 × 7% GST rate), and provincial sales tax of $800 ($10,000 × 8% PST rate), the entry is as follows:

Mar. 25	Cash	11,500	
	Sales		10,000
	GST Payable		700
	PST Payable		800
	To record daily sales and sales taxes.		

A	=	L	+	OE
+11,500		+700		+10,000
		+800		

Cash flows: +11,500

When the taxes are remitted to the Receiver General and Minister of Finance/Treasurer, the accounts GST Payable and PST Payable (or HST Payable) are debited and Cash is credited. The company does not report sales taxes as an expense. It simply forwards to the government the amount paid by the customer. Comeau Company serves only as a collection agent for the government.

Some businesses account for their sales on a tax-inclusive basis. They do not separate sales taxes from the price of the goods purchased. When this occurs, sales taxes must still be recorded separately from sales revenues. To extract the sales amount, divide total receipts by 100% plus the sales tax percentage.

To illustrate, assume that Comeau Company has total receipts of $11,500. The receipts from the sale are equal to 100% of the sales price plus 15% (7% + 8%) of sales, or 1.15 times the sales total. We can calculate the sales amount as follows: $11,500 ÷ 1.15 = $10,000. The sales tax amounts of $700 and $800 can be found by multiplying sales by the respective sales tax rates ($10,000 × 7% = $700, and $10,000 × 8% = $800).

In some provinces, PST is charged on the total purchase price plus GST. For example, in Quebec a $100 sale is subject to $7 GST ($100 × 7%) and $8.03 QST [($100 + $7) × 7.5%]. The escalated sales tax rate is 15% [($7 + $8.03) ÷ $100] rather than 14.5% (7% GST + 7.5% QST). Prince Edward Island also charges 10% PST on the purchase price plus GST. It is important to be careful when extracting sales tax amounts from total receipts because of the varying rate combinations that may be in use.

Helpful hint In Quebec the PST is called QST.

Property Taxes

Businesses that own property pay property taxes annually. These taxes are charged by the municipal and provincial governments, and are calculated at a specified rate for every $100 of assessed value of property (i.e., land and building). Property taxes generally cover a calendar year, although bills are not issued until the spring of each year.

To illustrate, assume that Tantramar Management owns land and a building in the city of Regina. Tantramar's year end is December 31. It receives its property tax bill for $6,000 on March 1, which is due to be paid on May 31.

In March, when Tantramar receives the property tax bill, it records the liability owed for its property taxes. At this point in time, two months have passed in the year, so Tantramar also records the property tax expense for the months of January and February. The property tax for the remaining ten months of the year is recorded as a prepayment. The entry is as follows:

A = L + OE
+5,000 +6,000 −1,000

Cash flows: no effect

Mar. 1	Property Tax Expense [($6,000 ÷ 12) × 2 months]	1,000	
	Prepaid Property Tax [($6,000 ÷ 12) × 10 months]	5,000	
	Property Tax Payable		6,000
	To record property tax payable.		

At this point in time, Tantramar has both a prepaid asset in the account Prepaid Property Tax and a liability in the account Property Tax Payable.

In May, when Tantramar pays the property tax bill, the entry is a simple payment of the liability:

A = L + OE
−6,000 −6,000

Cash flows: −6,000

May 31	Property Tax Payable	6,000	
	Cash		6,000
	To record payment of property tax.		

At this point, Tantramar has a zero balance in its liability account but still has a prepayment. Assuming Tantramar only makes adjusting entries annually, it would not adjust the prepaid property tax account until year end, December 31, with the following entry:

A = L + OE
−5,000   −5,000

Cash flows: no effect

Dec. 31	Property Tax Expense	5,000	
	Prepaid Property Tax		5,000
	To record property tax expense.		

There are other equally acceptable ways to record and adjust property taxes. Some companies would debit Prepaid Property Tax for $6,000 on March 1 and wait until adjusting entries are prepared to record any expense. Other companies would debit the Property Tax Expense initially when the bill is recorded on March 1 to save a later adjusting entry. In addition, companies may prepare monthly or quarterly adjusting entries. Regardless, at year end, the accounts Prepaid Property Tax and Property Tax Payable should each have a zero balance and Property Tax Expense should have a balance of $6,000.

Payroll and Employee Benefits

Every employer incurs liabilities related to employees' salaries or wages. One is the amount of salary or wages owed to employees. Managerial, administrative, and sales personnel are generally paid **salaries**. Salaries are often expressed as a specified amount per month or per year. Part-time employees, store clerks, factory employees, and manual labourers are normally paid **wages**. Wages are based on a rate per hour or on piecework (an amount per unit of product). The terms *salaries* and *wages* are frequently used interchangeably.

Another liability is the amount required by law to be withheld from employees' gross or total pay. Assume that Linfang Wang works 40 hours this week for the Pepitone Company, earning $10 per hour. Will Linfang receive a $400 cheque at the end of the week? No, she won't. The reason: Pepitone is required to withhold amounts known as **payroll deductions** from Linfang's wages to pay various other parties. For example, Pepitone must withhold amounts for federal and provincial income taxes, Canada Pension Plan (CPP) contributions, and employment insurance (EI) premiums. It might also withhold voluntary deductions for charitable, insurance, and other purposes.

Until these payroll deductions are remitted to the third parties Pepitone collected the amounts for, they are reported as a current liability in Pepitone's balance sheet. Illustration 10-1 summarizes the types of payroll deductions that most companies usually make.

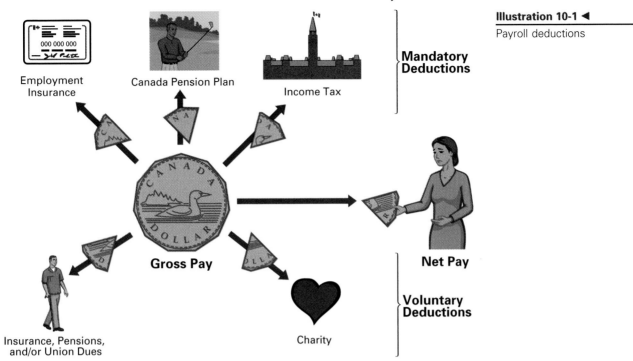

Illustration 10-1 ◄

Payroll deductions

The entries which follow are for the accrual and payment of a $100,000 payroll on which the Pepitone Company withholds assumed deductions from its employees' wages:

Mar. 7	Salaries and Wages Expense	100,000	
	CPP Payable		4,950
	EI Payable		2,100
	Income Taxes Payable		20,427
	United Way Payable		2,445
	Union Dues Payable		667
	Salaries and Wages Payable		69,411
	To record payroll and employee deductions for the week ending March 7.		
7	Salaries and Wages Payable	69,411	
	Cash		69,411
	To record payment of the March 7 payroll.		

A = L + OE
+4,950 −100,000
+2,100
+20,427
+2,445
+667
+69,411

Cash flows: no effect

A = L + OE
−69,411 − 69,411

↓ Cash flows: −69,411

The amount recorded in Salaries and Wages Expense, $100,000, is called **gross earnings**. The amount recorded in Salaries and Wages Payable, $69,411, is known as **net pay**. Net pay is calculated by deducting the employee payroll deductions from gross earnings.

In addition, Pepitone reports liabilities to its employees for the salaries and wages payable as well as liabilities to others, such as the government, United Way, and the union. Rather than pay its employees $100,000, Pepitone is instead required to withhold amounts such as income taxes, CPP, and EI and make these payments directly. In summary, Pepitone is essentially serving as a collection agency for the government and other third parties.

In addition to the liabilities incurred as a result of payroll deductions, employers also incur another type of payroll-related liability. With every payroll, the employer has liabilities to pay various payroll costs that are levied, such as the employer's share of CPP and EI. For example, employers have to pay one times each employee's CPP contribution and 1.4 times each employee's EI contribution. In addition, the provincial governments mandate employer funding of a Workplace Health, Safety, and Compensation Plan. These contributions, plus items such as paid vacations and employer-sponsored pensions, are referred to together as **employee benefits**.

While **employee** payroll deductions do not create an expense for employers, **employer** payroll contributions do. Based on the $100,000 payroll in our Pepitone example, the following entry would be made to record the employer's expense and liability for these employee benefits:

A	=	L	+	OE
		+4,950		−8,465
		+2,940		
		+575		

Cash flows: no effect

Mar. 7	Employee Benefits Expense	8,465	
	CPP Payable		4,950
	EI Payable		2,940
	Workers' Compensation Payable		575
	To record employer's payroll costs on March 7 payroll.		

The payroll and payroll liability accounts are classified as current liabilities because they must either be paid to employees or remitted to government authorities or other third parties periodically and in the near term.

Appendix 10A to this chapter explains how to calculate these amounts and account for payrolls.

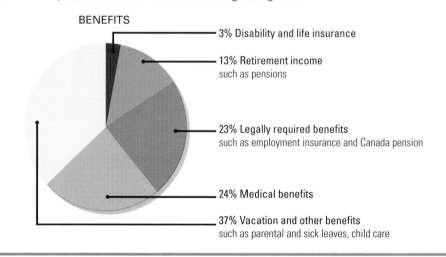

ACCOUNTING IN ACTION ▶ Business Insight

The battle over employee benefits has increased as benefit increases outpace wages and salaries. Growing faster than pay, benefits equalled 38% of salaries and wages in a recent year. While vacations and other forms of paid leave still take the biggest bite of the benefits pie, medical costs are the fastest-growing item.

BENEFITS

3% Disability and life insurance

13% Retirement income
such as pensions

23% Legally required benefits
such as employment insurance and Canada pension

24% Medical benefits

37% Vacation and other benefits
such as parental and sick leaves, child care

Current Maturities of Long-Term Debt

Companies often have a portion of long-term debt that will be due in the current year. That amount is considered a current liability. Assume that on January 1, 2005, Wynneck Construction issues a five-year, $25,000 note payable: Each January 1, starting January 1, 2006, $5,000 of the note is due to be paid. When financial statements are prepared on December 31, 2005, $5,000 should be reported as a current liability. The remaining $20,000 of the note should be reported as a long-term liability on the December 31, 2005, balance sheet.

It is not necessary to prepare an adjusting entry to recognize the current maturity of long-term debt. The proper statement classification of each liability account is recognized when the balance sheet is prepared.

BEFORE YOU GO ON . . .

►Review It

1. What are the two criteria for classifying a debt as a current liability?
2. What are some examples of current liabilities?
3. Name three items that are generally withheld from employees' wages or salaries.

►Do It

Prepare the journal entries to record the following transactions. Round any calculations to the nearest dollar.

1. Accrue interest on December 31 (year end) for a $10,000, 8%, three-month note payable issued on November 1.
2. The cash register total for a four-day craft sale is $256,000. This total includes sales taxes. The GST tax rate is 7% and the PST is 7.5%. Record the sales and sales taxes.
3. A property tax bill of $12,000 is received on May 1 and is due on June 21. Record the entry on May 1, assuming the company has a January 31 year end.
4. A company's gross wages amount to $10,000 per week. Amounts deducted from the employees' wages are CPP of $495, EI of $210, income tax of $3,965, and health insurance of $950. The employer's portion of CPP is $495 and of EI, $294. The wages have been paid to the employees, but the withholdings have not been remitted as yet. Record the weekly payroll and employee benefits, assuming cash is paid to the employees but the withholdings are still due.

Action Plan

- The formula for interest is as follows: face value × annual interest rate × time.
- Separate the sales tax from sales before recording any amounts. Divide the total proceeds by 100% plus the sales tax rates.
- Allocate the property tax bill between periods, determining the asset portion and the expense portion.
- Record both the employees' portion of the payroll and the benefits paid by the employer. Employee deductions are not an expense to the employer.

Solution

1.	Interest Expense ($10,000 × 8% × $\frac{2}{12}$)	133	
	Interest Payable		133
	To accrue interest on note payable.		
2.	Cash	256,000	
	Sales ($256,000 ÷ 114.5%)		223,581
	GST Payable ($223,581 × 7%)		15,651
	PST Payable ($223,581 × 7.5%)		16,768
	To record sales and sales taxes.		
3.	Prepaid Property Tax ($12,000 ÷ 12 × 9)	9,000	
	Property Tax Expense ($12,000 ÷ 12 × 3)	3,000	
	Property Tax Payable		12,000
	To record property tax.		
4.	Wages Expense	10,000	
	CPP Payable		495
	EI Payable		210
	Income Tax Payable		3,965
	Health Insurance Payable		950
	Cash		4,380
	To record payment of wages.		

Employee Benefits Expense	789	
CPP Payable		495
EI Payable		294
To record employee benefits.		

Related exercise material: BE10–1, BE10–2, BE10–3, BE10–4, BE10–5, BE10–6, BE10–7, E10–1, E10–2, E10–3, E10–4, E10–5, and E10–6.

Estimated Liabilities

study objective 3

Explain the accounting, and prepare the journal entries, for estimated liabilities.

An **estimated liability** is an obligation that exists but whose amount and timing are uncertain. However, the uncertainty is not so great that the company cannot reasonably estimate the liability. Commonly estimated liabilities include warranty liabilities and promotional liabilities. We discuss these two examples in the following sections. Other examples include employee benefits such as pensions and bonuses.

Product Warranties

Product warranty contracts may lead to future costs for replacement or repair of defective units. Generally, a manufacturer such as Black & Decker knows that it will have some warranty costs. From prior experience with the product, the company can usually reasonably estimate the anticipated cost of servicing (honouring) the warranty.

The accounting for warranty costs is based on the **matching principle**. The estimated cost of honouring product warranty contracts should be recognized as an expense in the period in which the sale occurs. To illustrate, assume that in 2005 Hermann Company sells 10,000 washers and dryers at an average price of $600. The selling price includes a one-year warranty on parts. Based on past experience, it is expected that 500 units (5%) will be defective, and that warranty repair costs will average $100 per unit. In 2005, warranty contracts are honoured on 300 units at a total cost of $30,000.

At December 31, it is necessary to accrue the estimated warranty costs on the 2005 sales. The calculation is as follows:

Number of units sold	10,000
Estimated rate of defective units	× 5%
Total estimated defective units	500
Average warranty repair cost	× $100
Estimated product warranty liability	$50,000

The adjusting entry, therefore, is as follows:

A = L + OE
    +50,000 −50,000

Cash flows: no effect

Dec. 31	Warranty Expense	50,000	
	Warranty Liability		50,000
	To accrue estimated warranty costs.		

The entry to record the actual repair costs in 2005 to honour warranty contracts on prior sales is shown below:

A = L + OE
−30,000 −30,000

Cash flows: no effect

Dec. 31	Warranty Liability	30,000	
	Repair Parts Inventory (and/or Wages Payable)		30,000
	To record honouring of 300 warranty contracts on 2005 sales.		

A warranty expense of $50,000 is reported as an operating expense in the income statement. The estimated warranty liability of $20,000 ($50,000 − $30,000) is classified as a current liability on the balance sheet.

In the following year, all expenses incurred to honour warranty contracts on 2005 sales should be debited to the Warranty Liability account. To illustrate, assume that 20 defective units are replaced in January 2006, at an average cost of $100. The summary entry for the month of January 2006 follows:

Jan. 31	Warranty Liability	2,000	
	Repair Parts Inventory (and/or Wages Payable)		2,000
	To record honouring of 20 warranty contracts		
	on 2005 sales.		

A = L + OE
−2,000 −2,000

Cash flows: no effect

It is quite likely that the actual expenses will not equal the estimated liability amount. Every year, similar to what is done with accounts receivable and the allowance for doubtful accounts, the warranty liability should be reviewed and adjusted as required.

Promotions

Many companies offer promotional items to attract or retain customers. These promotions take varying forms—cash rebates for returning a receipt, rebate coupon, and bar code or coupons which can be redeemed for a cash discount on items purchased, to name but two examples.

Promotional items are designed to stimulate sales. Much debate has taken place in recent years as to whether or not such promotional discounts should be recorded as an advertising expense or as a reduction of revenue. For example, assume a company sells software for $200, which has a $50 rebate coupon that allows the customer to send in proof of purchase and get $50 back. Should the company record sales revenue of $200 and advertising expense of $50, or should the company record net sales revenue of $150 and no expense? Both result in an increase to net income of $150, but the classification differs.

While there are exceptions, the consensus is that when a promotional item results in a reduced selling price, it should be accounted for as a reduction of revenue and not as an expense. Concerns have risen over the last few years that recording such rebates or discounts as an expense could result in artificially inflated revenue, which can have a significant impact on the valuation of a company.

A further complication of promotional items (such as mail-in cash rebates) is that companies do not know with any certainty at the time of sale the extent to which customers will redeem these rebates. Since it is unlikely that all mail-in cash rebates will be refunded, redemptions must be estimated in the same period the sale is recorded. This estimate should be recorded as a reduction to revenue and as a current liability.

To illustrate, assume that on January 10 Crunchy Cookies issues 60,000 store discount coupons which save customers $0.50 when they buy Crunchy Cookie Dough. The coupons expire on March 31. Based on past experience, Crunchy Cookies, which has a January 31 year end, estimates that 10% of the coupons will be redeemed.

The entry to record the initial liability when the promotion begins is as follows:

Jan. 10	Sales Discount for Coupon Redemptions	3,000	
	(60,000 × 10% × $0.50)		
	Coupon Liability		3,000
	To accrue estimated coupon liability.		

A = L + OE
  +3,000 −3,000

Cash flows: no effect

The Sales Discount for Coupon Redemptions is a contra sales account, deducted from sales to result in net sales in the same way that sales returns and allowances and sales discounts are deducted from sales as we learned in previous chapters. The coupon liability is reported as a current liability on the balance sheet.

The actual process of redeeming the coupon begins when the customer buys the dough and presents the coupon. The store then subtracts the cash amount of the coupon ($0.50) from the customer's bill, records a receivable, and submits the coupons to Crunchy Cookies to be repaid for the amounts the store has paid to customers. When it receives the coupons, Crunchy Cookies pays the grocery store cash for the value of the coupons redeemed.

If by month end in January, 5,000 coupons have been redeemed, Crunchy Cookies makes the following entry to record the redemption of these coupons:

A	=	L	+	OE
−2,500		−2,500		

Cash flows: −2,500

Jan. 31	Coupon Liability (5,000 × $0.50)	2,500	
	Cash		2,500
	To record redemption of coupons.		

The liability account should be reviewed periodically and adjusted for expired coupons. In addition, if Crunchy Cookies' original estimate of the liability differs from actual redemptions, the difference is adjusted in the period when it becomes known.

Accounting for promotional items has many additional complexities, which we have not addressed here. Further detail on this topic will be left to an intermediate accounting course.

ACCOUNTING IN ACTION ▶ Business Insight

New requirements to account for promotional incentives came about partly because of the number of companies caught using such incentives to artificially inflate revenue. For example, Bristol-Myers Squibb, the world's fifth-biggest drugmaker, restated more than US$2 billion in revenue after it was caught offering discounts to wholesalers to buy more goods than necessary to meet patients' needs. The drugmaker relied on these discounts to help sustain its own revenue growth until new heart and cancer medications were ready to introduce to the market.

Source: Joe Richter, "Drugmaker to Restate US$2B in Revenues: Boosted Sales by Offering Discounts to Wholesalers," *The National Post*, October 25, 2002, FP5.

BEFORE YOU GO ON...

▶Review It

1. Distinguish between definitely determinable liabilities and estimated liabilities.
2. How does estimating a warranty liability comply with the matching principle?
3. Why are promotional incentives debited to a contra revenue account rather than an expense account?

Related exercise material: BE10–8, BE10–9, E10–7, and E10–8.

Contingent Liabilities

study objective 4

Describe the accounting and disclosure requirements for contingent liabilities, and prepare the necessary journal entries.

The current liabilities in the preceding sections were either **definitely determinable** or **estimable**. There is no uncertainty about their existence. We knew when they were due and how much was owed, or we were able to reasonably estimate this. But suppose your company is currently involved in a dispute with the Canada Customs and Revenue Agency over the amount of the company's sales tax liability. Should you report the disputed amount as a liability on the balance sheet? Or suppose your company is involved in a lawsuit, which, if you lose, might result in bankruptcy. Liabilities such as these depend on the occurrence or non-occurrence of a future event. This event will confirm either the existence of the liability, the amount payable, the payee, and/or the date payable. These types of liabilities are called contingent liabilities.

A contingency exists when there is uncertainty about the outcome. Although contingent receivables exist, contingent liabilities are far more common. *Financial Reporting in Canada* reports that 79% of the 200 public companies surveyed disclosed contingent liabilities in a recent year. No company reported any contingent receivables.

Recording Contingent Liabilities

Recording contingent liabilities is difficult because these losses and liabilities are dependent—contingent—on some future event. The principle of conservatism requires that these contingencies be accrued by a debit to an expense (loss) account and a credit to a liability account if both of the following conditions are met:

1. The contingency is likely (the chance of occurrence is high);
2. The amount of the contingency can be reasonably estimated.

If you find it difficult to distinguish between a contingent liability and an estimated liability, remember that estimated liabilities are known to exist; it is only their amount or timing that is unknown. For example, a product warranty liability depends on the future failure of a product and that will definitely happen for some of the products sold. Estimates do not have the type of uncertainty which characterizes a contingency. Contingent liabilities are for unusual situations. They are not for ongoing and recurring activities such as product warranties.

ACCOUNTING IN ACTION ► Business Insight

Contingencies abound in the real world. Imperial Tobacco Canada's note on contingencies in its financial statements takes up more than three pages listing all the lawsuits against the company. Environmental contingencies are frequently reported by companies in the notes to their financial statements. Companies with underground storage tanks or toxic waste sites can end up with cleanup costs that may reach as high as $500 million depending on the type of contamination or waste.

Disclosure of Contingent Liabilities

When a contingent liability is likely but cannot be reasonably estimated, or if it is not determinable—neither likely nor unlikely—only disclosure of the contingency is required. Examples of contingencies that may require disclosure are pending or threatened lawsuits, a threat of expropriation of property, and loan guarantees. If a contingency is unlikely—the chance of occurrence is small—it should still be disclosed if the event could have a substantial negative effect on the company's financial position. Otherwise, it does not need to be disclosed.

After Imperial Tobacco Canada disclosed many ongoing and threatened lawsuits in its notes to the financial statements, the company concluded by stating how difficult it is for it to estimate the outcome of these contingent liabilities. Because these outcomes are not determinable, the details are fully disclosed to give decision-makers more information. A brief extract from this note is shown on the following page.

> ## IMPERIAL TOBACCO CANADA LIMITED
> ### Notes to the Consolidated Financial Statements
> ### December 31, 2002
>
> ### 16. Contingencies
>
> Several cases described herein involve several complicated and novel questions of law and fact that may take years to resolve. Accordingly, the Corporation is unable to meaningfully estimate the amount or range of loss that might possibly result from an unfavourable outcome in any of these matters.
>
> All the foregoing actions will be vigorously defended and, although some of these cases are at very early stages and the course and outcome of litigation are difficult to predict, the Corporation believes that a number of valid defences are available.

The following table summarizes the treatment of contingent liabilities:

	Contingent Liability	
Probability of Occurrence	Accrue	Disclose
Likely and reasonably estimable	X	
Likely but not estimable		X
Neither likely nor unlikely (not determinable)		X
Unlikely (but substantial negative effect possible)		X

BEFORE YOU GO ON . . .

▶Review It

1. What are the accounting guidelines for contingent liabilities?
2. Distinguish between estimated liabilities and contingent liabilities.
3. When should a contingent liability be recorded? Disclosed?

Related exercise material: BE10–10, E10–9, and E10–10.

Financial Statement Presentation

study objective 5

Explain and illustrate the financial statement presentation of current liabilities.

As indicated in Chapter 4, current liabilities are the first category under liabilities on the balance sheet. Each of the principal types of current liabilities is listed separately. In addition, the terms of operating lines of credit, notes payable, and other information concerning the individual items are disclosed in the notes to the financial statements.

Current liabilities are usually listed in order of liquidity, by maturity date. Sometimes it is difficult to determine which specific obligations should be listed in which order. A more common method of presenting current liabilities is to list them by order of magnitude, with the largest ones first. Many companies, as a matter of custom, show bank loans, notes payable, and accounts payable first, regardless of amount. The following excerpt from Imperial Tobacco's balance sheet illustrates this practice:

IMPERIAL TOBACCO CANADA LIMITED
Balance Sheet (partial)
December 31, 2002
(in millions)

	2002	2001
Current assets	$1,127	$1,290
Current liabilities		
Short-term borrowings		$ 63
Accounts payable and accrued liabilities	$ 400	474
Income, excise, and other taxes	382	388
Current portion of long-term debt	150	261
	$ 932	$1,186

Companies must carefully monitor the relationship of current liabilities to current assets. This relationship is critical in evaluating a company's short-term debt-paying ability. A company that has more current liabilities than current assets is usually the subject of some concern because it may not be able to make its payments when they become due.

In Imperial Tobacco's case, it has a positive, and improving, current ratio. You will recall from Chapter 2 that the current ratio is calculated by dividing current assets by current liabilities. Imperial Tobacco's current ratio is 1.2:1 ($1,127 million ÷ $932 million) in 2002 and 1.1:1 ($1,290 million ÷ $1,186 million) in 2001.

BEFORE YOU GO ON

▶**Review It**

1. How does The Forzani Group order its current liabilities in its balance sheet? The answer to this question is at the end of the chapter.
2. Describe the disclosure requirements for current liabilities.

Related exercise material: BE10–11 and E10–11.

the navigator

Demonstration Problem

Cornerbrook Company has the following selected transactions:

Feb. 1 Signs a $50,000, six-month, 9% note payable to the CIBC, receiving $50,000 in cash. Interest is payable at maturity.
　10 Cash register receipts total $43,200, which includes 7% GST and 8% PST.
　28 The payroll for the month consists of salaries of $50,000. CPP and EI contributions are $2,475 and $1,050, respectively. A total of $15,000 in income taxes is withheld. The salaries are paid on March 1.

The following adjustment data are noted at the end of the month:

1. Interest expense has been incurred on the note.
2. Employer payroll costs include CPP of $2,475 and EI of $1,470. The company also pays a monthly cost of $500 for a dental plan for its employees.
3. Some sales were made under warranty. Of the units sold under warranty this month, 350 are expected to become defective. Repair costs are estimated to be $40 per unit.

Additional
Demonstration
Problems

Instructions

(a) Journalize the February transactions. Round your calculations to the nearest dollar.
(b) Journalize the adjusting entries at February 28.

Action Plan

- Remember that interest rates are annual rates and must be adjusted for periods of time less than one year.
- Separate sales taxes from sales revenue before recording.
- Remember that employee deductions for CPP, EI, and income tax reduce the salaries payable.
- Employer contributions to CPP, EI, and the dental plan create an additional expense.
- Expense warranty costs in the period in which the sales occur.

Solution to Demonstration Problem

(a)

Feb. 1	Cash		50,000	
	Notes Payable			50,000
	Issued six-month, 9% note to the CIBC.			
10	Cash		43,200	
	Sales ($43,200 ÷ 115%)			37,565
	GST Payable ($37,565 × 7%)			2,630
	PST Payable ($37,565 × 8%)			3,005
	To record sales and sales taxes payable.			
28	Salaries Expense		50,000	
	CPP Payable			2,475
	EI Payable			1,050
	Income Taxes Payable			15,000
	Salaries Payable			31,475
	To record February salaries.			

(b)

Feb. 28	Interest Expense ($50,000 × 9% × $\frac{1}{12}$)		375	
	Interest Payable			375
	To record accrued interest for February.			
28	Employee Benefits Expense		4,445	
	CPP Payable			2,475
	EI Payable			1,470
	Dental Plan Payable			500
	To record employee benefit costs for February.			
28	Warranty Expense (350 × $40)		14,000	
	Warranty Liability			14,000
	To record estimated product warranty liability.			

the navigator

APPENDIX 10A ▶ PAYROLL ACCOUNTING

study objective 6

Calculate the payroll for a pay period.

Payroll and related fringe benefits make up a large percentage of current liabilities. Employee compensation is often the most significant expense that a company has. For example, before its restructuring, Air Canada reported 35,000 employees in total and labour costs of $2.5 billion, which was 25% of total operating expenses.

Payroll accounting involves more than paying employee wages. Companies are required by law to maintain payroll records for each employee, to report and remit payroll deductions, and to respect provincial and federal laws on employee compensation.

The term "payroll" covers all salaries and wages paid to employees. It does not include payments made for services of professionals such as accountants, lawyers, and architects. Such professionals are independent contractors rather than salaried employees. Payments to them are called fees, rather than salaries or wages. This distinction is important, because government regulations for the payment and reporting of payroll apply only to employees.

As we learned in the chapter, there are two types of payroll costs—employee costs and employer costs. The first, employee costs, involve amounts paid to employees (earnings) and amounts paid by employees (payroll deductions). The second, employer costs, involve amounts paid by the employer on behalf of the employee (employee benefits). We will explore employee and employer payroll costs in the following sections.

Determining Employee Payroll Costs

Determining the payroll costs for employees involves calculating (1) gross earnings, (2) payroll deductions, and (3) net pay.

Gross Earnings

Gross earnings is the total compensation earned by an employee. It consists of wages or salaries, plus any bonuses and commissions.

Total **wages** for an employee are determined by multiplying the hours worked by the hourly rate of pay. In addition to the hourly pay rate, most companies are required by law to pay hourly workers at least one and one-half times the minimum hourly wage for overtime work. The number of hours worked before overtime is payable is based on a standard work week, which can vary by industry and occupation.

Assume that Mark Jordan works for Academy Company as a shipping clerk. His authorized pay rate is $10 per hour. The calculation of Mark's gross earnings (total wages) for the 48 hours shown on his time card for the weekly pay period ending June 17 is as follows:

Type of Pay	Hours	×	Rate	=	Gross Earnings
Regular	44	×	$10	=	$440
Overtime	4	×	15	=	60
Total wages					$500

This calculation assumes that Jordan receives one and one-half times his regular hourly rate ($10 × 1.5) for any hours worked in excess of 44 hours per week (overtime). Overtime rates can be as much as twice the regular rates.

The **salary** for an employee is generally based on a monthly or yearly rate. These rates are then prorated to the payroll periods used by the company. Most executive and administrative positions are salaried and without overtime pay.

Many companies have bonus agreements for management and other employees. Bonus arrangements may be based on such factors as increased sales or net income. Bonuses may be paid in cash and/or by granting executives and employees the opportunity to acquire shares in the company at favourable prices (called stock option plans).

Payroll Deductions

As anyone who has received a paycheque knows, gross earnings are usually very different from the amount actually received. The difference is due to payroll deductions. Such deductions do not result in an expense to the employer. The employer is merely a collection agent. It subsequently transfers the deductions to the government or other agency (such as a union, an insurance company, or the United Way). The designated collection agency for the federal government is known as the Receiver General, a division of the Canada Customs and Revenue Agency (CCRA).

Payroll deductions may be mandatory or voluntary. Mandatory deductions are required by law and include Canada Pension Plan contributions, employment insurance premiums, and personal income tax. Voluntary deductions are at the option of the employee.

Canada Pension Plan (CPP)

All employees between the ages of 18 and 70, except those employed in the province of Quebec, must contribute to the Canada Pension Plan. Quebec administers its own similar program, the Quebec Pension Plan (QPP). These plans provide supplemental disability, retirement, and death benefits to qualifying Canadians.

Contribution rates are set by the federal government and are adjusted every January if there are increases in the cost of living. At the time of writing, employee contributions under the *Canada Pension Plan Act* were 4.95% of pensionable earnings. Pensionable earnings are gross earnings less a basic yearly exemption (currently $3,500). A maximum ceiling or limit ($39,900 in 2003) is imposed on pensionable earnings. The exemption and ceiling are prorated to the relevant pay period.

Mark Jordan's CPP contribution for the weekly pay period ending June 17 is $21.42, calculated as follows:

> Gross earnings: $500
> Basic yearly CPP exemption: $3,500
> Prorate basic exemption per week: $3,500 ÷ 52 = $67.31
> Weekly deduction: $500 − $67.31 = $432.69 × 4.95% = $21.42

In addition to withholding employee deductions for remittance to the Receiver General, companies must contribute on behalf of their employees. We will discuss the employer's contributions later in this appendix.

Employment Insurance (EI)

The Canada Pension Plan applies to all employees, whether self-employed or employed by others. Employment insurance is paid only by people who are not self-employed. Employment insurance is designed to provide income protection for a limited period of time to employees who are temporarily laid off, who are on parental leave, or who lose their jobs.

Under the provisions of the *Employment Insurance Act*, an employee is currently required to pay a premium of 2.1% on insurable earnings, to a maximum earnings ceiling of $39,000. In most cases, insured earnings are gross earnings plus any taxable benefits. There is no specified yearly exemption. The employment insurance premium for Mark Jordan for the June 17 payroll is $10.50 ($500 × 2.1%).

Personal Income Tax

In accordance with the *Income Tax Act*, employers are required to withhold income tax from employees for each pay period. The amount to be withheld is determined by three variables: (1) the employee's gross earnings, (2) the number of credits claimed by the employee, and (3) the length of the pay period. To indicate to the CCRA the number of credits claimed, the employee must complete a Personal Tax Credits Return (TD1). There is no limit on the amount of gross earnings subject to income tax withholdings. The higher the earnings, the higher the amount of taxes withheld.

The calculation of personal income tax withholdings is complicated. The best way to determine how much should be withheld from an employee's wages for federal and provincial income taxes is to use payroll deductions tables supplied by the CCRA.

Payroll Deductions Tables

Payroll deductions tables indicate the amount of income tax that should be withheld from gross wages based on the number of credits claimed. Separate tables are provided for weekly, biweekly, semimonthly, and monthly pay periods. Income tax deductions vary by province. CPP and EI also vary, but by wage level. The easiest way to determine all of these payroll deductions is to use tables, rather than to try to calculate the deductions. Tables can be requested from your local CCRA office or downloaded from the CCRA's website <www.ccra-adrc.gc.ca/tax/business/tod>. Simply download the "Tables on Diskette for Windows." This program, which can also be used directly on the CCRA's website, performs the lookup function and accurately calculates payroll information. Information returns can also be sent electronically through this site.

Illustration 10A-1 shows the results of payroll information entered for Mark Jordan. For a weekly wage of $500, with an assumed TD1 claim code of 4, the federal and Ontario income taxes to be withheld total $51.75. CPP and EI contributions are $21.42 and $10.50, respectively.

Payroll Deductions for Regular Salary				
Employee's name (optional)	Mark Jordan			
Pay period ending date (optional)	2005-06-17			
Gross salary (or pension income) for the pay period				500.00
Total EI insurable earnings for the pay period				500.00
Taxable salary or pension income				500.00
Canada Pension Plan (CPP) deductions			21.42	
Employment insurance (EI) deductions			10.50	
Federal tax deductions		37.50		
Provincial or territorial tax deductions		14.25		
Total tax		51.75	51.75	
Requested additional tax deduction			0.00	
Total deductions			83.67	83.67
Net amount				416.33
Total claim amount (from TD1 federal)	Claim Code 4 (11,198.01 - 12,919.00)			
Total claim amount (from TD1 prov or terr)	Claim Code 4 (11,185.01 - 12,869.00)			
Employer's pay period	Weekly payments (52)			
Province of employment	Ontario			

Illustration 10A-1 ◄

Payroll deductions

These are the same amounts calculated manually earlier. Whether you calculate employee payroll deductions manually or by using the tables, be careful to use the appropriate guide, as rates, exemptions, and other regulations can and do change often.

Voluntary Deductions

Employees may choose to authorize withholdings for charitable, retirement, and other purposes. All voluntary deductions from gross earnings should be authorized in writing by the employee. The authorization may be made individually or as part of a group plan. Deductions for charitable organizations such as the United Way, or for financial arrangements such as Canada Savings Bonds and the repayment of loans from company credit unions, are made individually. In contrast, deductions for union dues, extended health insurance, life insurance, and pension plans are often made on a group basis. In the calculation of net pay in the next section, we assume that Jordan has voluntary deductions of $10 for the United Way and $5 for union dues.

Net Pay

Net pay is determined by subtracting payroll deductions from gross earnings. For Mark Jordan, net pay for the weekly pay period ending June 17 is $401.33, calculated as follows:

Gross earnings		$500.00
Payroll deductions:		
CPP	$21.42	
EI	10.50	
Income tax	51.75	
United Way	10.00	
Union dues	5.00	98.67
Net pay		$401.33

Before we learn how to journalize employee payroll costs and deductions, we will turn our attention to specific *employer* payroll costs. After this discussion, we will record the total employee and employer payroll costs for Academy Company, where Mark Jordan works.

Determining Employer Payroll Costs

Employee payroll deductions do not create an expense for the employer. Employer payroll contributions do. Payroll costs result from costs levied on employers by the federal and provincial governments. The federal government requires CPP and EI employer contributions. The provincial governments require employer funding of a Workplace Health, Safety, and Compensation Plan. Some provinces also levy an education or health tax on employers. These contributions, plus such items as paid vacations and pensions, are referred to as employee benefits.

Canada Pension Plan

We have seen that each employee must contribute to the Canada Pension Plan. The employer must match each employee's CPP contribution. The matching contribution results in an employee benefits expense to the employer. The employer's contributions are subject to the same rate and maximum earnings that apply to the employee. The account CPP Payable is used for both the employee's and the employer's CPP contributions.

Employment Insurance

Employers are required to contribute 1.4 times an employee's EI deductions during a calendar year. The account Employee Benefits Expense is debited for this contribution and EI Payable is credited to recognize this liability.

Workplace Health, Safety, and Compensation

Helpful hint CPP and EI premiums are paid by both the employer and the employee. Workers' compensation is paid entirely by the employer.

The Workplace Health, Safety, and Compensation Plan provides supplemental benefits for workers who are injured or disabled on the job. The cost of this program is paid entirely by the employer; the employee is not required to make contributions to this plan. Employers are assessed a rate—usually between 1% and 10% of their gross payroll—based on the risk of injury to employees and past experience.

Additional Employee Benefits

In addition to the three payroll contributions described above, employers have other employee benefit costs. Two of the most important are paid absences and post-employment benefits. In addition to these, some provinces impose other payroll costs on businesses of certain sizes. For example, Ontario and Quebec have a health tax. Manitoba and Newfoundland have both a health and a post-secondary education tax.

Paid Absences

Employees are given rights to receive compensation for absences when certain conditions of employment are met. The compensation may be for paid vacations, sick pay benefits, and paid holidays. A liability should be estimated and accrued for future paid absences. When the amount cannot be estimated, the potential liability should be disclosed. Ordinarily, vacation pay is the only paid absence that is accrued. Other types of paid absences are only disclosed in notes to the statements.

Post-Employment Benefits

Post-employment benefits are payments by employers to retired or terminated employees. These payments are for (1) supplemental health care, dental care, and life insurance, and (2) pensions.

Employers must use the **accrual basis** in accounting for post-employment benefits. It is important to **match** the cost of these benefits with the periods in which the employer benefits from the services of the employee.

Recording the Payroll

Recording the payroll involves maintaining payroll department records, recognizing payroll expenses and liabilities, paying the payroll, and filing and remitting payroll deductions.

Maintaining Payroll Department Records

Employers must provide each employee with a Statement of Remuneration Paid (Form T4), following the end of each calendar year, to file with his or her personal income tax return. This statement shows employment income, CPP contributions, EI premiums, and income tax deducted for the year, in addition to other voluntary deductions. The record that provides this information and other essential data is the employee earnings record. An extract from Mark Jordan's employee earnings record for the month of June is shown in Illustration 10A-2. This record includes the pay details calculated in Illustration 10A-1 for the week ending June 17.

ACADEMY COMPANY
Employee Earnings Record
Year Ended December 31, 2005

Name — Mark Jordan   Address — 162 Bowood Avenue

Social Insurance Number — 113-114-469   Toronto

Date of Birth — December 24, 1962   Ontario, M4N 1Y6

Date Employed — September 1, 2004   Telephone — 416-486-0669

Date Employment Ended — _____   E-mail — jordan@sympatico.ca

Job Title — Shipping Clerk   Claim Code — 4

| 2005 Period Ending | Total Hours | Gross Earnings | | | | Deductions | | | | | | Payment | |
		Regular	Overtime	Total	Cumulative	CPP	EI	Income Tax	United Way	Union Dues	Total	Net Amount	Cheque #
06/03	46	440.00	30.00	470.00	10,470.00	19.93	9.87	46.35	10.00	5.00	91.15	378.85	974
06/10	47	440.00	45.00	485.00	10,955.00	20.18	10.19	49.00	10.00	5.00	94.37	390.63	1028
06/17	48	440.00	60.00	500.00	11,455.00	21.42	10.50	51.75	10.00	5.00	98.67	401.33	1077
06/24	46	440.00	30.00	470.00	11,925.00	19.93	9.87	46.35	10.00	5.00	91.15	378.85	1133
June Total		1,760.00	165.00	1,925.00		81.46	40.43	193.45	40.00	20.00	375.34	1,549.66	

Illustration 10A-2 ▲

Employee earnings record

A separate earnings record is kept for each employee and updated after each pay period. The cumulative payroll data on the earnings record are used by the employer to (1) determine when an employee has reached the maximum earnings subject to CPP and EI premiums, (2) file information returns with the CCRA (as explained later in this section), and (3) provide each employee with a statement of gross earnings and withholdings for the year on the T4 form.

In addition to employee earnings records, many companies find it useful to prepare a payroll register. This record accumulates the gross earnings, deductions, and net pay per employee for each pay period and provides the documentation for preparing a paycheque for each employee. Academy Company's payroll register is presented in Illustration 10A-3. It shows the data for Mark Jordan in the wages section. In this example, Academy Company's total weekly payroll is $17,210, as shown in the gross earnings column.

Illustration 10A-3 ▼

Payroll register

ACADEMY COMPANY
Payroll Register
Week Ending June 17, 2005

| Employee | Total Hours | Gross Earnings | | | Deductions | | | | | | Payment | |
		Regular	Overtime	Gross	CPP	EI	Income Tax	United Way	Union Dues	Total	Net Pay	Cheque #
Office Salaries												
Aung, Ng	44	638.00		638.00	28.25	13.40	177.75	15.00		234.40	403.60	998
Canton, Mathew	44	649.00		649.00	28.79	13.63	146.40	20.00		208.82	440.18	999
Mueller, William	44	583.00		583.00	25.53	12.24	107.45	11.00		156.22	426.78	1000
Subtotal		5,200.00		5,200.00	226.20	109.20	1,750.54	120.00		2,205.94	2,994.06	
Wages												
Caron, Réjean	44	440.00	30.00	470.00	19.93	9.87	76.30	18.00	5.00	129.10	340.90	1025
Jordan, Mark	48	440.00	60.00	500.00	21.42	10.50	51.75	10.00	5.00	98.67	401.33	1077
Milroy, Lee	47	440.00	45.00	485.00	20.68	10.19	80.50	10.00	5.00	126.37	358.63	1089
Subtotal		11,000.00	1,010.00	12,010.00	522.44	252.21	3,896.36	301.50	215.00	5,187.51	6,822.49	
Total		16,200.00	1,010.00	17,210.00	748.64	361.41	5,646.90	421.50	215.00	7,393.45	9,816.55	

Note that this record is a listing of each employee's payroll data for the pay period. In some companies, the payroll register is a special journal. Postings are made directly to ledger accounts. In other companies, the payroll register is a supplementary record that provides the data for a general journal entry and later posting to the ledger accounts. At Academy Company, the latter procedure is followed.

In a computerized accounting system, the payroll register is automatically updated from inputted information on the employees' earnings records. The register also provides the supporting documentation for electronic funds transfers between the company's bank account and those of its employees. Alternatively, the register is used to generate electronically printed payroll cheques. Automatic outputs from a computerized payroll system also include monthly reports for the CCRA and annual T4 slips.

Recognizing Payroll Expenses and Liabilities

Payroll costs are incurred only for the employees' salaries and wages and the employer's contributions. Employee payroll deductions are not an expense to the company, since they have been collected for the government or another third party. They remain a current liability to the company until remitted.

Employee Payroll Costs

A journal entry is made to record the employee portion of the payroll. For the week ending June 17, the entry for Academy Company using total amounts from the company's payroll register for the period as shown in Illustration 10A-3, is as follows:

June 17	Salaries Expense	5,200.00	
	Wages Expense	12,010.00	
	CPP Payable		748.64
	EI Payable		361.41
	Income Tax Payable		5,646.90
	United Way Payable		421.50
	Union Dues Payable		215.00
	Salaries and Wages Payable		9,816.55
	To record payroll for the week ending June 17.		

A = L + OE

+748.64 −5,200.00
+361.41 −12,010.00
+5,646.90
+421.50
+215.00
+9,816.55

Cash flows: no effect

Specific liability accounts are credited for the mandatory and voluntary deductions made during the pay period as shown above. Separate expense accounts are used for gross earnings because office workers are on salary and other employees are paid an hourly rate. The amount credited to Salaries and Wages Payable is the sum of the individual cheques the employees will receive when the payroll is paid.

Employer Payroll Costs

Employer payroll costs are usually recorded when the payroll is journalized. The entire amount of gross pay is subject to four of the employer payroll costs mentioned earlier: CPP, EI, Workers' Compensation, and vacation pay. For the June 17 payroll, Academy Company's CPP is $748.64 ($748.64 × 1). Its EI premium is $505.97 ($361.41 × 1.4).

Assume that Academy Company is also assessed for Workers' Compensation at a rate of 1%. Its compensation expense for the week would therefore be $172.10 [($5,200 + $12,010) × 1%]. For vacation pay, assume that Academy Company employees accrue vacation days at an average rate of 4% of the gross payroll (equivalent to two weeks of vacation). The accrual for vacation benefits in one pay period—one week—is $688.40 [($5,200 + $12,010) × 4%].

The Province of Ontario levies an additional employer payroll cost—a health tax to help fund health care. The rate is 1.95% of payroll, however, the first $400,000 is exempt from this tax. Academy's payroll for the year has not yet reached this level so it is exempt from this health tax.

Accordingly, the entry to record the payroll costs or employee benefits associated with the June 17 payroll is as follows:

A	=	L	+	OE
+748.64				−2,115.11
		+505.97		
		+172.10		
		+688.40		

Cash flows: no effect

June 17	Employee Benefits Expense	2,115.11	
	CPP Payable		748.64
	EI Payable		505.97
	Workers' Compensation Payable		172.10
	Vacation Pay Payable		688.40
	To record employer payroll costs on June 17 payroll.		

The liability accounts are classified as current liabilities since they will be paid within the next year. Employee Benefits Expense is often combined with Salaries and Wages Expense on the income statement and classified as an operating expense.

Recording Payment of the Payroll

Payment by cheque or electronic funds transfer is made from either the employer's regular bank account or a payroll bank account. Each paycheque or EFT is usually accompanied by a **statement of earnings** document. This shows the employee's gross earnings, payroll deductions, and net pay for the period and for the year to date.

Following payment of the payroll, the cheque numbers are entered in the payroll register. The entry to record payment of the payroll for Academy Company follows:

A	=	L	+	OE
−9,816.55		−9,816.55		

Cash flows: −9,816.55

June 17	Salaries and Wages Payable	9,816.55	
	Cash		9,816.55
	To record payment of payroll.		

Many companies use a separate bank account for payroll. Only the total amount of each period's payroll is transferred, or deposited, into that account prior to distribution. This helps the company determine if there are any unclaimed amounts. This is another example of an imprest fund, first introduced with petty cash in Chapter 7.

Filing and Remitting Payroll Deductions

Preparation of information returns is the responsibility of the payroll department. Deductions are paid by the comptroller's department. Much of the information for the returns is obtained from employee earnings records.

For the purposes of reporting and remitting, companies combine withholdings of CPP, EI, and income tax. **The withholdings must be reported and remitted monthly** on a Statement of Account for Current Source Deductions (Form PD7A), no later than the 15th day of the month following the month's pay period. There are allowable variations from the pattern of monthly remittances. For example, large employers must remit more often, and smaller companies with perfect payroll deduction remittance records can remit quarterly. Workplace Health, Safety, and Compensation is remitted quarterly to the Workplace Health, Safety, and Compensation Commission. Remittances can be made by mail or through deposits at any Canadian financial institution. When payroll deductions are remitted, payroll liability accounts are debited and cash is credited.

The entry to record the remittance of payroll deductions by Academy Company, in the following month, is as follows:

July 13	CPP Payable ($748.64 + $ 748.64)	1,497.28	
	EI Payable ($361.41 + $505.97)	867.38	
	Income Tax Payable	5,646.90	
	United Way Payable	421.50	
	Union Dues Payable	215.00	
	Workers' Compensation Payable	172.10	
	Cash		8,820.16
	To record payment of payroll deductions for June 17 payroll.		

A	=	L	+	OE
-8,820.16		-1,497.28		
		-867.38		
		-5,646.90		
		-421.50		
		-215.00		
		-172.10		

▼ Cash flows: -8,820.16

Note that the vacation pay liability, recorded on June 17, is not debited or "paid" until the employees actually take their vacation.

Other information returns must be filed by the last day of February each year. In addition, as noted previously, employers must provide employees with a Statement of Remuneration Paid (T4) by the same date.

Summary of Study Objectives

1. *Explain a current liability and distinguish between the major types of current liabilities.* A current liability is a debt that is likely to be paid as follows: (1) within one year, and (2) from existing current assets or through the creation of other current liabilities. There are three major types of liabilities. Definitely determinable liabilities are those with no uncertainty as to existence, amount, or timing. Estimated liabilities exist, but their amount or timing is uncertain. Contingent liabilities depend on a future event to confirm their existence (and possibly the amount and timing).

2. *Explain the accounting, and prepare the journal entries, for definitely determinable current liabilities.* Operating lines of credit are repayable on demand. Interest is normally paid and recorded monthly on these demand loans.

When an interest-bearing promissory note payable is issued, interest expense is accrued over the life of the note. At maturity, the amount paid is equal to the face value of the note plus any accrued interest.

Sales taxes payable are recorded at the time the related sales occur. The company serves as a collection agent for the taxing authority. Sales taxes are not an expense to the company.

Property taxes cover a calendar year and are recorded when the bill is received, or they are estimated and accrued until the actual property tax amount is known. Companies can end up with both a prepayment and a liability for property taxes at the same time in the year as adjustments are made to record the expense in the proper periods.

In recording payroll, wage or salary expense is debited for the gross payroll. Employee deductions are credited to current liability accounts until remitted. The employer's share of the withholdings is debited to an Employee Benefits Expense account and credited to current liability accounts until remitted.

The current maturities of long-term debt should be reported as a current liability in the balance sheet.

3. *Explain the accounting, and prepare the journal entries, for estimated liabilities.* Product warranties and promotional costs are estimated and recorded either as an expense (for warranties) or as a reduction of revenue (for promotional costs) and a liability in the period in which the sales occur. These liabilities are reduced as repairs under warranty or redemptions occur. They are adjusted annually for outstanding or expired warranties or coupons.

4. *Describe the accounting and disclosure requirements for contingent liabilities, and prepare the necessary journal entries.* If it is likely that the contingency will occur and the amount is reasonably estimable, the liability should be recorded in the accounts. However, if the contingency is probable but the amount is not estimable, or if the likelihood is not determinable, then the contingency should be disclosed in the notes to the statements.

5. *Explain and illustrate the financial statement presentation of current liabilities.* The nature and amount of each current liability and contingency should be reported in the balance sheet or in the notes accompanying the financial statements.

6. *Calculate the payroll for a pay period (Appendix 10A).* In recording employee payroll costs, Salaries (or Wages) Expense is debited for gross earnings, individual liability accounts are credited for payroll deductions, and Salaries (Wages) Payable is credited for net pay. In recording employer payroll costs, Employee Benefits Expense is debited for the employer's share of CPP, EI, Workers' Compensation, vacation pay, and any other benefits provided. Each benefit is credited to its respective current liability account.

Glossary

Key Term Matching Activity

Collateral Property pledged as security for a loan. (p. 485)

Contingent liability A potential liability that may become an actual liability in the future. (p. 495)

Definitely determinable liability A liability whose existence, amount, and timing are known with certainty. (p. 485)

Employee benefits Payments made by an employer, in addition to wages and salaries, to provide pension, insurance, medical, or other benefits for its employees. (p. 489)

Estimated liability An existing liability whose amount or timing is uncertain and must be estimated. (p. 492)

Gross earnings Total compensation earned by an employee. Also known as gross pay. (p. 489)

Net pay Gross earnings less payroll deductions. (p. 489)

Notes payable Obligations in the form of written promissory notes. (p. 485)

Operating line of credit Pre-authorized approval to borrow money at a bank, up to a pre-set limit, when required. (p. 485)

Payroll deductions Deductions from gross earnings to determine the amount of a paycheque. (p. 488)

Salaries Specified amounts per period (e.g., month or year) paid to executive and administrative personnel. (p. 488)

Wages Amounts paid to employees based on a rate per hour or on piecework. (p. 488)

Note: All Questions, Exercises, and Problems below with an asterisk (∗) relate to material in Appendix 10A.

Self-Study Questions

Chapter 10 Self-Test

Answers are at the end of the chapter.

(SO 1) K 1. To be classified as a current liability, a debt must be expected to be paid:
(a) out of existing current assets.
(b) by creating other current liabilities.
(c) within three months.
(d) Either (a) or (b)

(SO 2) AP 2. Gilbert Company borrows $88,500 on September 1, 2004, from the Bank of Nova Scotia by signing a 6% note due September 1, 2005. Interest is payable at maturity. What is the accrued interest at December 31, 2004?
(a) $1,327.50   (c) $1,770.00
(b) $1,760.00   (d) $5,310.00

(SO 2) AP 3. Reeves Company has $4,515 in total proceeds from sales. If the proceeds include GST of 7% and PST of 8%, the amount (rounded to the nearest dollar) to be credited to Sales is:
(a) $3,838.   (c) $4,515.
(b) $3,926.   (d) $5,192.

(SO 2) AP 4. On March 1, Swift Current Company receives its property tax assessment of $13,200 for 2005. The property tax bill is due May 1. If Swift Current prepares quarterly financial statements, how much property tax expense should the company report for the quarter ended March 31, 2005?
(a) $1,100   (c) $4,400
(b) $3,300   (d) $13,200

(SO 2) AP 5. Rebecca works for The Blue Company at a salary of $550 per week. Canada Pension Plan contributions are $23.89 for the employee and the same for the employer. Income taxes are $88.75. Employment insurance premiums are $11.55 for the employee and $16.17 for the employer. How much is Rebecca's weekly net (take-home) pay?
(a) $385.75   (c) $514.56
(b) $425.81   (d) $550.00

(SO 2) K 6. Employer payroll costs do not include:
(a) employment insurance.
(b) Canada Pension Plan contributions.
(c) income tax deducted from employee earnings.
(d) workers' compensation.

(SO 3) K 7. Recording estimated warranty expense in the year of the sale best follows which accounting principle or convention?
(a) Consistency   (c) Matching
(b) Full disclosure (d) Materiality

(SO 3) AP 8. The Frost Cereal Company started a sales promotion at the beginning of the year. Each consumer who sends in five UPC symbols (bar codes) from cereal box tops receives a valuable "prize." Frost sells 300,000 boxes of cereal during the year. The company estimates that 20% of the UPC symbols of the cereal boxes sold will eventually be returned for the premium. In all, 35,000 box tops are returned and redeemed for 7,000 prizes during the current year. Each "prize" costs Frost $2. What is the estimated liability for this promotion at the end of the year?
(a) $10,000   (c) $16,000
(b) $14,000   (d) $24,000

(SO 4) K 9. If a contingent liability is reasonably estimable and it is likely that the contingency will occur, the contingent liability:
   (a) should be accrued in the accounts.
   (b) should be disclosed in the notes accompanying the financial statements.
   (c) should not be recorded or disclosed until the contingency actually happens.
   d. must be paid immediately.

(SO 5) K 10. Current liabilities are listed in the balance sheet:
   (a) in order of liquidity (due date).
   (b) in order of magnitude.
   (c) in no particular order.
   (d) All of the above

*11. During a recent week Emilie Marquette worked 35 hours, at an hourly wage of $10 per hour. Her weekly CPP exemption is $67.31, and the CPP contribution rate is 4.95%. Her EI premium is calculated at 2.1%. The employee's and employer's share of CPP and EI are: (SO 6) AP
   (a) employee CPP, $13.99; EI, $7.35; employer CPP $13.99; EI, $7.35.
   (b) employee CPP, $13.99; EI, $7.35; employer CPP, $13.99; EI, $10.29.
   (c) employee CPP, $17.32; EI, $7.35; employer CPP, $17.32; EI, $10.29.
   (d) employee CPP, $13.99; EI, $7.35; employer CPP, $19.59; EI, $7.35.

the navigator

Questions

(SO 1) K 1. Li Feng believes a current liability is a debt that is likely to be paid in one year. Is Li correct? Explain.

(SO 1) K 2. What is the difference between accounts payable and notes payable? How is a note payable different from an operating line of credit?

(SO 2) C 3. Your roommate says, "Sales taxes are reported as expenses in the income statement." Do you agree? Explain.

(SO 2) C 4. Explain how recording property taxes can result in both a liability (property tax payable) and an asset (prepaid property tax) in the same year.

(SO 2) C 5. What are unearned revenues and why are they classified as a liability? Describe an example of unearned revenue.

(SO 2) C 6. What is the difference between gross pay and net pay? Which amount (gross or net) should a company record as wages or salaries expense?

(SO 2) C 7. Is the income tax withheld from an employee paycheque an expense for the employer? Explain.

(SO 2) C 8. Distinguish between the types of employee payroll deductions, and give examples of each.

(SO 2) K 9. Identify the main types of employer payroll costs.

(SO 2) C 10. Anwar Company incurred a long-term liability of $100,000 on January 1, 2005. Of this debt, $25,000 must be repaid annually, each January 1. Explain how Anwar should classify this liability on its December 31, 2005, balance sheet.

(SO 3) C 11. The accountant for Amiable Appliances feels that warranty expense should not be recorded unless an appliance is returned for repair. "Otherwise, how do you know if the appliance will be returned, and if so, how much it will cost to fix?" he says. Do you agree? Explain.

12. A motion picture company recently released a DVD of a popular movie with a $5 mail-in rebate if the customer sends proof of purchase. How should the motion picture company account for these rebates? (SO 3) C

13. How are estimated and contingent liabilities alike? How do they differ? (SO 3, 4) K

14. What is a contingent liability? Give an example of a contingent liability that is likely but not estimable, and an example of a contingency that is not determinable. (SO 4) C

15. Under what circumstances is a contingent liability recorded in the accounts? Under what circumstances is a contingent liability disclosed only in the notes to the financial statements? (SO 4) C

16. St. Lawrence Company obtains $25,000 cash on July 1 by signing a 7%, six-month, $25,000 note payable to the National Bank. St. Lawrence's fiscal year ends on September 30. What information should be reported for the note payable in the financial statements? (SO 5) C

17. In what order should current liabilities be listed on the balance sheet? (SO 5) K

*18. What are the primary uses of the employee earnings record and payroll register? (SO 6) K

*19. To whom, and how often, are payroll deductions remitted? (SO 6) C

*20. What are paid absences? How are they accounted for? (SO 6) K

Brief Exercises

Identify current liabilities.
(SO 1) K

BE10–1 Identify which of the following items would be classified as a current liability. For those that are not current liabilities, identify where they should be classified.

1. A product warranty
2. Cash received in advance for airline tickets
3. HST collected on sales
4. Cash receipts from sales
5. Interest owing on an overdue account payable
6. Interest due on an overdue account receivable
7. A lawsuit pending against the company. The company is not sure of the likely outcome.
8. Amounts withheld from the employees' weekly pay
9. Property tax payable
10. A mortgage payable with $5,000 due within one year

Record note payable.
(SO 2) AP

BE10–2 On August 1, 2005, Passera Company borrows $55,000, signing a three-month, 7.5% note payable. Prepare journal entries for Passera Company on August 1, 2005, and on the maturity date. Assume interest is payable at maturity and monthly adjusting entries are not prepared.

Record note payable.
(SO 2) AP

BE10–3 Bourque Company borrows $60,000 from First Bank on July 1, 2004, signing a nine-month, 8% note payable. Interest is payable at maturity. Prepare journal entries for Bourque Company to record the following: (a) receipt of the proceeds of the note; (b) accrual of interest at Bourque's year end, December 31, 2004; and (c) payment of the note at maturity. Assume adjusting entries are made only at the end of the year.

Record sales taxes.
(SO 2) AP

BE10–4 Auto Supply Company does not separate sales and sales taxes at the time of sale. The register total for March 16 is $8,050. All sales are subject to 7% GST and 8% PST. PST is not charged on GST. Calculate the sales taxes payable, and make the entry to record the sales and the sales taxes payable.

Record unearned revenue and prepaid rent.
(SO 2) AP

BE10–5 Centennial Property Company collects $6,500 cash for five months' rent in advance from Rikard's Menswear on October 1, 2004. Both companies have a December 31 fiscal year end. Prepare journal entries for both companies on October 1 and December 31, 2005.

Record property tax.
(SO 2) AP

BE10–6 Dresner Company has a December 31 fiscal year end. It receives a $7,500 property tax bill for 2005 on March 31, 2005. The bill is payable on May 31. Prepare entries for March 31, May 31, and December 31, assuming the company adjusts its accounts annually.

Record payroll.
(SO 2) AP

BE10–7 Zerbe Consulting Company's gross salaries in August were $15,000. Deductions included $730 for CPP, $315 for EI, and $4,305 for income taxes. The company's payroll costs were $730 for CPP and $441 for EI. Prepare journal entries to record (a) the payment of salaries on August 31, and (b) the company's payroll costs for August.

Record warranty.
(SO 3) AP

BE10–8 On December 1, Ng Company introduces a new product that includes a one-year warranty on parts. In December, 1,000 units are sold. Management believes that 5% of the units will be defective and that the average warranty cost will be $75 per unit. (a) Prepare the adjusting entry at December 31 to accrue the estimated warranty cost. (b) In January of the following year, the cost of defective parts replaced under the warranty was $375. Prepare an entry to record the replacement of the parts.

Record cash rebate.
(SO 3) AP

BE10–9 In August 2005, the Mega-Big Motion Picture Company sells 100,000 copies of a recently released DVD of a popular movie. Each DVD contains a $6 rebate if the consumer sends in proof of purchase with the completed rebate form. Mega-Big estimates that 15% of the purchasers will claim the rebate. Prepare an adjusting entry at August 31 to accrue the estimated rebate liability. What will be the entry to record each rebate when it is redeemed?

Record contingent liability.
(SO 4) AP

BE10–10 Athabasca Toil & Oil Company is a defendant in a lawsuit for improper discharge of pollutants and waste into the Athabasca River. Athabasca's lawyers have advised that the company will likely lose this lawsuit and that it could settle out of court for $50,000. How should Athabasca record this current liability? What are the arguments for and against recording this contingent liability?

BE10–11 **Sleeman Breweries Ltd.** reported the following selected liabilities (in thousands) at December 28, 2002. The liabilities are listed in alphabetical order.

Prepare current liabilities
section.
(SO 5) AP

Accounts payable and accrued liabilities	$27,495
Bank indebtedness	10,461
Current portion of long-term debt	9,672
Long-term debt	73,950

Prepare the current liabilities section of Sleeman's balance sheet, in good format, at December 28, 2002.

*BE10–12 Becky Sherrick's regular hourly wage rate is $16, and she receives an hourly rate of $24 for work in excess of 40 hours. During a January pay period, Becky works 45 hours. Becky's income tax withholding is $143.70. CPP deductions total $34.29. EI deductions total $15.96. Calculate Becky's gross earnings and net pay for the pay period.

Calculate gross earnings
and net pay.
(SO 6) AP

*BE10–13 Data for Becky Sherrick are presented in BE10–12. Prepare the journal entries to record (a) Becky's pay for the period, and (b) the payment of Becky's wages. Use January 15 for the end of the pay period and the payment date.

Record payroll.
(SO 6) AP

*BE10–14 In January gross earnings in the **Bri Company** totalled $70,000, from which $3,330 was deducted for the Canada Pension Plan, $1,470 for employment insurance, and $19,360 for income tax. Prepare the entries to record the January payroll, including the employee benefit costs.

Record payroll.
(SO 6) AP

*BE10–15 At **Sublette.Com**, employees are entitled to one day's vacation for each month worked. In January, 50 employees worked the full month. Record the vacation pay liability for January, assuming the average daily pay for each employee is $180.

Record vacation pay.
(SO 6) AP

Exercises

E10–1 **Briffet Construction** borrows $200,000 from the TD Bank on October 1, 2005. It signs a two-year, 8% note payable. Interest is payable monthly.

Record note payable and
note receivable.
(SO 2) AP

Instructions

(a) Prepare the journal entries to record the transactions on October 1, 2005, and the first interest payment on November 1 for Briffet Construction. Round your answers to the nearest dollar.
(b) Prepare the journal entries to record the transactions on October 1, 2005, and the first interest receipt on November 1 for the TD Bank. (*Hint*: You might find it helpful to review accounting for notes receivable in Chapter 8.)

E10–2 On May 31, **Microchip Company** borrows $70,000 from Northeastern Bank and issues a six-month, 7% note, due on November 30. Interest is payable at maturity. Neither Microchip Company nor Northeastern Bank prepares monthly adjusting entries.

Record note payable and
note receivable.
(SO 2) AP

Interactive Homework

Instructions

(a) Microchip Company has a July 31 fiscal year end. Prepare journal entries for Microchip on May 31, July 31, and November 30.
(b) Northeastern Bank has an October 31 fiscal year end. Prepare journal entries for Northeastern Bank on May 31, October 31, and November 30.

E10–3 In providing accounting services to small businesses, you encounter the following situations:

Record sales taxes.
(SO 2) AP

1. **Sainsbury Company** rings up sales and sales taxes separately on its cash register. On April 10, the register totals are sales $26,500, GST $1,855, and PST $2,120.
2. **Hockenstein Company** does not segregate sales and sales taxes. Its register total for April 15 is $19,950, which includes 7% GST and 7% PST.

Instructions

Prepare the entry to record the sales transactions and related taxes for each client. Assume that PST is not charged on a tax inclusive basis (i.e., not charged on GST) in either of these situations.

Record unearned subscription revenue.
(SO 2) AP

E10–4 Westwood Company publishes a monthly sports magazine, *Adventure Time*. Subscriptions to the magazine cost $45 per year. During November 2004, Westwood sells 7,000 subscriptions which begin with the December issue. Westwood prepares financial statements quarterly and recognizes subscription revenue earned at the end of each quarter. Westwood's year end is December 31.

Instructions

(a) Prepare the entry in November for the receipt of the subscriptions.
(b) Prepare the adjusting entry at December 31, 2004, to record subscription revenue earned in December.
(c) Prepare the adjusting entry at March 31, 2005, to record subscription revenue earned in the first quarter of 2005.

Record property tax; determine financial statement impact.
(SO 2) AP

E10–5 Seaboard Company receives its annual property tax bill for the calendar year on April 30, payable on June 30. The bill for 2004 was $25,800; for 2005, $26,640. Seaboard has a May 31 fiscal year end.

Instructions

(a) Prepare journal entries for Seaboard on June 30, 2004, April 30, 2005, and May 31, 2005, assuming the company does not prepare monthly adjusting entries.
(b) What is recorded on Seaboard's May 31, 2004, balance sheet with respect to property taxes? On the May 31, 2005, balance sheet?
(c) Calculate Seaboard's property tax expense for the year ended May 31, 2005.

Record payroll.
(SO 2) AP

Interactive Homework

E10–6 The Hidden Dragon Restaurant's gross payroll for August is $40,500. The company deducted $1,715 for CPP, $850 for EI, and $8,010 for income taxes from the employees' cheques. Employees are paid monthly at the end of each month. Hidden Dragon's related payroll costs for August are $1,715 for CPP and $1,190 for EI.

Instructions

(a) Prepare a journal entry for Hidden Dragon on August 31 to record the payment of the August payroll to employees.
(b) Prepare a journal entry on August 31 to accrue for Hidden Dragon's payroll costs.
(c) On September 15 Hidden Dragon pays the government the appropriate amounts for August's payroll. Prepare a journal entry to record this remittance.

Record warranty costs.
(SO 3) AP

E10–7 Sinclair Company sells automatic can openers under a 90-day warranty for defective merchandise. Based on past experience, Sinclair estimates that 3% of the units sold will become defective during the warranty period. Management estimates that the average cost of replacing or repairing a defective unit is $15. The units sold and units defective during the last two months of 2004 are as follows:

Month	Units Sold	Units Defective
November	30,000	600
December	32,000	400

Instructions

(a) Determine the estimated warranty liability at December 31 for the units sold in November and December.
(b) Prepare the journal entries to record (1) the estimated liability for warranties, and (2) the costs (assume actual costs of $15,000) incurred in honouring the 1,000 warranty claims as of December 31.
(c) Give the entry to record the honouring of 500 warranty claims in January, at an average cost of $15 per claim.

Calculate coupon liability.
(SO 3) AP

Interactive Homework

E10–8 Crispy Cookies sells cookies for $2.50 per box. Starting in 2004 as a way to boost sales, the company included inside each box a 50-cent rebate coupon that can be returned and redeemed, along with proof of purchase. There is no expiry date on these coupons. Crispy Cookies estimates that 15% of these coupons will eventually be redeemed. Crispy Cookies has a December 31 fiscal year end. Sales are 150,000 boxes of cookies in 2004 and 190,000 in 2005. Redemptions total 20,000 coupons in 2004 and 23,000 in 2005.

Instructions

(a) What amount should be recorded as contra revenue (sales discounts for coupon redemptions) in 2004? In 2005?
(b) What is the coupon liability that should be reported at December 31, 2004? At December 31, 2005?
(c) How much cash was paid out by Crispy Cookies for the coupons in 2004? In 2005?
(d) Was the cash paid for redemptions the same amount as that recorded for the sales discount for coupon redemptions? Explain why or why not.

E10–9 The Sleep-a-Bye Baby Company is the defendant in a lawsuit alleging that its portable baby cribs are unsafe. The company has offered to replace the crib free of charge for any concerned parent. Nonetheless, it has been sued for damages and distress amounting to $500,000. The company plans to vigorously defend its product safety record in court.

Analyse contingent liability. (SO 4) AP

Instructions

(a) What should the company record or report in its financial statements for this situation? Explain why.
(b) What if Sleep-a-Bye Baby Company's lawyers advise that it is very likely the company will have to pay damages of $100,000? Does this change what should be recorded or reported in the financial statements? Explain.

E10–10 Presented below is a list of transactions.

Determine financial statement impact of transactions. (SO 2, 3, 4) AP

1. Purchased inventory (perpetual system) on account.
2. Extended payment terms of account payable in item 1 above by issuing a 5%, six-month note payable.
3. Recorded accrued interest on the note payable from item 2 above.
4. Recorded cash sales of $74,750 which included HST of 15%.
5. Recorded wage expense of $35,000. Paid employees $25,000; the difference was for various payroll deductions withheld.
6. Recorded employer's share of employee benefits.
7. Accrued property taxes payable.
8. Disclosed a contingent loss on a lawsuit whose likely outcome the company cannot determine.
9. Recorded estimated liability for product rebates outstanding.
10. Paid product rebate claims that were accrued in item 9 above.
11. Recorded the receipt of cash for services that will be performed in the future.

Instructions

Set up a table using the format shown below. Indicate the effect ("+" for increase, "–" for decrease, and "NE" for no effect) of each of the above transactions on the financial statement categories indicated. The first one has been done for you as an example.

	Assets	Liabilities	Owner's Equity	Revenues	Expenses	Net Income
1.	+	+	NE	NE	NE	NE

E10–11 Larkin Online Company has the following liability accounts at August 31, 2005, after posting adjusting entries:

Prepare current liabilities section of balance sheet. Calculate current ratio. (SO 5) AP

Interactive Homework

Accounts payable	$67,000	Mortgage payable	$120,000
Bank indebtedness	50,000	Notes payable	80,000
Coupon liability	4,000	Property taxes payable	8,000
GST payable	12,000	Unearned revenue	24,000
Interest payable	8,000	Warranty liability	18,000

Additional information:

1. Bank indebtedness is from an operating line of credit which is due on demand.
2. On August 31, 2005, the unused operating line of credit is $25,000.
3. Coupon and warranty costs are expected to be incurred within one year.
4. Of the mortgage, $10,000 is due each year.
5. The note payable matures in three years.

Instructions

(a) Prepare the current liabilities section of the balance sheet.
(b) Calculate Larkin's current ratio, assuming total current assets are $300,000.

Record payroll.
(SO 6) AP

*E10–12 Kate Gough's regular hourly wage rate is $13, and she receives a wage of 1.5 times the regular hourly rate for work in excess of 40 hours. During a September weekly pay period, Kate worked 43 hours. Kate lives in Alberta and has a claim code of 1 for tax deductions.

After this information is inputted, the following information is generated:

Payroll Deductions for Regular Salary			
Employee's name (optional)	Kate Gough		
Pay period ending date (optional)	2005-09-16		
Gross salary (or pension income) for the pay period			578.50
Total EI insurable earnings for the pay period			578.50
Taxable salary or pension income			578.50
Canada Pension Plan (CPP) deductions		25.30	
Employment insurance (EI) deductions		12.15	
Federal tax deductions	62.65		
Provincial or territorial tax deductions	28.15		
Total tax	90.80	90.80	
Requested additional tax deduction		0.00	
Total deductions		128.25	128.25
Net amount			450.25
Total claim amount (from TD1 federal)	Claim Code 1 (Minimum - 7,756.00)		
Total claim amount (from TD1 prov or terr)	Claim Code 1 (Minimum - 13,525.00)		
Employer's pay period	Weekly payments (52)		
Province of employment	Alberta		

Instructions

(a) Prepare a journal entry to record the accrual of Kate's salary on September 16.
(b) Prepare a journal entry to record the employer's related payroll costs.
(c) Prepare a journal entry to record the payment of Kate's salary on September 16.

Record payroll.
(SO 6) AP

*E10–13 Ahmad Company has the following data for the weekly payroll ending January 31:

Employee	Hours Worked M Tu W Th F S	Hourly Rate	Income Tax Withheld	Health Insurance
A. Kassam	8 8 9 8 10 3	$11	$ 81	$10
H. Faas	8 8 8 8 8 2	13	87	15
D. Liteplo	9 10 8 8 9 0	14	107	15

Employees are paid 1.5 times the regular hourly rate for all hours worked in excess of 40 hours per week. CPP is deducted at a rate of 4.95% on earnings over the $67.31 weekly exemption, and EI is deducted at a rate of 2.1% of gross earnings. Ahmad Company must make payments to the Workers' Compensation Plan equal to 2% of the gross payroll. In addition, Ahmad matches the employees' health insurance contributions.

Instructions

(a) Prepare the payroll register for the weekly payroll.
(b) Prepare the journal entry to record the payroll and Ahmad's employee benefits.

Calculate missing payroll amounts. Record payroll.
(SO 6) AP

*E10–14 Selected data from the February 28 payroll register for Yue Company are presented below, with some amounts intentionally omitted:

Gross earnings:

		Deductions:	
Regular	$ (1)	Canada Pension Plan	$ (3)
Overtime	1,050	Employment insurance	294
Total	(2)	Income tax	3,389
		Union dues	139
		United Way	225
		Total deductions	(4)
		Net pay	(5)
		Accounts debited:	
		Warehouse wages	5,070
		Store wages	(6)

Pensionable earnings are $11,800. CPP premiums are 4.95% of pensionable earnings. EI premiums are 2.1% of gross earnings.

Instructions

(a) Fill in the missing amounts. Round all answers to the nearest dollar.
(b) Calculate the company's contributions for the Canada Pension Plan (1 time) and employment insurance (1.4 times).
(c) Journalize all aspects of the February 28 payroll and its payment.
(d) Journalize the payment of amounts withheld on March 10.

Problems: Set A

P10–1A The following transactions occurred in Wendell Company. Wendell's fiscal year end is December 31.

Identify liabilities.
(SO 1, 3, 4, 5) AP

1. Wendell purchased goods for $120,000 on December 23, terms n/30.
2. Wendell's chief executive is to be paid a bonus of $35,000 six months after year end.
3. Weekly salaries of $6,000 are paid every Friday for a five-day (Monday to Friday) work week. This year, December 31 is a Wednesday. Payroll deductions include CPP of 4.95% and EI of 2.1% of gross salaries, and income tax withholdings of $1,800.
4. Property taxes of $40,000 were assessed on November 1 for the upcoming calendar year. They are payable by March 1.
5. Wendell is the defendant in a negligence suit. Wendell's legal counsel estimates that Wendell may suffer a $75,000 loss if it loses the suit. In legal counsel's opinion, the likelihood of success in the case is not determinable at this time.
6. Wendell entered into a $500,000, 9% note payable on July 1. The note requires payment of the principal in instalments of $100,000, each June 30, for the next five years. Interest is due monthly on the first of each month.
7. Wendell issued a mail-in purchase rebate on one of its specialty inventory items sold between September 1 and November 30. Each item was sold for $45 and had a $4 rebate attached to it. A total of 4,500 items were sold during that period. Wendell estimates that 25% of the customers will request a rebate. By December 31 Wendell had issued $2,900 in rebates.

Instructions

(a) Identify which transactions above should be presented in the current liabilities section and which in the long-term liabilities section of Wendell's balance sheet on December 31. Identify the account title(s) and amount(s) for each reported liability.
(b) Indicate any information that should be disclosed in the notes to Wendell's financial statements.

P10–2A Included in the current liabilities section of the December 31, 2004, balance sheet of Learnstream Company were Notes Payable $12,000 and Interest Payable $465. The note payable was issued on June 30, 2004, and has a maturity date of February 28, 2005, and an interest rate of 7.75% payable at maturity. The note is payable to Tanner Company. The following are selected transactions of Learnstream Company during 2005. Learnstream prepares financial statements quarterly and uses a perpetual inventory system.

Record and post note transactions. Show financial statement presentation.
(SO 2, 5) AP

Jan. 12 Purchased merchandise on account from McCoy Company for $20,000, terms n/30.
  31 Issued a three-month, 9%, $20,000 note to McCoy Company in payment of an account. Interest is payable monthly.
Feb. 28 Paid monthly interest charges on the McCoy note.
  28 Paid the Tanner note in full including all interest owing.
Mar. 31 Paid monthly interest charges on the McCoy note.
Apr. 30 Paid the face value and one month's interest on the McCoy note.
July   1 Purchased equipment from Scottie Equipment by paying $11,000 cash and signing a three-month, 8% note for $30,000. Interest is payable at maturity.
Sept.30 Accrued interest on the Scottie note.
Oct.   1 Paid the face value and interest on the Scottie note.

Dec. 1 Borrowed $15,000 from the Toronto-Dominion Bank by issuing a three-month, 8% note. Interest is payable monthly on the first of each month.
      31 Recognized interest expense on the Toronto-Dominion Bank note.

Instructions

(a) Prepare journal entries for the above transactions.
(b) Post to the accounts Notes Payable, Interest Payable, and Interest Expense.
(c) Show the balance sheet presentation of notes payable and interest payable at December 31, 2005, and the income statement presentation of interest expense for the year ended December 31, 2005.

Record current liability transactions and adjusting entries, and prepare current liabilities section.
(SO 2, 3, 5) AP

P10–3A On January 1, 2005, the ledger of Shumway Software Company contains the following liability accounts:

Accounts payable	$42,500
Coupon liability	4,500
CPP payable	1,340
EI payable	756
Goods and Services Tax payable	5,800
Income taxes payable	2,515
Provincial Sales Tax payable	6,600
Unearned service revenue	15,000

During January the following selected transactions occurred:

Jan. 1 Borrowed $15,000 cash on a four-month, 8%, note. Interest is payable at maturity.
      5 Sold merchandise for cash totalling $8,820, which included 7% GST and 8% PST. The cost of this sale was $4,600. Shumway Software uses a perpetual inventory system.
      12 Provided services for customers who had made advance payments of $8,500.
      14 Paid $5,800 to the Receiver General and $6,600 to Provincial Treasurer for sales taxes collected in December 2004.
      15 Paid $4,611 to the Receiver General amounts owing from the December payroll for CPP, EI, and income taxes.
      20 Sold 500 units of a new product on credit at $54 per unit, plus 7% GST and 8% PST. This new product is subject to a one-year warranty. The cost of this sale was $25 per unit.
      25 Sold merchandise for cash totalling $15,525, which included sales taxes (7% GST and 8% PST). The cost of this sale was $9,000.
      29 Paid $2,900 for coupons redeemed during the month.
      31 Recorded and paid the monthly payroll. Gross salaries were $16,000. Amounts withheld included CPP $720, EI $336, and income taxes $3,215.
      31 Recorded the employer's share of CPP and EI. (*Note*: Employers are required to contribute $1 to CPP for each $1 of CPP withheld from employees and $1.40 to EI for each $1 of EI withheld from employees.)

Instructions

(a) Journalize the January transactions.
(b) Journalize the adjusting entries at January 31 for (1) interest on the outstanding note payable, and (2) estimated warranty liability, assuming warranty costs are expected to equal 9% of sales of the new product.
(c) Prepare the current liabilities section of the balance sheet at January 31, 2005. Assume no change in Accounts Payable.

Record warranty.
(SO 3) AP

P10–4A On January 1, 2004, Hopewell Company began a three-year warranty program designed to stimulate sales. The warranty costs are estimated at 4% of sales in 2004 and 5% of sales in 2005. The sales and warranty figures for the years ended December 31, 2004 and 2005, are as follows:

Year	Sales	Warranty Expenditures
2004	$740,000	$21,000
2005	820,000	33,000

Instructions

Prepare journal entries to record the estimated warranty liability and warranty expenditures (all cash) for 2004 and 2005.

P10–5A The Safe Computing Company produces and sells an anti-virus software program to retail stores for $30. The retail stores sell the software to consumers for $40. In March 2005, Safe Computing advertised the software in *PC Magazine* and included a $5 coupon that consumers can use to reduce the price of the software. The coupon has an expiry date of September 30, 2005. Retail stores must submit all redeemed coupons to Safe Computing by the tenth day of the month following the sale. Based on past experience, Safe Computing estimates that 10,000 of these coupons will be redeemed before the expiry date.

Record coupon transactions. (SO 3) AP

Instructions

(a) Prepare journal entries, as required, for Collegiate Computer Store—one of Safe Computing Company's customers—for the following:

  1. During April 2005, Collegiate Computer Store sells 50 software packages for cash. Twenty customers pay the full price and 30 present the $5 coupon and pay the reduced price. Assume Collegiate uses a perpetual inventory system. (Record one summary entry dated April 30.)
  2. On April 30, 2005, Collegiate sends Safe Computing the coupons redeemed to date and requests a refund.
  3. On May 10, 2005, Collegiate receives the requested refund from Safe Computing.

(b) Prepare journal entries, as required, for Safe Computing for the following:

  1. The March 31, 2005, adjusting entry to record the estimated coupon liability
  2. Receipt of the 30 coupons presented for redemption from Collegiate Computer Store on April 30, 2005
  3. Payment to Collegiate on May 10, 2005, for the redeemed coupons

(c) On October 15, 2005, Safe Computing determines that in total 10,250 coupons have been redeemed. What entry, if any, should Safe Computing prepare?

P10–6A The Northern Affairs Program of the Government of Canada manages waste and contaminated sites in Nunavut, the Northwest Territories, and the Yukon. There are currently 1,818 contaminated waste sites in northern Canada. At 976 sites, cleanup has already been completed.

Discuss contingency reporting. (SO 4) AP

  A total of 394 sites are receiving active attention. The cost to clean up these sites is estimated at $723 million. At 16 sites, the government has been notified that it may have to assume some level of financial responsibility for the sites in the future. The estimated cost of cleaning up these sites is $79 million.

  The remaining 432 sites have been assessed and are of low risk.

Instructions

(a) What journal entries, if any, should the Government of Canada prepare to record this situation?
(b) What should the government disclose in its financial statements for this situation, if anything?

*P10–7A Sure Value Hardware has four employees who are paid on an hourly basis plus time-and-a-half for all hours worked in excess of 40 hours a week. Payroll data for the week ended March 15, 2005, are presented below:

Prepare payroll register and record payroll. (SO 6) AP

Employee	Hours Worked	Hourly Rate	CPP	EI	Income Tax Withheld	United Way
I. Dahl	40	$15.00	$26.37	$12.60	$ 91.10	$5.00
F. Gualtieri	42	15.00	28.60	13.55	101.95	5.00
G. Ho	44	14.50	29.69	14.01	108.35	8.00
A. Israeli	46	14.50	31.84	14.92	122.55	5.00

The first three employees are sales clerks (store wages expense) and the other employee does administrative duties (office wages expense).

Instructions

(a) Prepare a payroll register for the weekly payroll.
(b) Journalize the payroll on March 15, 2005, and the accrual of employee benefits expenses.
(c) Journalize the payment of the payroll on March 16, 2005.
(d) Journalize the payment on April 15, 2005, of the amounts payable to the Receiver General and United Way.

Record and post payroll
transactions. Calculate
liability balances.
(SO 6) AP

*P10–8A The following payroll liability accounts are included in the ledger of Drumheller
Company on January 1, 2005:

Canada Pension Plan payable	$ 5,454	Union dues payable	$1,250
Employment insurance payable	2,923	Canada Savings Bonds payable	2,500
Income tax payable	18,600	Vacation pay payable	6,450
Workers' compensation payable	5,263	Disability insurance payable	1,050

In January, the following transactions occurred:

Jan.   8 Sent a cheque to the insurance company for the disability insurance.
       10 Sent a cheque for $1,250 to the union treasurer for union dues.
       12 Issued a cheque to the Receiver General for the amounts due.
       15 Purchased Canada Savings Bonds for employees by writing a cheque for $2,500.
       20 Paid the amount due to the Workers' Compensation Plan.
       31 Completed the monthly payroll register, which shows office salaries $26,400, store wages
          $37,400, CPP withheld $3,014, EI withheld $1,340, income tax withheld $16,760,
          union dues withheld $950, Canada Savings Bond deductions $1,200, and long-term
          disability insurance premiums $1,100.
       31 Prepared payroll cheques for the net pay and distributed the cheques to the employees.

At January 31, the company also makes the following accruals for employee compensation:

1. CPP in an amount equal to the employees' contributions, and EI in an amount equal to 1.4
   times the employees' contributions
2. Workers' Compensation Plan at 7% of the gross payroll
3. Vacation pay at 4% of gross earnings

Instructions

(a) Enter the beginning balances in general ledger accounts.
(b) Journalize and post the January transactions and adjustments to the liability accounts.
(c) Present the payroll liability accounts in the current liabilities section of the balance sheet
    as at January 31, 2005.

Calculate and record
payroll.
(SO 6) AP

*P10–9A For the year ended December 31, 2005, Western Electric Company reports the fol-
lowing summary payroll data:

Gross earnings:	
Administrative salaries	$180,000
Electricians' wages	470,000
Total	$650,000
Deductions:	
CPP contributions	$ 28,710
Income tax	143,000
EI contributions	13,650
United Way contributions	5,000
Dental insurance premiums	2,400
Long-term disability insurance	1,500
Total	$194,260

Western Electric Company's payroll costs include CPP, EI, and workers' compensation. The workers' compensation costs are $13,000 for the current year.
     In addition, the company matches the employees' contributions to the long-term disability
insurance plan, and pays the entire cost of a medical insurance plan. The latter amounts to $26,600
for the current year.

Instructions

(a) Prepare a summary journal entry, at December 31, for the full year's payroll.
(b) Journalize the entry at December 31 to record the employee benefit expense for the year.
(c) Calculate the company's total payroll-related expense for the year.

Problems: Set B

P10–1B The following transactions occurred in Iqaluit Company. Iqaluit's fiscal year end is April 30.

Identify liabilities.
(SO 1, 3, 4, 5) AP

1. Iqaluit purchased goods for $12,000 on April 29, terms n/30, FOB destination. The goods arrived on May 3.
2. Six months after year end, the company chief executive officer is to be paid a bonus equal to 5% of net income. Net income is expected to be $600,000.
3. Weekly salaries of $10,000 are paid every Friday for a five-day (Monday to Friday) work week. This year, April 30 is a Thursday. Payroll deductions include CPP of 4.95% and EI of 2.1% of gross salaries, and income tax withholdings of $3,000.
4. Iqaluit received $25,000 from customers on April 27 for services to be performed in May.
5. Iqaluit was named in a lawsuit alleging negligence for oil spillage that leaked into the neighbouring company's water system. Iqaluit's legal counsel estimates that the company will likely lose the suit. Restoration costs are expected to total $250,000.
6. The company purchased equipment for $35,000 on April 1. It issued a 7.5%, six-month note in payment. Interest is payable monthly on the first of each month.
7. Iqaluit offered a one-year replacement warranty on one of its new products. It estimated it would cost $45 to honour each warranty and that 5% of the units sold would be returned for replacement within the warranty period. By April 30, 10,000 units of the product had been sold, and customers had returned 100 units under the warranty.

Instructions

(a) Identify which transactions above should be presented in the current liabilities section and which in the long-term liabilities section of Iqaluit's balance sheet on April 30. Identify the account title(s) and amount(s) for each reported liability.
(b) Indicate any information that should be disclosed in the notes to Iqaluit's financial statements.

P10–2B MileHi Mountain Bikes markets mountain-bike tours to clients vacationing in various locations in the mountains of British Columbia. On February 28, 2005, the company had a balance of $15,000 in Notes Payable and $375 in Interest Payable. This six-month, 6% note was issued on September 30, 2004, and is payable to Eifert Company. Interest is payable at maturity. The balance in the interest expense account on February 28, 2005, was $1,115. To prepare for the upcoming summer biking season, MileHi entered into the following transactions related to notes payable:

Record and post note transactions. Show financial statement presentation.
(SO 2, 5) AP

Mar. 2 Purchased Mongoose bikes for use as rentals by issuing a $9,000, 9% note payable that is due in three months. Interest is due at maturity.
   31 Recorded accrued interest for the Mongoose note.
   31 Paid the Eifert note, plus interest.
Apr. 1 Issued a $25,000 note to Mountain Real Estate for the purchase of mountain property on which to build bike trails. The note bears 10% interest and is due in nine months. Interest on this note is payable the first of each month.
   30 Recorded accrued interest for the Mongoose and Mountain Real Estate notes.
May 1 Paid interest on Mountain Real Estate note.
   2 Issued a 6% note to Western Bank for an $18,000 loan. The funds will be used for working capital for the beginning of the season. The note and the interest are due in four months.
   31 Recorded accrued interest for all three notes.
June 1 Paid principal and interest on the Mongoose note.
   1 Paid interest on the Mountain Real Estate note.
   30 Recorded accrued interest for the Mountain Real Estate note and the Western Bank note.

Instructions

(a) Prepare journal entries for the above transactions.
(b) Post the above entries to the accounts Notes Payable, Interest Payable, and Interest Expense starting with the balances from February 28, 2005.
(c) Assuming that MileHi's year end is June 30, 2005, show the balance sheet presentation of notes payable and interest payable at that date and the income statement presentation of interest expense relating to notes payable for the year.

Record current liability transactions and adjusting entries, and prepare current liabilities section.
(SO 2, 3, 5) AP

P10–3B On January 1, 2005, the ledger of Zaur Company contained these liability accounts:

Accounts payable	$52,000	Income taxes payable	$ 4,640
Coupon liability	2,150	PST payable	6,430
CPP payable	1,905	Unearned service revenue	16,000
EI payable	1,058	Warranty liability	5,750
GST payable	7,500		

During January, the following selected transactions occurred. Zaur uses a periodic inventory system.

Jan.   2 Issued 50,000 coupons for $1.00 each with an expiry date of April 30, 2005. Based on prior experience, estimated that 10% of these will be redeemed.

5 Sold merchandise for cash totalling $15,820, which includes 7% GST and 6% PST.

12 Provided services for customers who had made advance payments of $7,000.

14 Paid the Receiver General and Provincial Treasurer for sales taxes collected in December 2004, $7,500 and $6,430, respectively.

15 Paid the Receiver General amounts owing from the December payroll for CPP, EI, and income taxes.

17 Paid $12,000 to creditors on account.

20 Sold 500 units of a new product on credit at $60 per unit, plus 7% GST and 6% PST. This new product is subject to a two-year warranty. The cost of the unit sold is $25 per unit.

21 Borrowed $18,000 from HSBC Bank on a three-month, 7% note. Interest is payable monthly on the twenty-first of each month.

25 Sold merchandise for cash totalling $14,125, which includes 7% GST and 6% PST.

30 Paid $2,400 for coupons redeemed during the month.

31 Determined that the company had used $875 of parts inventory during January to honour warranty contracts.

31 Recorded and paid the monthly payroll. Gross salaries were $22,500. Amounts withheld included CPP $1,027, EI $472, and income taxes $5,135.

31 Recorded the employer's share of CPP and EI. (*Note:* Employers are required to contribute $1 to CPP for each $1 of CPP withheld from employees and $1.40 to EI for each $1 of EI withheld from employees.)

Instructions

(a) Journalize the January transactions. Round all amounts to the nearest dollar.

(b) Journalize adjusting entries for the following:
   1. Interest on the note payable. Use one-third of a month for the period January 21–31.
   2. Estimated warranty liability on the new product sales on January 20. Use 6% of sales.

(c) Prepare the current liabilities section of the balance sheet at January 31, 2005.

Record warranty.
(SO 3) AP

P10–4B On January 1, 2004, Logue Company began a two-year warranty program designed to stimulate sales. The warranty costs are estimated at 5% of sales in 2004 and 2005. The sales and warranty figures for the years ended December 31, 2004 and 2005, are as follows:

Year	Sales	Warranty Expenditures
2004	$ 60,000	$1,900
2005	105,000	4,300

Instructions

Prepare journal entries to record the estimated warranty liability and warranty expenditures (credit Repair Parts Inventory) for 2004 and 2005.

Record coupon transactions.
(SO 3) AP

P10–5B The Easy Tax Company produces and sells a personal income tax software program to retail stores for $15. The retail stores sell the software to consumers for $25. In January 2005, Easy Tax promoted the software in Office Supply Mart's national advertising flyer and included a $4 coupon that consumers can use to reduce the price of the software. The coupon has an expiry date of April 30, 2005. Stores must submit all redeemed coupons to Easy Tax by the tenth day of the month following the sale. Based on past experience, Easy Tax estimates that 15,000 of these coupons will be redeemed before the expiry date.

Instructions

(a) Prepare journal entries, as required, for the Nipissing branch of Office Supply Mart for the following:

1. During January 2005, the Nipissing Office Supply Mart sells 100 software packages for cash. Forty-five customers pay the full price and 55 present the $4 coupon and pay the reduced price. Assume all branches of Office Supply Mart use a perpetual inventory system. (Record one summary entry dated January 31.)
2. On January 31, 2005, the Nipissing Office Supply Mart sends Easy Tax the coupons redeemed to date and requests a refund.
3. On February 10, 2005, the Nipissing Office Supply Mart receives the requested refund from Easy Tax.

(b) Prepare journal entries, as required, for Easy Tax for the following:

1. Recording of the estimated coupon liability in January
2. Receipt of 55 coupons presented for redemption from Nipissing Office Supply Mart on January 31, 2005
3. Payment to Nipissing Office Supply Mart on February 10, 2005, for the redeemed coupons

(c) On May 15, 2005, Easy Tax determines that in total 15,750 coupons have been redeemed. What entry, if any, should Easy Tax prepare?

P10–6B On September 20, 2005, White-Wall Tire Co. recalls 10.2 million defective White-Wall tires. The White-Wall tires have been linked to numerous deaths, injuries, and incidents of tire separation and blowouts. White-Wall offers to provide free tire inspections and replace suspect tires through its dealership network. When a dealer replaces the recalled tires with a White-Wall brand, the company reimburses the dealer for the wholesale price of the tires, plus $20 per tire to cover mounting and balancing and the extra paperwork involved. When non-White-Wall brands are used to replace the recalled tire, White-Wall reimburses the dealer up to $100 per tire, which gives the dealer the usual profit margin.

Discuss contingency reporting.
(SO 4) AP

Instructions

What should the company record or disclose in its December 31, 2005, financial statements for this situation? Explain why.

*P10–7B Scoot Scooters has four employees who are paid on an hourly basis, plus time-and-a-half for hours in excess of 35 a week. Payroll data for the week ended February 15, 2005, are presented below:

Prepare payroll register and record payroll.
(SO 6) AP

Employee	Hours Worked	Hourly Rate	CPP	EI	Income Tax Withheld	United Way
P. Kilchyk	39	$9.50	$15.95	$8.18	$47.45	$ 0.00
B. Quon	32	10.00	12.51	6.72	33.35	5.00
C. Pospisil	34	11.50	16.02	8.21	48.05	7.50
B. Verwey	36	10.50	15.64	8.05	46.45	5.00

Instructions

(a) Prepare a payroll register for the weekly payroll.
(b) Journalize the payroll on February 15, 2005, and the accrual of employee benefits expenses.
(c) Journalize the payment of the payroll on February 15, 2005.
(d) Journalize the payment of the employee benefits on March 14, 2005.

*P10–8B The following payroll liability accounts are included in the ledger of Amora Company on January 1, 2005:

Record and post payroll transactions. Calculate liability balances.
(SO 6) AP

Canada Pension Plan payable	$ 8,788	Canada Savings Bonds payable	$ 2,420
Income tax payable	25,510	Vacation pay payable	10,704
Employment insurance payable	4,768	United Way donations payable	750
Workers' compensation payable	5,676	Salaries and wages payable	0
Union dues payable	1,200		

In January, the following transactions occurred:

Jan. 10 Sent a cheque to the union treasurer for union dues.

12 Issued a cheque to the Receiver General for the amounts due.
17 Issued a cheque to United Way.
20 Paid the Workers' Compensation Plan.
31 Completed the monthly payroll register, which showed office salaries $40,800, store wages $48,400, CPP withheld $4,127, EI withheld $1,873, income tax withheld $23,400, union dues withheld $1,250, United Way contributions $750, and Canada Savings Bonds deductions $1,210.
31 Prepared payroll cheques for the net pay and distributed them to employees.

At January 31, the company also made the following adjustments pertaining to employee benefits:

1. One times the employees' CPP contributions and 1.4 times the employees' EI contributions
2. Workers' Compensation Plan in an amount equal to 6% of the gross payroll
3. Vacation pay at 4% of gross earnings

Instructions

(a) Enter the beginning balances in general ledger accounts.
(b) Journalize and post the January transactions and adjustments.
(c) Calculate the balances in the payroll liability accounts as at January 31.

Calculate missing payroll amounts and record.
(SO 6) AN

P10–9B Selected data from a payroll register for the week ended June 30 for Slovac Company are presented below, with some amounts intentionally omitted:

Store wages expense	$ (1)
Warehouse wages expense	9,800
CPP deductions	1,165
EI deductions	(2)
Group insurance plan	400
Union dues	260
United Way	600
Income tax	(3)
Net pay	11,410
Overtime earnings	1,490
Regular earnings	23,150
Total gross earnings	(4)

EI premiums are 2.1% of the gross payroll.

Instructions

(a) Fill in the missing amounts.
(b) Journalize the payroll, including the employer's portion of CPP and EI, for the week ended June 30.
(c) Journalize the payment of the payroll to the employees on June 30, and the remittance of the amounts due to the Receiver General on July 15.

Continuing Cookie Chronicle

(Note: This is a continuation of the Cookie Chronicle from Chapters 1 through 9.)

Part 1

A customer has asked Natalie about returning a mixer for repair under warranty. According to the warranty granted to customers by Kzinski, Natalie's supplier of the fine European mixers, the terms are as follows:

Kzinski warrants the fine European mixer to be free of defects in material and workmanship for a period of one year from the date of original purchase. If the mixer has such a defect, Kzinski will repair or replace the mixer free of charge for parts and labour. The product must be shipped prepaid to an authorized Kzinski service centre. The cost to ship the mixer is paid by the consumer. The cost to return the product to the consumer is paid by Kzinski.

Natalie contacts Kzinski and is told that the authorized service centre in Canada is in Toronto. Because Natalie values servicing her customers, she decides that Cookie Creations will offer its own warranty, effective for sales made after January 1, 2005. This warranty will assume the responsibility of paying for shipping to Toronto for any mixers needing repair under Kzinski's warranty terms.

Kzinski advises Natalie that based on its past experience approximately 10% of mixers are returned for repair or replacement. Natalie estimates the average cost to ship a mixer to Toronto will be $50.

The following transactions take place in 2005 and 2006:

1. A total of 30 mixers are sold in 2005.
2. Four of the mixers sold in 2005 are returned for repair in 2006. The total shipping cost for returning these four mixers to Toronto is $210.
3. A total of 40 mixers are sold in 2006.
4. Two of the mixers sold in 2006 are returned for repair in 2006. The total shipping cost for returning these two mixers to Toronto is $96.

Instructions

(a) Determine the warranty liability at December 31, 2005.
(b) Prepare the journal entry to record the estimated warranty liability at December 31, 2005.
(c) Prepare the summary journal entry (or entries) to record the shipment of the six mixers (four from the 2005 sales and two from the 2006 sales) for warranty repair in 2006.
(d) Determine the warranty liability at December 31, 2006. (Hint: Note that there is no longer any liability outstanding for the mixers sold in 2005. The one-year warranty period has expired.)
(e) Prepare the journal entry to record the estimated warranty liability at December 31, 2006. (*Hint:* Similar to accounting for bad debts, consider any existing balance in the warranty liability account when you prepare your entry. You will find it helpful to prepare a general ledger account for the warranty liability and to post the above transactions.)

Part 2

Natalie is thinking of repaying all amounts outstanding to her grandmother. Recall that Cookie Creations borrowed $2,000 on November 16, 2004, from Natalie's grandmother. Interest on the note is 6% per annum and the note plus interest was to be repaid in 24 months. Recall that a monthly adjusting journal entry was prepared for the months of November, 2004 (1/2 month); December, 2004; and January, 2005.

Instructions

(a) Calculate the interest payable that was accrued and recorded to January 31, 2005.
(b) Calculate the total interest expense and interest payable to August 31, 2005. Prepare the journal entry at August 31, 2005, to bring the accounting records up to date.
(c) Natalie repays her grandmother on September 15, 2005—ten months after her grandmother extended the loan to Cookie Creations. Prepare the journal entry for the loan repayment.

Cumulative Coverage—Chapters 3 to 10

The unadjusted trial balance of LeBrun Company at its year end, July 31, 2005, is as follows:

LEBRUN COMPANY
Trial Balance
July 31, 2005

	Debit	Credit
Cash	$ 18,000	
Petty cash	200	
Accounts receivable	35,000	
Allowance for doubtful accounts		$ 2,000
Notes receivable (due December 31, 2008)	10,000	
Merchandise inventory	59,500	
Prepaid expenses	16,000	
Land	50,000	
Building	105,000	
Accumulated amortization—building		10,800
Equipment	25,000	
Accumulated amortization—equipment		12,200
Patent (net of $15,000 accumulated amortization)	60,000	
Accounts payable		81,000
Mortgage payable (due August 1, 2026)		121,190
LeBrun, capital		127,690
LeBrun, drawings	15,000	
Sales		750,000
Cost of goods sold	600,000	
Operating expenses	100,000	
Interest expense	11,180	
Totals	$1,104,880	$1,104,880

Adjustment Data:

1. The July 31 bank statement included a debit memo for service charges of $30 and an NSF cheque received from a customer on account of $450.
2. Estimated uncollectible accounts receivable at July 31 are $3,500.
3. The 6% note receivable was issued on January 1, 2005. Interest has not previously been received or accrued.
4. A physical count of inventory determined that $57,000 of inventory was actually on hand.
5. Prepaid expenses of $5,500 expired during the year (use Operating Expenses summary account).
6. Amortization is calculated on the long-lived assets using the following methods and useful lives:

   Building: straight-line, 25 years, $15,000 residual value
   Equipment: double declining-balance, five years, $2,000 residual value
   Patent: straight-line, 15 years, no residual value

7. The 8% mortgage payable was issued on August 1, 2001. Interest is paid monthly at the beginning of each month for the previous month's interest. Of the mortgage principal, $1,680 is currently due.
8. Accrued liabilities at July 31 are $1,350 (use Accounts Payable).

Instructions

(a) Prepare the adjusting journal entries required at July 31, 2005. Round your calculations to the nearest dollar.
(b) Prepare an adjusted trial balance at July 31, 2005.
(c) Prepare a multiple-step income statement and statement of owner's equity for the year ended July 31, and a classified balance sheet as at July 31, 2005.

Financial Reporting and Analysis

Practice
Tools

Financial Reporting Problem

BPY10–1 Refer to the financial statements of **The Forzani Group Ltd.** and the Notes to Consolidated Financial Statements in Appendix A.

Instructions

Answer the following questions about the company's current and contingent liabilities:

(a) What were Forzani's total current liabilities at February 2, 2003? What was the increase/decrease in total current liabilities from the prior year?
(b) What were the components of total current liabilities on February 2, 2003?
(c) Calculate Forzani's current ratio for 2003 and 2002. Did it improve or deteriorate in 2003?
(d) Does Forzani report any contingent liabilities? If so, where are they disclosed? Explain the nature, amount, and significance of Forzani's contingent liabilities, if any.

Interpreting Financial Statements

BYP10–2 **Saputo Inc.** produces and distributes fluid and powdered milk, yogurt, mozzarella, cheddar, and other speciality cheeses, as well as snack cakes, muffins, and tarts. The company reported the following information about contingencies in the notes to its March 31, 2003, financial statements:

> **SAPUTO INC.**
> **Notes to the Consolidated Financial Statements**
> **March 31, 2003**
>
> The company is defendant to certain claims arising from the normal conduct of its business. The Company believes that the final resolution of these claims will not have a material adverse effect on its earnings or financial position.
>
> The Company from time to time enters into agreements in the normal course of its business, such as service agreements and leases, and in connection with business or asset acquisitions or dispositions, which agreements by their nature may provide for indemnifications of counterparties. These indemnification provisions may be in connection with breach of representations and warranties and for future claims for certain liabilities, including liabilities related to tax and environmental matters. The terms of these indemnification provisions vary in duration. Given the nature of such indemnifications, the Company is unable to reasonably estimate its maximum potential liability under these agreements.

Instructions

(a) Why would Saputo Inc. disclose information about these legal disputes in the notes to the financial statements instead of accruing these as liabilities in its accounting records?
(b) Where should Saputo Inc. record the legal costs incurred to date on the disputes (i.e., the costs before going to trial)?

Accounting on the Web

BYP10–3 Payroll deductions for CPP contributions, EI premiums, and income tax withheld are remitted periodically to the Canada Customs and Revenue Agency. This case explores the CCRA website, viewing payroll deduction guides and forms.

Instructions

Specific requirements for this Internet case are available on the Weygandt website.

Critical Thinking

Collaborative Learning Activity

BYP10–4 Every major airline has a frequent-flyer program to encourage passenger loyalty. Various types of awards are available for points accumulated under the program, including the right to free travel. There is great debate about how airlines should record the cost of this "free" seat when frequent-flyer points are redeemed.

Some airlines believe that frequent flyer-liabilities should be disclosed as contingent liabilities, arguing that the probability of the air miles being redeemed is not quantifiable.

Others believe that the liability should be estimated and accrued, but have different views on how the amount to record should be determined. Some argue that only the increased or incremental costs associating with rewarding frequent-flyer members should be recorded. These costs would include the costs of food, drink, and ticket delivery costs. Other costs, such as fuel for the airplane and labour to staff it, are going to be incurred whether frequent-flyer passengers travel or not.

The other point of view is that the cost to be recorded should be a percentage of the ticket price originally eligible for point accumulation. This usually results in a cost allocation for each seat redeemed using frequent-flyer points that is roughly equal to a discounted or seat-sale price. Full fare is not usually a consideration, because it is unlikely that full-fare passengers will be displaced by passengers using free travel awards.

Instructions

With the class divided into groups, assign a debate position for the following issues:
(a) Recording the liability: One group should provide the arguments for disclosing the liability as a contingent liability, rather than recording it. Another group should provide the arguments for estimating and accruing the liability.
(b) Determining the amount of the liability: One group should provide the arguments in support of using incremental costs. Another group should provide the arguments for using a seat-sale fare. Another group should provide arguments for other cost allocations that should also be considered.

Communication Activity

BYP10–5 The Show Time movie theatre sells thousands of gift certificates every year. The certificates can be redeemed at any time since they have no expiry date. Some of them may never be redeemed (because they are lost or forgotten, for example).

The owner of the theatre has raised a number of questions on how to account for these gift certificates.

Instructions

Write a memo to answer the following questions from the owner:

(a) Why is a liability recorded when these certificates are sold? After all, they bring customers into the theatre where they spend money on snacks and drinks, etc. Why should something which helps generate additional revenue be treated as a liability?

(b) How should the gift certificates which are never redeemed be treated? At some point in the future, can the liability related to them be eliminated? If so, what type of journal entry would be made?

Ethics Case

BYP10–6 The Nice Nuke Company, which owns and operates a nuclear plant, recently received notice from the provincial government that it has to find a new disposal site for its radioactive waste. The company is also told it is responsible for the environmental cleanup of the old site. The vice-president of engineering and the vice-president of finance meet to discuss the situation. The engineer says that it could take many years to clean up the site and that the cost could be considerable—a minimum of $50 million and perhaps as much as $100 million.

The vice-president of finance, says that there's no way that the company can afford to record this liability. He says he's not even sure he wants to disclose the potential liability for fear of the effect on the company's share price.

Instructions

(a) Who are the stakeholders in this situation?

(b) What are the alternative reporting options the company can use?

(c) What is the likely impact of each alternative on the company's financial position?

(d) Is there anything unethical in what the vice-president proposes to do about this potential liability?

(e) What do you recommend the company do?

Answers to Self-Study Questions

1. d   2. c   3. b   4. b   5. b   6. c   7. c   8. a   9. a   10. d   *11. b

Answer to Forzani Review It Question 1

The Forzani Group reports bank indebtedness first, followed by accounts payable and accrued liabilities, and the current portion of long-term debt. Current liabilities are not listed in order of magnitude. They may be listed in order of maturity.

Remember to go back to the Navigator Box at the beginning of the chapter to check off your completed work.

appendix A

Specimen Financial Statements:

The Forzani Group Ltd.

www.forzanigroup.com

In this appendix we illustrate current financial reporting with a comprehensive set of corporate financial statements that are prepared in accordance with generally accepted accounting principles. We are grateful for permission to use the actual financial statements of The Forzani Group Ltd.—Canada's largest sporting goods retailer. Forzani's financial statement package features a statement of management's responsibilities for financial reporting, auditors' report, balance sheet, combined statement of operations (or income statement as we know it) and retained earnings, cash flow statement, and notes to the financial statements.

We encourage students to use these financial statements in conjunction with relevant material in the textbook, and to solve the Review It questions in the Before You Go On section within the chapter and the Financial Reporting Problem in the Broadening Your Perspective section of the end-of-chapter material.

Annual reports, including the financial statements, are reviewed in detail on the interactive Student Navigator CD that accompanies this textbook.

Annual Report
Walkthrough

MANAGEMENT'S RESPONSIBILITIES FOR FINANCIAL REPORTING

The Annual Report, including the consolidated financial statements, is the responsibility of the management of the Company. The consolidated financial statements were prepared by management in accordance with generally accepted accounting principles. The significant accounting policies used are described in Note 1 to the consolidated financial statements. The integrity of the information presented in the financial statements, including estimates and judgments relating to matters not concluded by year-end, is the responsibility of management. Financial information presented elsewhere in this Annual Report has been prepared by management and is consistent with the information in the consolidated financial statements.

Management is responsible for the development and maintenance of systems of internal accounting and administrative controls. Such systems are designed to provide reasonable assurance that the financial information is accurate, relevant and reliable, and that the Company's assets are appropriately accounted for and adequately safeguarded. The Board of Directors is responsible for ensuring that management fulfills its responsibilities for final approval of the annual consolidated financial statements. The Board appoints an Audit Committee consisting of three directors, none of whom is an officer or employee of the Company or its subsidiaries. The Audit Committee meets at least four times each year to discharge its responsibilities under a written mandate from the Board of Directors. The Audit Committee meets with management and with the independent auditors to satisfy itself that they are properly discharging their responsibilities, reviews the consolidated financial statements and the Auditors' Report, and examines other auditing, accounting and financial reporting matters. The consolidated financial statements have been reviewed by the Audit Committee and approved by the Board of Directors of The Forzani Group Ltd. The consolidated financial statements have been examined by the shareholders' auditors, Deloitte & Touche, LLP, Chartered Accountants. The Auditors' Report outlines the nature of their examination and their opinion on the consolidated financial statements of the Company. The independent auditors have full and unrestricted access to the Audit Committee, with and without management present.

Bob Sartor, C.A.
Chief Executive Officer

Bill Gregson, C.A.
President & Chief Operating Officer

AUDITORS' REPORT

TO THE SHAREHOLDERS OF THE FORZANI GROUP LTD.

We have audited the consolidated balance sheets of **The Forzani Group Ltd.** as at February 2, 2003 and January 27, 2002 and the consolidated statements of operations and retained earnings and cash flows for the years then ended. These consolidated financial statements are the responsibility of the Company's management. Our responsibility is to express an opinion on these consolidated financial statements based on our audits.

We conducted our audits in accordance with Canadian generally accepted auditing standards. Those standards require that we plan and perform an audit to obtain reasonable assurance whether the financial statements are free of material misstatement. An audit includes examining, on a test basis, evidence supporting the amounts and disclosures in the financial statements. An audit also includes assessing the accounting principles used and significant estimates made by management, as well as evaluating the overall financial statement presentation.

In our opinion, these consolidated financial statements present fairly, in all material respects, the financial position of the Company as at February 2, 2003 and January 27, 2002 and the results of its operations and its cash flows for the years then ended in accordance with Canadian generally accepted accounting principles.

Calgary, Alberta
March 7, 2003

Deloitte & Touche LLP

Chartered Accountants

A FOCUSED DIRECTION

CONSOLIDATED BALANCE SHEETS
(in thousands)
(audited)

As at	February 2, 2003	January 27, 2002
ASSETS		
Current		
Cash	$ 523	$ 494
Accounts receivable	38,275	35,988
Inventory	268,519	229,270
Prepaid and other expenses	11,123	4,481
	318,440	270,233
Capital assets (Note 3)	142,236	120,525
Goodwill and other intangibles (Note 4)	38,684	37,394
Other assets (Note 5)	7,452	8,112
	$506,812	$ 436,264
LIABILITIES		
Current		
Indebtedness under revolving credit facility (Note 6)	$ 4,204	$ 17,094
Accounts payable and accrued liabilities	209,873	188,995
Current portion of long-term debt	3,638	14,032
	217,715	220,121
Long-term debt (Note 7)	32,062	35,454
Deferred lease inducements	52,251	46,623
Future income tax liability (Note 10)	1,061	2,021
	303,089	304,219
SHAREHOLDERS' EQUITY		
Share capital (Note 9)	124,866	83,719
Retained earnings	78,857	48,326
	203,723	132,045
	$506,812	$ 436,264

On behalf of the Board:

Roman Doroniuk, C.A.

John M. Forzani

CONSOLIDATED STATEMENTS OF OPERATIONS AND RETAINED EARNINGS

(in thousands, except share data)

(audited, except where otherwise noted)

	For the 53 weeks ended February 2, 2003	For the 52 weeks ended January 27, 2002
Corporate and Franchise Retail Sales (unaudited – Note 12)	$ 1,053,449	$ 876,434
Revenue		
Corporate	$ 715,003	$ 579,196
Franchise	208,792	179,061
	923,795	758,257
Cost of sales	603,326	497,758
Gross margin	320,469	260,499
Operating and administrative expenses		
Store operating	177,252	142,788
General and administrative	60,230	55,215
	237,482	198,003
Operating earnings before undernoted items	82,987	62,496
Amortization	29,624	22,574
Interest	4,354	4,901
Gain on sale of investments (Note 13)	(1,454)	-
	32,524	27,475
Earnings before income taxes	50,463	35,021
Provision for (recovery of) income taxes (Note 10)		
Current	22,133	6,434
Future	(2,201)	7,958
	19,932	14,392
Net earnings	30,531	20,629
Retained earnings, opening	48,326	27,697
Retained earnings, closing	$ 78,857	$ 48,326
Earnings per share	$ 1.01	$ 0.76
Diluted earnings per share	$ 0.96	$ 0.74
Total number of common shares outstanding	30,787,179	27,622,447
Weighted average number of common shares outstanding	30,082,408	27,085,234

CONSOLIDATED STATEMENTS OF CASH FLOWS

(in thousands)

(audited)

	For the 53 weeks ended February 2, 2003	For the 52 weeks ended January 27, 2002
Cash provided by (used in) operating activities		
Net earnings	$30,531	$ 20,629
Items not involving cash		
Amortization	29,624	22,574
Amortization of finance charges	571	181
Amortization of deferred lease inducements	(8,767)	(6,394)
Gain on sale of investment	(1,445)	-
Future income tax expense	(2,201)	7,958
Cash flow from operations (Note 9 (c))	48,313	44,948
Changes in non-cash elements of working capital (Note 8)	(27,300)	(24,161)
	21,013	20,787
Cash provided by (used in) financing activities		
Proceeds from issuance of share capital	40,416	1,311
Principal repayment of long-term debt	(13,786)	(2,683)
(Decrease) increase in revolving credit facility	(12,890)	17,094
Proceeds from deferred lease inducements	14,395	11,559
	28,135	27,281
Cash provided by (used in) investing activities		
Addition of capital assets	(50,085)	(40,791)
Addition of other assets	(1,186)	(1,710)
Acquisition of wholly owned subsidiary, net of cash acquired (Note 14)	-	(18,518)
Sale of investments	1,690	-
Disposal of capital assets	276	347
Disposal of other assets	186	68
	(49,119)	(60,604)
Increase (decrease) in cash	29	(12,536)
Net cash position, opening	494	13,030
Net cash position, closing	$ 523	$ 494

Supplementary cash flow information (Note 8)

NOTES TO CONSOLIDATED FINANCIAL STATEMENTS (Tabular amounts in thousands, except share data)

1. Nature of Operations

The Forzani Group Ltd. "FGL" or "the Company" is Canada's largest sporting goods retailer. FGL currently operates 215 corporate stores under the banners: Sport Chek, Sport Mart, Coast Mountain Sports, and Forzani's. The Company is also the franchisor of 161 stores under the banners: Sports Experts, Intersport, R'n'R, Econosports and Atmosphere. FGL operates two websites, dedicated to the Canadian online sporting goods market, at www.sportchek.ca and www.sportmart.ca.

2. Significant Accounting Policies

The consolidated financial statements have been prepared by management in accordance with Canadian generally accepted accounting principles. The financial statements have, in management's opinion, been prepared within reasonable limits of materiality and within the framework of the accounting policies summarized below:

(a) Organization

The consolidated financial statements include the accounts of The Forzani Group Ltd. and its subsidiaries, all of which are wholly owned.

(b) Inventory

Inventory is valued at the lower of laid-down cost and net realizable value. Laid-down cost is determined using the weighted average cost method and includes invoice cost, duties, freight, and distribution costs. Net realizable value is defined as the expected selling price.

Volume rebates and other supplier discounts are included in income when earned.

(c) Capital assets

Capital assets are recorded at cost and are amortized using the following methods and rates:

- Building - 4% declining-balance basis
- Building on leased land - 20 years straight-line basis
- Furniture, fixtures, equipment and automotive - straight-line basis over 3-5 years
- Leasehold improvements - straight-line basis over the lesser of the length of the lease and estimated useful life of the improvements, not exceeding 10 years

(d) Goodwill and other intangibles

Goodwill represents the excess of the purchase price over the fair market value of the identifiable net assets acquired. Goodwill and other intangible assets, with indefinite lives, are not amortized, but tested for impairment at least annually, at year end, and, if required, asset values reduced accordingly.

The method used to assess impairment is a review of the profitability of the assets acquired.

Non-competition agreement costs are being amortized, on a straight-line basis, over the five-year life of the agreements.

(e) Other assets (see Note 5)

Other assets include financing costs, system and interactive development costs, long-term receivables, and an investment in a wholesale distribution company.

Interactive development costs relate to the development of the sportchek.ca interactive web site, designed as a part of the Company's multi-channel retailing and branding strategy. These costs are being amortized over five years following the commencement of the web site's operations in June, 2001.

Financing costs represent fees incurred in establishing the Company's revolving credit facility. These costs are being amortized over the term of the facility.

System development costs relate to the implementation of software. Upon activation, costs are amortized over the estimated useful lives of the systems.

Long-term receivables are carried at cost less a valuation allowance.

The investment in shares of a wholesale distribution company is carried at cost and periodically reviewed for impairment. The method used to assess impairment is a review of the operation's profitability.

(f)   Deferred lease inducements

Deferred lease inducements represent cash and non-cash benefits that the Company has received from landlords pursuant to store lease agreements. These lease inducements are amortized against rent expense over the term of the lease, not exceeding 10 years.

(g)   Revenue recognition

Revenue includes sales to customers through corporate stores operated by the Company and sales to, and service fees from, franchise stores. Sales to customers through corporate stores operated by the Company are recognized at the point of sale, net of an estimated allowance for sales returns. Sales of merchandise to franchise stores are recognized at the time of shipment. Royalties and administration fees are recognized when earned, in accordance with the terms of the franchise agreements.

(h)   Store opening expenses

Operating costs incurred prior to the opening of new stores are expensed as incurred.

(i)   Fiscal year

The Company's fiscal year follows the retail calendar. The fiscal years for the consolidated financial statements presented are the 53-week period ended February 2, 2003 and the 52-week period ended January 27, 2002.

(j)   Foreign currency translation

Foreign currency accounts are translated to Canadian dollars as follows:

At the transaction date, each asset, liability, revenue or expense is translated into Canadian dollars by the use of the exchange rate in effect at that date. At the year-end date, monetary assets and liabilities are translated into Canadian dollars by using the exchange rate in effect at that date and the resulting foreign exchange gains and losses are included in income in the current period. The amendments to Foreign Currency Translation, of the Canadian Institute of Chartered Accountants, "CICA", Handbook Section 1650, applicable January 1, 2002, did not have an impact on the Company's operations.

(k)   Financial instruments (see Notes 7 and 16)

Accounts receivable, accounts payable and accrued liabilities, long-term debt and derivative transactions, constitute financial instruments. The Company also, in the normal course of business, enters into leases in respect of real estate and certain point-of-sale equipment.

The Company enters into forward contracts and options, with financial institutions, as hedges of other financial transactions and not for speculative purposes. The Company's policies do not allow leveraged transactions and are designed to minimize foreign currency risk. The Company's policies require all hedges to be linked with specific liabilities on the balance sheet and to be assessed, both at inception, and on an ongoing basis, as to their effectiveness in offsetting changes in the fair values or cash flows of the hedged liabilities.

(l)   Measurement uncertainty

The amounts recorded for amortization of capital assets, the provision for shrinkage and obsolescence of inventory are based on estimates. By their nature, these estimates are subject to measurement uncertainty and the impact on the consolidated financial statements of future periods could be material.

(m)   Stock Option Plan

The Company has a stock option plan as described in Note 9 (d). No compensation expense is recognized when stock options are issued to employees. Any consideration paid by employees on the exercise of stock options is credited to share capital.

(n)   Income taxes (see Note 10)

The Company follows the liability method under which future income taxes and obligations are determined based on differences between the financial reporting and tax basis of assets and liabilities, measured using tax rates substantively enacted at the balance sheet date.

FORZANI ANNUAL REPORT F2003

(o) **Employee Profit Sharing Plan (see Note 9(e))**

The Company has an Employee Profit Sharing Plan that causes an amount no less than 1%, and no greater than 5%, of consolidated earnings before income taxes, to be paid to a Trustee for the purchase of shares of the Company. These shares are distributed to participating employees on a predetermined basis, upon retirement from the Company. Compensation expense is recognized when such contributions are made.

(p) **Comparative Figures**

Certain 2002 comparative figures have been reclassified to conform with the current year's presentation.

3. Capital Assets

	2003			2002		
	Cost	Accumulated Amortization	Net Book Value	Cost	Accumulated Amortization	Net Book Value
Land	$ 638	$ -	$ 638	$ 638	$ -	$ 638
Buildings	6,280	1,637	4,643	6,036	1,406	4,630
Building on leased land	3,159	1,186	1,973	3,159	1,029	2,130
Furniture, fixtures, equipment and automotive	97,117	52,438	44,679	74,330	39,778	34,552
Leasehold improvements	145,150	54,847	90,303	119,079	40,504	78,575
	$ 252,344	$ 110,108	$ 142,236	$ 203,242	$ 82,717	$ 120,525

4. Goodwill and Other Intangible Assets

	2003	2002
Goodwill	$21,319	$19,438
Trademarks/Tradenames	16,702	16,702
Non-competition agreements	3,000	3,000
	41,021	39,140
Less accumulated amortization	2,337	1,746
	$38,684	$37,394

During the prior fiscal year, the Company adopted new CICA standards on "Goodwill and Other Intangible Assets". Under the new accounting standards, goodwill and other intangible assets with indefinite lives are no longer amortized, but are tested for impairment at least annually. At year end, there was no impairment of goodwill and other intangible assets. Prior to the January 29, 2002 adoption of CICA Handbook requirements for goodwill and other intangible assets, the Company amortized pre-existing trademarks over ten years and pre-existing goodwill over five years, each on a straight-line basis.

In accordance with the transitional provisions of the new standards, CICA 3062, the following is a summary of the fiscal 2002 comparable 52-week period, net earnings and earnings per share, had the new standards been applied retroactively to January 29, 2001.

	For the 52-week Period ended 27-Jan-02 (previously reported)	For the 52-week Period ended 27-Jan-02 (restated)
Earnings before income taxes	$35,021	$35,021
Amortization of goodwill	-	552
Earnings before income taxes	$35,021	$35,573
Provision for income taxes	14,392	14,619
Net earnings	$20,629	$20,954
Earnings per share	$0.76	
Earnings per share adjusted		$0.77

5.   Other Assets

	2003	2002
Interactive development	$2,649	$2,649
Deferred financing charges	2,124	1,397
System development	1,471	1,121
	6,244	5,167
Less accumulated amortization	2,246	960
	3,998	4,207
Long-term receivables	950	1,005
Investment in shares of a wholesale distribution company	2,504	2,900
	$7,452	$8,112

6.   Indebtedness

The Company has a $140 million credit facility with General Electric Capital Canada Inc. (G.E.) and National Bank of Canada, comprised of a $115 million revolving loan and a $25 million term loan repayable at maturity on December 20, 2003. Under the terms of the credit agreement, the interest rate payable on both the revolving and term loans is based on the Company's financial performance as determined by its interest coverage ratio. As at February 2, 2003, the interest rate paid was 4.5%. The facility is secured by general security agreements against all existing and future acquired assets of the Company. As at February 2, 2003, the Company is in compliance with all covenants.

Subsequent to the fiscal year end, on February 3, 2003, the Company extended its existing credit agreement to February 3, 2006. This agreement with G.E. was amended to: assign a 21.43% pro rata share of the revolving credit facility and term loan to each of National Bank of Canada and The Royal Bank of Canada and; grant an increase of the maximum revolving credit commitment to $150 million via the exercising of a single, irreversible option.

7.   Long-term Debt

	2003	2002
G.E. term loan (see Note 6)	$25,000	$25,000
Vendor take-back re: Sport Mart acquisition, with interest rates from prime plus 1% to prime plus 2% (see Note 14)	7,039	15,000
Various long-term debts, with interest rates from prime plus 1.5% to prime plus 2%	-	5,490
Mortgages, with monthly blended payments of $52,611, including interest at rates from approximately 7% to 10%, compounded semi-annually, supported by land and buildings, renewable July 1, 2004 and August 1, 2005.	3,631	3,966
Security Deposits	30	30
	35,700	49,486
Less current portion	3,638	14,032
	$32,062	$35,454

Principal payments on the above mortgages due in the next five years, assuming the mortgages continue to be renewed on similar terms, are as follows:

2004	$370
2005	$404
2006	$296
2007	$169
2008	$182

Based on estimated interest rates currently available to the Company for mortgages with similar terms and maturities, the fair value of the mortgages at February 2, 2003 amounted to approximately $3,600,000 (2002 - $3,966,000). Interest costs incurred for the 53-week period ended February 2, 2003 on long-term debt amounted to $2,330,983 (2002 - $2,312,906). The fair value of the other long-term debt components above, approximates book value.

8. Supplementary Cash Flow Information

	2003	2002
Changes in non-cash elements of working capital		
Accounts receivable	$ (2,287)	$ (3,044)
Inventory	(39,249)	(50,130)
Prepaid and other expenses	(6,642)	942
Accounts payable	20,878	28,071
	$(27,300)	$(24,161)
Cash interest paid	$ 5,195	$ 5,190
Cash taxes paid	$ 14,897	$ 790

9. Share Capital

(a) Authorized

An unlimited number of Class A shares

An unlimited number of Preferred shares, issuable in series

(b) Issued

Class A shares

	Number	Consideration
Balance, January 28, 2001	26,918,448	$ 82,408
Shares issued upon employees exercising stock options	703,999	1,311
Balance, January 27, 2002	**27,622,447**	**83,719**
Shares issued upon employees exercising stock options	**664,732**	**2,817**
Shares issued March 26, 2002 upon public stock offer		
(net of issuance costs and related future income tax)	**2,500,000**	**38,330**
	30,787,179	**$124,866**

(c) Earnings and Cash Flow Per Share [1]

	2003	2002
Earnings Per Share		
Basic	$1.01	$0.76
Diluted	$0.96	$0.74
Cash Flow Per Share		
Basic	$1.61	$1.66
Diluted	$1.53	$1.61
Weighted average number of common shares outstanding		
Basic	30,082,408	27,085,234
Diluted	31,678,044	27,944,114
Common shares outstanding		
Basic	30,787,179	27,622,447
Diluted	32,382,815	28,481,327

Diluted calculations assume that options under the stock option plan have been exercised at the later of the beginning of the year or date of issuance, and that the funds derived therefrom would have been used to repurchase shares at the average market value of the Company's stock, 2003 - $19.55 (2002 - $8.33).

(1) Cash flow per share is a not a recognized measure under Canadian generally accepted accounting principles. Cash flow per share is defined to be cash flow from operations before non-cash changes in working capital divided by the weighted average shares outstanding. Management believes that cash flow per share is a key measure, as it demonstrates the Company's ability to generate cash flow necessary to fund future growth.

(d) Stock Option Plan

The Company has granted stock options to directors, officers and employees to purchase 2,437,968 Class A shares at prices between $3.00 and $22.06 per share. These options expire on dates between March 31, 2003 and June 5, 2007.

A summary of the status of the Company's stock option plan as of February 2, 2003 and January 27, 2002, and any changes during the year ending on those dates is presented in the following table:

Stock Options	2003		2002	
	Shares	Weighted Average Exercise Price	Shares	Weighted Average Exercise Price
Outstanding, beginning of year	1,997,700	$4.84	2,109,233	$3.13
Granted	1,105,000	$8.88	595,800	$7.37
Exercised	664,732	$4.24	703,999	$1.86
Forfeited	-	-	3,334	$3.81
Outstanding, end of year	2,437,968	$6.81	1,997,700	$4.84
Options exercisable at year end	1,103,482		935,247	

The following table summarizes information about stock options outstanding at February 2, 2003:

Range of Exercise Prices	Options Outstanding			Options Exercisable	
	Number Outstanding	Weighted Average Remaining Contractual Life	Weighted Average Exercise Price	Number of Shares Exercisable	Weighted Average Exercise Price
$3.00 - $3.90	1,162,000	0.9 years	$3.25	682,000	$3.40
$4.16 - $4.26	393,501	1.3 years	$4.23	193,500	$4.20
$6.18 - $14.65	697,467	3.8 years	$11.21	227,982	$11.36
$16.49 - $22.06	185,000	4.2 years	$18.00	-	-
	2,437,968			1,103,482	

The Company does not recognize an expense in the financial statements, for share options granted to employees and directors, when issued at market value.

Effective January 1, 2002 , Canadian generally accepted accounting principles require disclosure of the impact on net earnings, using the fair-value method, for stock options issued on or after January 1, 2002. If the fair-value method had been used, the effect on the Company's net earnings and earnings per share, for the 53-week period ended February 2, 2003, would have been as follows, if the expense had been realized based on the number of stock options granted in the period (the pro forma amounts):

	For the 53-week period ended February 2, 2003
Net earnings - as reported	$30,531
- pro forma	$30,201
Earnings per share - as reported	$1.01
- pro forma	$1.00
Diluted earnings per share - as reported	$0.96
- pro forma	$0.95

(e)   **Employee Profit Sharing Plan**

Under the terms of the Employee Profit Sharing Plan the Company has accrued $1,000,000 for the purchase of shares, in trust, for distribution to participating employees.

10. Income Taxes

The components of the future income tax asset (liability) amount as at February 2, 2003 and January 27, 2002, are as follows:

	2003	2002
Current assets	$ (4,610)	$ (3,567)
Capital and other assets	(14,776)	(14,733)
Tax benefit of share issuance costs	556	-
Deferred lease inducements	17,769	16,279
Future income tax liability	$ (1,061)	$ (2,021)

A reconciliation of income taxes at the combined statutory federal and provincial tax rate to the actual income tax rate is as follows:

	2003		2002	
Federal and provincial income taxes	$19,222	38.10%	$ 13,856	39.60%
Increase (decrease) resulting from:				
Effect of substantively enacted tax rate changes	451	0.90%	48	0.10%
Permanent differences	(60)	(0.10)%	317	0.90%
Other, net	319	0.60%	171	0.50%
Provision for income taxes	$19,932	39.50%	$ 14,392	41.10%

Federal Part I.3 tax and provincial capital tax expense in the amount of $960,000 (2002 - $790,000) is included in operating expenses.

11. Commitments

(a) The Company is committed, at February 2, 2003, to minimum payments under long-term real property leases for the next five years as follows:

		Gross
	2004	$55,251
	2005	$51,638
	2006	$50,165
	2007	$47,827
	2008	$47,005

In addition, the Company may be obligated to pay percentage rent under certain of the leases.

(b) As at February 2, 2003, the Company has open letters of credit for purchases of inventory of approximately $3,031,000 (2002 - $3,735,000).

The Company has entered into long-term lease agreements for the rental of data processing hardware and software equipment. The leases, expiring at various dates until 2007, call for minimum lease payments of, $3,799,413 in 2004, $2,456,400 in 2005, $1,793,500 in 2006, and $218,700 in 2007.

12. Corporate and Franchise Retail Sales

Total corporate and franchise retail sales have been shown on the Consolidated Statements of Operations and Retained Earnings to indicate the size of the Company's total retail sales level (on an unaudited basis). Only revenue from corporately owned stores, wholesale sales to, and fees from, franchisees are included in the Consolidated Statements of Operations and Retained Earnings.

13. Sale of Investment

During the year, the Company sold its investment in a wholesale distribution operation. The Company held 668,668 common and 334,334 series C preferred shares, which were valued at $2,899,800. The Company received consideration of $1,690,100 and 234,771 shares in a publicly traded wholesale distribution company, resulting in a pre-tax gain of $1,445,000. Subsequent to the initial transaction, 13,400 shares of the 234,771 received were sold, for a gain of $9,000, resulting in an overall pre-tax gain on sale of investments, of $1,454,000.

14.   Acquisition

Effective August 1, 2001, the Company acquired all of the outstanding shares of Sport Mart Inc. This acquisition has been accounted for using the purchase method and accordingly the consolidated financial statements include the results of operations since the date of acquisition.

The purchase of all of the outstanding common; class B and preference shares, 9,891,267; 368 and 17,761,718 shares respectively, was made for a consideration of $35 million, consisting of $20 million cash and a vendor take-back loan of $15 million payable as to $8.5 million on August 1, 2002, $3.0 million on August 1, 2003 and $3.5 million on August 1, 2006. The loan is secured by a general security agreement and bears interest at rates of prime plus 2% on the first and second installments and prime plus 1% on the final installment. The assigned fair values of the underlying assets and liabilities acquired by the Company, as at August 1, 2001, are summarized as follows:

Current assets	$ 24,939
Capital assets	8,704
Trademarks/trade names	16,443
Goodwill	17,938
Non-competition agreements	3,000
Total assets acquired	$ 71,024
Current liabilities	$(24,060)
Long-term liabilities	(8,710)
Future income tax liability	(3,254)
Total liabilities assumed	(36,024)
Total consideration	$ 35,000

15.   Contingencies

(a)   As part of its operations, the Company has entered into agreements with certain franchisees to buy back inventory in the event that the franchisees' bank realizes on related security. The maximum exposure to the Company is limited to the lesser of 75% of the book value of inventory or the franchisees' bank indebtedness. As at February 2, 2003, the maximum exposure was $25,874,232 (2002 - $20,320,000).

(b)   Claims and suits have been brought against the Company in the ordinary course of business. In the opinion of management, all such claims and suits are adequately covered by insurance, or if not so covered, the results are not expected to materially affect the Company's financial position. Any costs to the Company arising from these claims and suits will be charged to earnings in the year in which they occur.

16.   Financial Instruments

The carrying value of the Company's accounts receivable and accounts payable and accrued liabilities approximates, based on available information, fair value as at February 2, 2003.

The Company is exposed to credit risk on its accounts receivable from franchisees. The accounts receivable are net of applicable allowance for doubtful accounts, which are established based on the specific credit risks associated with individual franchisees and other relevant information. Concentration of credit risk with respect to receivables is limited, due to the large number of franchisees.

The Company purchases a portion of its inventory from foreign vendors with payment terms in non-Canadian dollars. To manage the foreign exchange risk associated with these purchases, the Company hedges its exposure to foreign currency by purchasing foreign exchange options and forward contracts to fix exchange rates and protect planned margins. The Company has the following derivative instruments outstanding at February 2, 2003 and January 27, 2002:

FORZANI ANNUAL REPORT F2003

	Notional amounts maturing in			
	Less than 1 year	Over 1 year	**2003 total**	2002 total
Foreign exchange contracts ($CAD)				
United States dollar contracts	**12,712**	-	**12,712**	10,958
EURO contracts	**367**	-	**367**	1,812
Swiss Franc contracts	**-**	-	**-**	8
Total	**13,079**	-	**13,079**	12,778

As at February 2, 2003, these instruments had unrealized losses of $0.2 million (2002 - $0.1 million gain).

The Company is exposed to interest risk on its credit facility and the term loan. Interest rate risk reflects the sensitivity of the Company's financial condition to movements in interest rates. For fiscal year 2003, a +/-1% change in interest rates would change interest expense by +/- $292 (2002 +/- $421).

17. Segmented Financial Information

The Company operates principally in two business segments: corporately-owned and operated retail stores and as franchisor of retail stores. Identifiable assets, depreciation and amortization, interest expense and capital expenditures are not disclosed by segment as they are substantially corporate in nature.

	2003	2002
Revenues:		
Corporate	**$ 715,003**	$ 579,196
Franchise	**208,792**	179,061
	923,795	758,257
Operating Profit:		
Corporate	**87,201**	65,426
Franchise	**16,163**	12,396
	103,364	77,822
Non-segment specific administrative expenses	**20,377**	15,326
Amortization	**29,624**	22,574
Interest expense	**4,354**	4,901
Gain on sale of investments	**(1,454)**	-
	52,901	42,801
Earnings before income taxes	**50,463**	35,021
Income tax expense	**19,932**	14,392
Net Earnings	**$ 30,531**	$ 20,629

18. Related Party Transaction

The Company has advanced $320,567 (2002-$398,750) to an officer for housing purchase assistance. The advance is being repaid over a four-year term commencing on January 28, 2002 and bears interest at bank prime rate.

49

appendix B
Sales Taxes

All businesses operating in Canada need to understand how sales taxes apply to their particular business in their particular province or territory. Sales taxes may take the form of the **Goods and Services Tax (GST)**, **Provincial Sales Tax (PST)**, or **Harmonized Sales Tax (HST)**. GST is levied by the federal government. PST is levied by the provinces and territories, with the exception of Alberta, the Northwest Territories, Nunavut, and Yukon, where no provincial sales tax is charged. Nova Scotia, New Brunswick, and Newfoundland and Labrador have combined the GST and PST into one harmonized sales tax, known as the HST.

As an agent of the federal and provincial governments, a business is required to collect sales taxes on the sale of certain goods and services. In addition, businesses pay sales taxes on most disbursements. We will discuss the collection, payment, recording, and remittance of each of these types of sales taxes in the following sections.

Types of Sales Taxes

Goods and Services Tax

The GST is a federal sales tax on most goods and services provided in Canada. A business must register for the GST if it provides taxable goods or services in Canada and if it has revenues of more than $30,000 in any year. Businesses that have to, or decide to, voluntarily register for the GST are called registrants. Registrants can claim a credit—called an **input tax credit (ITC)**—to offset the GST they pay or owe on purchases of goods or services against the GST they collect or are owed. GST returns are submitted quarterly for most registrants (monthly for large registrants) to the Canada Customs and Revenue Agency (CCRA). The taxes are payable to the Receiver General, who is the collection agent for the federal government.

The GST applies at a rate of 7% on most transactions. Transactions subject to GST are called **taxable supplies**. There are two other categories of goods and services with respect to the GST:

- zero-rated supplies, such as basic groceries and prescription drugs
- exempt supplies, such as educational services, health-care services, and financial services

No GST applies to zero-rated or exempt supplies. However, zero-rated suppliers can claim input tax credits.

Illustration B-1 provides the GST status of some typical goods and services.

Taxable Supplies	Zero-Rated Supplies	Exempt Supplies
Building materials	Prescription drugs	Used house
Ready-to-eat pizza	Uncooked pizza	Dental services
Two doughnuts	Six or more doughnuts	Insurance policy

The reason ready-to-eat pizza and two doughnuts have GST added to the purchase price is because they are considered convenience items and not basic groceries.

Provincial Sales Tax

Provincial sales taxes are charged on retail sales of certain goods and services. In the provinces charging sales tax, except Quebec and Prince Edward Island, this tax is applied to the selling price of the item before GST is applied. Similarly, GST is charged on the selling price of the item before PST is applied, thus avoiding GST being charged on PST. In Quebec and Prince Edward Island, however, the provincial sales tax is cascaded—that is, applied to the total of the selling price plus GST. Quebec's sales tax is also known as the QST (Quebec Sales Tax).

The following example shows the calculation of cascaded sales tax, using a taxable item sold in Quebec for $100:

Selling price	$100.00
GST ($100 × 7%)	7.00
QST [($100 + $7) × 7.5%]	8.03
Total	$115.03

Provincial sales taxes are remitted periodically to the Minister of Finance or Provincial Treasurer in each province.

PST rates vary by province and can change with each provincial budget. It is important to understand that the PST may not be applied at the same rate to all taxable goods and services. For example, in Ontario, the rates vary for insurance premiums and alcoholic beverages. Certain goods are exempt, such as children's clothing, textbooks, and residential rent, and may be purchased with no PST. Examples of exempt services that are not taxable include personal services such as dental and medical services. Because rates and exemptions vary by province, it is important, when starting a business, to check with provincial officials for details on how to calculate the provincial tax that must be applied to sales.

Harmonized Sales Tax

The provinces of Newfoundland and Labrador, Nova Scotia, and New Brunswick charge Harmonized Sales Tax, or HST. Instead of charging GST and PST separately, only the HST is charged at a combined rate of 15%.

Similar to GST, HST returns are submitted quarterly for most registrants (monthly for large registrants) to the CCRA. The federal government then gives the provincial portion of the tax to the province.

To summarize, four provinces—British Columbia, Manitoba, Ontario, and Saskatchewan—apply PST and GST to the selling price of a taxable good or service. Two provinces—Prince Edward Island and Quebec—apply PST to the total of the purchase price and the GST. Three provinces—New Brunswick, Newfoundland and Labrador, and Nova Scotia—charge a combined GST and PST (harmonized) rate of 15% on the selling price. Four provinces and territories do not charge PST—Alberta, the Northwest Territories, Nunavut, and Yukon. In addition to the different ways of applying sales taxes, the rates of sales tax differ in each province and territory, as shown below:

Illustration B-2 ◀
Sales tax rates

Province/Territory	GST (HST) Rate	PST Rate	Combined Rate
Alberta	7.0%	0.0%	7.0%
British Columbia	7.0%	7.5%	14.5%
Manitoba	7.0%	7.0%	14.0%
New Brunswick	15.0%	N/A	15.0%
Newfoundland and Labrador	15.0%	N/A	15.0%
Northwest Territories	7.0%	0.0%	7.0%
Nova Scotia	15.0%	N/A	15.0%
Nunavut	7.0%	0.0%	7.0%
Ontario	7.0%	8.0%	15.0%
Prince Edward Island	7.0%	10.0%	17.7%[1]
Quebec	7.0%	7.5%	15.025%[1]
Saskatchewan	7.0%	6.0%	13.0%
Yukon	7.0%	0.0%	7.0%

[1] In Prince Edward Island and Quebec only, the GST is included in the provincial sales tax base.

Sales Taxes Collected on Receipts

Sales taxes are collected by businesses from consumers on taxable goods and services. It is important to understand that sales taxes are not a source of revenue for a company. Sales taxes are collected by a company on behalf of the federal and provincial governments. Consequently, collected sales tax is a current liability to the company until remitted to the respective government at regular intervals.

Services

Now let's look at how service companies record sales taxes on the services they provide. Assume that a law firm bills a client for legal services. Some service providers, such as law firms, do not have to charge PST in some provinces. In these provinces, the law firm would only charge 7% GST on the legal services provided.

The following entry would be made to record the billing of a client for $500 of services provided by a law firm in Ontario on May 28. In Ontario, legal services are exempt from PST, so only 7% GST would be charged on these services.

May 28	Accounts Receivable	535	
	Legal Fees Earned		500
	GST Payable ($500 × 7%)		35
	To record revenue earned from legal fees.		

A	=	L	+	OE
+535		+35		+500

Cash flows: no effect

Note that the revenue recorded is $500, and not $535. The legal fees earned are exclusive of the GST amount collected, which is recorded as a current liability.

Assume instead that $250 of cleaning services were provided by a company in Saskatchewan for cash on July 24. These services are subject to both PST (6%) and GST (7%), and would be recorded as follows:

A = L + OE
+282.50 +15.00 +250.00
       +17.50

↑ Cash flows: +282.50

July 24	Cash	282.50	
	Cleaning Service Revenue		250.00
	PST Payable ($250 × 6%)		15.00
	GST Payable ($250 × 7%)		17.50
	To record cleaning service revenue.		

If these same services were provided by a company in New Brunswick, where HST is 15%, the entry would be as follows:

A = L + OE
+287.50 +37.50 +250.00

↑ Cash flows: +287.50

July 24	Cash	287.50	
	Cleaning Service Revenue		250.00
	HST Payable ($250 × 15%)		37.50
	To record cleaning service revenue.		

Goods

Entries are needed to record the sales taxes owed when goods are sold, or to reduce sales taxes payable when goods are returned.

Sales

Assume that Staples sells $1,000 of office furniture, on credit, in the province of Ontario, where PST is 8%. GST is 7%. Staples uses a perpetual inventory system and the cost of the furniture to Staples was $800. The following two entries are required to record the sale and the cost of the sale on May 20:

A = L + OE
+1,150 +70 +1,000
       +80

Cash flows: no effect

A = L + OE
−800   −800

Cash flows: no effect

May 20	Accounts Receivable	1,150	
	Sales		1,000
	GST Payable ($1,000 × 7%)		70
	PST Payable ($1,000 × 8%)		80
	To record sale of office furniture on account.		
20	Cost of Goods Sold	800	
	Merchandise Inventory		800
	To record cost of merchandise sold.		

Under the periodic inventory system, the second entry would not be recorded.

Sales Returns and Allowances

If a $300 sales return and allowance were granted by Staples on May 25 for returned merchandise from the above sale, the entry to record the credit memorandum would appear as follows:

A = L + OE
−345 −21 −300
      −24

Cash flows: no effect

A = L + OE
+240   +240

Cash flows: no effect

May 25	Sales Returns and Allowances	300	
	GST Payable ($300 × 7%)	21	
	PST Payable ($300 × 8%)	24	
	Accounts Receivable		345
	To record returned goods.		
25	Merchandise Inventory ($300 ÷ $1,000 × $800)	240	
	Cost of Goods Sold		240
	To record cost of merchandise returned.		

Note that the GST and PST payable accounts are debited, rather than debiting a receivable account, to indicate that this is a return of previously collected sales tax. This entry assumes that the merchandise was in good condition and returned to inventory. Note also that the GST and PST did not form part of the original cost of the merchandise, and therefore are not considered in restoring the cost of the merchandise to the inventory account.

Under the periodic inventory system, the second entry would not be recorded.

Sales Taxes Paid on Disbursements

As a consumer of goods and services, a business must pay the applicable PST and GST charged by its suppliers on taxable goods and services.

Purchase of Merchandise for Resale

When purchasing merchandise for resale, the treatment of the PST is different than that of the GST. PST is a single-stage tax collected from the final consumers of taxable goods and services. Consequently, wholesalers do not charge the tax to the retailer who will in turn resell the merchandise, at a higher price, to the final consumer. By presenting a vendor registration number, retailers are able to buy merchandise for resale, exempt of the PST.

Businesses must pay GST on the purchase of merchandise but can then offset the GST paid against any GST collected. Consequently, **when merchandise is purchased, the GST paid by a business is *not* part of the inventory cost**. The GST paid on purchases is debited to an account called GST Recoverable and is called an input tax credit.

In Quebec, the QST works somewhat like the GST. Businesses can offset QST paid against any QST collected. The QST paid on purchases is debited to an account called QST Recoverable and is called an input tax refund. Other differences also exist in the treatment of QST. This appendix will focus on PST and does not discuss the QST in any detail.

Purchases

The following is an entry to record the purchase of goods for resale on May 4 at a price of $4,000, on account, using a perpetual inventory system:

May 4	Merchandise Inventory	4,000	
	GST Recoverable ($4,000 × 7%)	280	
	Accounts Payable		4,280
	To record goods purchased on account.		

A = L + OE
+4,000 +4,280
+280

Cash flows: no effect

The cost of the merchandise, $4,000, is not affected by the GST, which is recorded as a receivable.

Under a periodic inventory system, the $4,000 debit would have been recorded to the Purchases account.

Purchase Returns and Allowances

The entry to record a $300 return of merchandise on May 8 is as follows:

May 8	Accounts Payable	321	
	GST Recoverable ($300 × 7%)		21
	Merchandise Inventory		300
	To record the return of goods.		

A = L + OE
−21 −321
−300

Cash flows: no effect

Note that the GST Recoverable account is credited instead of the GST Payable account because this is a return of previously recorded GST.

Under the periodic inventory system, the credit of $300 would have been recorded to the Purchase Returns and Allowances account.

To summarize, PST is not paid on purchases of merchandise for resale. GST paid on purchases is normally recoverable and recorded as a current asset in the GST Recoverable account. Purchase returns and allowances require an adjustment of GST only, since PST was not paid on the original purchase.

Operating Expenses

Although PST is not charged on goods purchased for resale, it is charged to businesses that use taxable goods and services in their operations. For example, a business must pay GST and PST when it buys office supplies. As with all purchases made by a registered business, the GST is recoverable (can be offset as an input tax credit against GST collected). Because the PST is not recoverable, the PST forms part of the asset or expense that is being acquired.

The following is the entry for a cash purchase of office supplies on May 18 in the amount of $200 in the province of Ontario where PST is 8% and GST is 7%:

```
A    =    L    +    OE
+216
 +14
-230

Cash flows: -230
```

May 18	Office Supplies ($200 + $16[1] PST)	216	
	GST Recoverable ($200 × 7%)	14	
	Cash		230
	To record purchase of office supplies.		

[1] $200 × 8% = $16

In this situation, the cost of the supplies includes both the supplies and the PST. Because GST is recoverable, it does not form part of the asset cost.

This same purchase would be recorded as follows if it occurred in the province of Prince Edward Island, where GST is 7% and PST is charged on GST at 10%:

```
A    =    L    +    OE
+221.40
 +14.00
-235.40

Cash flows: -235.40
```

May 18	Office Supplies ($200 + $21.40[2] PST)	221.40	
	GST Recoverable ($200 × 7%)	14.00	
	Cash		235.40
	To record purchase of office supplies.		

[2] $200 + $14 = $214 × 10% = $21.40

Remember that in Prince Edward Island the provincial sales tax base includes both the cost of the item and the GST. That is, the PST is determined by multiplying 10% by $214 ($200 + $14).

When HST is applied, it is treated in the same manner as GST. HST is recoverable and does not form part of the cost of the item purchased. The purchase of office supplies would be recorded as follows if it had occurred in the province of Newfoundland and Labrador where HST is 15%:

```
A    =    L    +    OE
+200
 +30
-230

Cash flows: -230
```

May 18	Office Supplies	200	
	HST Recoverable ($200 × 15%)	30	
	Cash		230
	To record purchase of office supplies.		

Note that the same amount is paid for the supplies in Ontario and Newfoundland and Labrador, $230, but the amount recorded as the cost of the office supplies differs ($216 and $200).

Property, Plant, and Equipment

Businesses incur costs other than those for merchandise and operating expenses, such as for the purchase of property, plant, and equipment. The PST and GST apply to these purchases in the same manner as described in the operating expenses section above. All

GST (or HST) paid is recoverable and is not part of the cost of the asset. The PST, however, is part of the cost of the asset being purchased as it is not recoverable.

The following is the entry for the purchase of office furniture on May 20 from Staples, on account, for $1,000 plus applicable sales taxes in Ontario. PST is 8% and GST is 7%.

May 20	Office Furniture ($1,000 + $80[1] PST)	1,080	
	GST Recoverable ($1,000 × 7%)	70	
	Accounts Payable		1,150
	To record purchase of office furniture.		
[1] $1,000 x 8% = $80			

A = L + OE
+1,080 +1,150
+70

Cash flows: no effect

Because the PST is not recoverable, the cost of the furniture is $1,080, inclusive of the PST.

Compare this entry made by the buyer to record the purchase, to the entry made by the seller to record the sale on page B4. Both companies record accounts payable and accounts receivable in the same amount, $1,150. However, the seller records both GST and PST payable while the buyer records only GST recoverable. The PST paid by the buyer is not recoverable, so it becomes part of the cost of the office furniture, $1,080.

In Prince Edward Island, where GST is 7% and PST is charged on GST at 10%, the same entry would be recorded as follows:

May 20	Office Furniture ($1,000 + $107[2] PST)	1,107	
	GST Recoverable ($1,000 x 7%)	70	
	Accounts Payable		1,177
	To record purchase of office furniture.		
[2] $1,000 + $70 = $1,070 × 10% = $107			

A = L + OE
+1,107 +1,177
+70

Cash flows: no effect

In P.E.I., PST is calculated on a cost base which includes the GST. Therefore, PST is calculated on $1,070 ($1,000 + $70).

In Nova Scotia, where HST is 15%, the entry would be recorded as follows:

May 20	Office Furniture	1,000	
	HST Recoverable ($1,000 × 15%)	150	
	Accounts Payable		1,150
	To record purchase of office furniture.		

A = L + OE
+1,000 +1,150
+150

Cash flows: no effect

As we have noted before, the amount paid for the PST changes the amount recorded as the cost of the office furniture in each province: $1,080 in Ontario, $1,107 in Prince Edward Island, and $1,000 in Nova Scotia.

Remittance of Sales Taxes

As mentioned in the introduction, businesses act as agents of the federal and provincial governments in charging and later remitting taxes charged on sales and services. For example, Staples, the seller of office furniture illustrated on page B4, must remit GST to the CCRA and PST to the Treasurer of Ontario. Notice that even if Staples has not received payment from a customer buying on account before the due date for the remittance, the tax must still be paid to the government authorities. As a registrant, however, Staples will also benefit from claiming input tax credits and recording a reduction in amounts payable from applying GST on sales.

GST (HST)

When remitting the amount owed to the federal government at the end of a reporting period for GST (or HST), the amount of GST payable is reduced by any amount in the GST Recoverable account. Any difference is remitted, as shown in the following journal entry, using assumed amounts payable and recoverable:

A	=	L	+	OE
−2,500		−6,250		
−3,750				

Cash flows: −3,750

June 30	GST Payable	6,250	
	GST Recoverable		2,500
	Cash		3,750
	To record remittance to CCRA for GST.		

The GST (HST) remittance form requires the registrant to report at specified dates, depending on the business's volume of sales. That is, the amount of the sales and other revenue as well as the amount of GST charged on these sales, whether collected or not. The amount of the input tax credits claimed is also entered on the form to reduce the amount owing to CCRA. If the GST recoverable exceeds the GST payable, the remittance form should be sent as soon as possible in order to ask for a refund. The entry to record the cash receipt from a GST refund will be similar to the entry shown above, except that there will be a debit to Cash, instead of a credit.

The above discussion of the remittance of GST explains why all registrants need two general ledger accounts. One account, GST Payable, is used to keep track of all GST charged on sales and revenues. The second account, GST Recoverable, is used to keep track of the GST input tax credits that have been paid on all of the business's purchases. Failure by a business to capture the proper amounts of input tax credits has a significant impact on income and on cash flows.

PST

The remittance of PST to the Treasurer or Minister of Finance of the applicable province or territory is similar to that of GST except that, since no credit can be claimed, the amount paid at the end of each reporting period is the amount of the balance in the PST Payable account.

Consequently, the entry to record a remittance of PST, using an assumed amount payable, would appear as follows:

A	=	L	+	OE
−7,400		−7,400		

Cash flows: −7,400

June 30	PST Payable	7,400	
	Cash		7,400
	To record remittance of PST.		

Conclusion

Be careful when you record the amounts of taxes charged or claimed in the business accounts. Numbers must be rounded carefully. If the amount of the tax calculated is less then half a cent, the amount should be rounded down. If the amount of the tax as calculated comes to more than half a cent, the amount should be rounded up. For example, applying 7% GST on an amount of $44.20 would give you $2.954. The tax amount to be recorded can be rounded down to $2.95. Rounding might seem insignificant, but with many transactions the amounts can add up and the registrant is responsible to the government authorities for any shortfall created in error.

Sales tax law is intricate. It has added a lot of complexity to the accounting for most transactions flowing through today's businesses. Fortunately, computers that are programmed to automatically determine and record the correct sales tax rate for each good or service provided have simplified matters somewhat. Before recording sales tax transactions, however, it is important to understand all of the relevant sales tax regulations. Check the federal and provincial laws in your jurisdiction.

Brief Exercises

BEB–1 Journalize the purchase on account of $7,000 of merchandise for resale in the province of Manitoba. The company uses a perpetual inventory system and the purchase is PST exempt.

Journalize inventory purchase with GST—perpetual inventory system.

BEB–2 Journalize the return of $1,000 of the merchandise purchased in BEB–1.

Journalize purchase return—perpetual inventory system.

BEB–3 Journalize the cash purchase of $500 of office supplies in the province of Saskatchewan, where PST is 6%.

Journalize purchase of supplies with GST and PST.

BEB–4 Journalize the purchase on account of a $15,000 delivery truck in the province of Nova Scotia, where HST is 15%.

Journalize truck purchase with HST.

BEB–5 Journalize the purchase on account of $100 of office supplies and $4,000 of merchandise for resale in the province of Ontario. The company uses a perpetual inventory system and the purchase of merchandise is PST exempt. The PST rate is 8%.

Journalize purchase of supplies and inventory, with GST and PST—perpetual inventory system.

BEB–6 Journalize the sale on account, for $1,800, of merchandise costing $1,200 in the province of Prince Edward Island. Assume the company uses a perpetual inventory system. The PST is 10% and the GST is included in the provincial sales tax base.

Journalize sales with GST and PST—perpetual inventory system.

BEB–7 Half of the shipment described in BEB–6 is returned as the incorrect sizes have been shipped. Journalize the credit memorandum of the business selling the goods.

Journalize sales return, with GST and PST—perpetual inventory system.

BEB–8 Journalize the sale in BEB–6 and the credit memorandum in BEB–7 assuming the business uses a periodic inventory system.

Journalize sales and sales return with GST and PST—periodic inventory system.

BEB–9 Journalize the billing for $250 of services by R. R. Dennis, dentist, in the province of British Columbia. Dental services are exempt from GST and PST.

Journalize exempt services.

BEB–10 Journalize the billing of accounting fee revenue of $600 for the preparation of personal income tax returns in the province of Alberta. GST is applicable on this service. Alberta does not charge PST.

Journalize fees with GST.

BEB–11 Journalize two payments: one cheque to the Receiver General for GST and one to the Treasurer of Ontario for PST. The balances in the accounts are as follows: GST Payable $4,450, GST Recoverable $1,900, and PST Payable $4,870.

Journalize the remittance of GST and PST.

BEB–12 Journalize the deposit of a cheque from the Receiver General for a refund of $690 following the filing of an HST return. The balances in the accounts are as follows: HST Payable $2,920 and HST Recoverable $3,610.

Journalize HST refund.

Exercises

EB–1 Stratton Company is a merchant operating in the province of Ontario where the PST rate is 8%. Stratton uses a perpetual inventory system. Transactions for the business are shown below:

Journalize sales transactions with sales taxes—perpetual inventory system.

Mar. 1 Paid March rent to the landlord for the rental of a warehouse. The lease calls for monthly payments of $5,500 plus 7% GST.

3 Sold merchandise on account and shipped merchandise to Marvin Ltd. for $20,000, terms n/30, FOB shipping point. This merchandise cost Stratton $11,000.

Interactive Homework

Mar. 5 Granted Marvin a sales allowance of $500 for defective merchandise purchased on March 3. No merchandise was returned.

7 Purchased on account from Tiller Ltd. merchandise for resale at a list price of $14,000, plus applicable tax.

12 Made a cash purchase at Home Depot of a desk for the shipping clerk. The price of the desk was $600 before applicable taxes.

31 Paid the monthly remittance of GST to the Receiver General. The balances in the accounts were as follows: GST Payable $4,280 and GST Recoverable $1,917.

Instructions

(a) Prepare the journal entries to record these transactions on the books of Stratton Company.
(b) Assume instead that Stratton operates in the province of Alberta, where PST is not applicable. Prepare the journal entries to record these transactions on the books of Stratton.
(c) Assume instead that Stratton operates in the province of Prince Edward Island, where PST is charged on GST at 10%. Prepare the journal entries to record these transactions on the books of Stratton.
(d) Assume instead that Stratton operates in the province of New Brunswick, where HST is 15%. Prepare the journal entries to record these transactions on the books of Stratton.

Journalize sales transactions with sales taxes—periodic inventory system.

EB–2 Using the information for the transactions of Stratton Company in EB–1, assume now that Stratton uses a periodic inventory system.

Instructions

(a) Prepare the journal entries to record these transactions on the books of Stratton Company.
(b) Assume now that Stratton operates in the province of Alberta, where PST is not applicable. Prepare the journal entries to record these transactions on the books of Stratton.
(c) Assume now that Stratton operates in the province of Prince Edward Island, where PST is charged on GST at 10%. Prepare the journal entries to record these transactions on the books of Stratton.
(d) Assume now that Stratton operates in the province of New Brunswick, where HST is 15%. Prepare the journal entries to record these transactions on the books of Stratton. Assume that the GST balances on March 31 provided in EB–1 are the balances in the HST accounts.

Journalize service transactions with sales taxes.

EB–3 Tom LeBrun is a sole practitioner providing accounting services in the province of Manitoba. The provincial sales tax rate in Manitoba is 6%, but accounting services are exempt of provincial sales tax. Transactions for the business are shown below:

June 8 Purchased a printer on account at a cost of $1,200. The appropriate sales taxes were added to this purchase price.

10 Purchased toner for the printer for $50 cash from a local stationery store. The store added the appropriate sales taxes to the purchase price.

12 Billed a client for accounting services provided. The fee charged was $750 and GST was added to the fee billed.

15 Collected $107 on account. The original fee was $100 and the GST charged was $7.

30 Paid the monthly remittance of GST to the Receiver General. The balances in the accounts were as follows: GST Payable $1,520.60 and GST Recoverable $820.45.

Instructions

Prepare the journal entries to record these transactions on the books of Tom LeBrun's accounting business.

Problems

Journalize transactions with sales taxes—perpetual inventory system.

PB–1 Mark's Music is a store that buys and sells musical instruments in Ontario, where the provincial sales tax is charged at a rate of 8%. Mark's Music uses a perpetual inventory system. Transactions for the business are shown below:

Nov. 2 Purchased two electric guitars from Fender Supply Limited, on account, at a cost of $700 each.

Nov. 4 Made a cash sale of two keyboards for a total invoice price of $2,200, plus applicable taxes. The cost of each keyboard was $750.

5 Received a credit memorandum from Western Acoustic Inc. for the return of an acoustic guitar which was defective. The original invoice price before taxes was $400 and the guitar had been purchased on account.

7 One of the keyboards from the cash sale of Nov. 4 was returned to the store for a full cash refund because the customer was not satisfied with the instrument.

8 Purchased store supplies from a stationery store. The price of the supplies is $100 before all applicable taxes.

10 Sold one Omega trumpet to the Toronto Regional Band, on account, for an invoice price of $2,700 before applicable taxes. The trumpet had cost Mark's Music $1,420.

13 Purchased two saxophones from Yamaha Canada Inc. on account. The invoice price was $2,100 for each saxophone, excluding applicable taxes.

14 Collected $4,025 on account. The payment included GST of $245 and PST of $280.

16 Returned to Yamaha Canada Inc. one of the saxophones purchased on Nov. 13, as it was the wrong model. Received a credit memorandum from Yamaha for the full purchase price.

20 Made a payment on account for the amount owing to Fender Supply Limited for the purchase of Nov. 2.

30 Paid the monthly remittance of GST to the Receiver General. The balances in the accounts were as follows: GST Payable $5,540 and GST Recoverable $1,860.

30 Paid the monthly remittance of PST to the Treasurer of Ontario. The balance in PST Payable is $5,920.

Instructions

Prepare the journal entries to record the Mark's Music transactions.

PB–2 Transaction data for Mark's Music are available in PB–1. Assume Mark's Music uses a periodic inventory system instead of a perpetual inventory system.

Journalize transactions with sales taxes—periodic inventory system.

Instructions

Prepare the journal entries to record the Mark's Music transactions.

PB–3 David Simmons, LL.B., is a lawyer operating as a sole practitioner in Nunavut. Nunavut does not charge provincial sales taxes. Transactions for the business are shown below:

Journalize service transactions with sales taxes.

May 1 Signed a two-year lease for the office space and immediately paid the first and last months' rent. The lease calls for the monthly rent of $1,500 plus applicable taxes.

4 Purchased an office suite of furniture, on account, from Leon's at a cost of $3,400. The appropriate sales taxes were added to this purchase price.

5 Returned one chair to Leon's due to a defect. The cost of the chair before taxes was $400.

6 Billed a client for the preparation of a will. The client was very pleased with the product and immediately paid David's invoice for fees of $1,000 plus taxes.

10 Purchased paper for the photocopier for $200 cash from a local stationery store. The store added the appropriate sales taxes to the purchase price.

13 Billed Manson Ltd. for legal services rendered connected with the purchase of land. The fee charged is $900 plus applicable taxes.

18 Paid Leon's for the furniture purchase of May 4, net of returned items.

19 Paid $5 cash to a local grocery store for coffee for the office coffee machine. Groceries are GST exempt.

21 In accordance with the lease agreement with the landlord, David must pay for water supplied by the municipality. The water invoice was received and the services amounted to $100 plus GST.

May 25 Collected a full payment from Manson Ltd. for the May 13 bill.

27 Completed the preparation of a purchase and sale agreement for Edwards Inc. and billed fees of $1,200.

June 20 Deposited a cheque from the Receiver General for a refund of $270 following the filing of the May GST return. The balances in the accounts were as follows: GST Payable $990 and GST Recoverable $1,260.

Instructions

Prepare the journal entries to record these transactions on the books of David Simmons' law practice.

appendix C
Accounting Systems

In the textbook, we learned how to record accounting transactions in a general journal. Each journal entry was then individually posted to its respective general ledger account. However, such a practice is only useful in a company where the volume of transactions is low. In most companies, it is necessary to use additional journals (called special journals) and ledgers (called subsidiary ledgers) to record transaction data.

We will look at subsidiary ledgers and special journals in the next sections. Both subsidiary ledgers and special journals can be used in either a manual accounting system or a computerized accounting system.

Subsidiary Ledgers

Imagine a business that has several thousand customers who purchase merchandise from it on account. It records the transactions with these customers in only one general ledger account—Accounts Receivable. It would be virtually impossible to determine the balance owed by an individual customer at any specific time. Similarly, the amount payable to one creditor would be difficult to locate quickly from a single accounts payable account in the general ledger.

Instead, companies use subsidiary ledgers to keep track of individual balances. A **subsidiary ledger** is a group of accounts that share a common characteristic (for example, all accounts receivable). The subsidiary ledger frees the general ledger from the details of individual balances. A subsidiary ledger is an addition to, and an expansion of, the general ledger.

Two common subsidiary ledgers are:

1. The accounts receivable (or customers') ledger, which collects transaction data for individual customers
2. The accounts payable (or creditors') ledger, which collects transaction data for individual creditors

Other subsidiary ledgers include an inventory ledger, which collects transaction data for each inventory item purchased and sold, as was described in Chapter 5. Some companies also use a payroll ledger, detailing individual employee pay records. In each of these subsidiary ledgers, individual accounts are arranged in alphabetical, numerical, or alphanumerical order.

The detailed data from a subsidiary ledger are summarized in a general ledger account. For example, the detailed data from the accounts receivable subsidiary ledger are summarized in Accounts Receivable in the general ledger. The general ledger account that summarizes subsidiary ledger data is called a **control account**.

Each general ledger control account balance must equal the total balance of the individual accounts in the related subsidiary ledger. This is an important internal control function.

Example

An example of an accounts receivable control account and subsidiary ledger is shown in Illustration C-1 for Mercier Enterprises.

Illustration C-1 ▶

Accounts receivable general ledger control account and subsidiary ledger

Accounts Receivable is a control account.

GENERAL LEDGER

Accounts Receivable   No. 112

Date	Explanation	Ref.	Debit	Credit	Balance
2005					
Jan. 31			12,000		12,000
31				8,000	4,000◀

ACCOUNTS RECEIVABLE SUBSIDIARY LEDGER

The subsidiary ledger is separate from the general ledger.

Aaron Co.   No. 112-172

Date	Explanation	Ref.	Debit	Credit	Balance
2005					
Jan. 11	Invoice 336		6,000		6,000
19	Payment			4,000	2,000●

Branden Inc.   No. 112-173

Date	Explanation	Ref.	Debit	Credit	Balance
2005					
Jan. 12	Invoice 337		3,000		3,000
21	Payment			3,000	0●

Caron Co.   No. 112-174

Date	Explanation	Ref.	Debit	Credit	Balance
2005					
Jan. 20	Invoice 339		3,000		3,000
29	Payment			1,000	2,000●

The example is based on the following transactions:

Credit Sales			Collections on Account		
Jan. 11	Aaron Co.	$ 6,000	Jan. 19	Aaron Co.	$4,000
12	Branden Inc.	3,000	21	Branden Inc.	3,000
20	Caron Co.	3,000	29	Caron Co.	1,000
		$12,000			$8,000

The total debits ($12,000) and credits ($8,000) in Accounts Receivable in the general ledger match the detailed debits and credits in the subsidiary accounts. The balance of $4,000 in the control account agrees with the total of the balances in the individual accounts receivable accounts (Aaron $2,000 + Branden $0 + Caron $2,000) in the subsidiary ledger.

Rather than relying on customer or creditor names in a subsidiary ledger, a computer system expands the account number of the control account. For example, if the general ledger control account Accounts Receivable was numbered 112, the first customer account in the accounts receivable subsidiary ledger might be numbered 112-001, the second 112-002, and so on. Most systems allow inquiries about specific customer accounts in the subsidiary ledger (by account number) or about the control account.

As shown, postings are made monthly to the control account in the general ledger. We will learn, in the next section, how special journals facilitate monthly postings. We will also learn how to fill in the posting references (in the Ref. column) in both the general ledger and subsidiary ledger accounts. Postings to the individual accounts in the subsidiary ledger are made daily. The rationale for posting daily is to ensure that account information is current. This enables Mercier Enterprises to monitor credit limits, send statements to customers, and answer inquiries from customers about their account balances. In a computerized accounting system, transactions are simultaneously recorded in journals and posted to both the general and subsidiary ledgers.

Advantages of Subsidiary Ledgers

Subsidiary ledgers have several advantages:

1. **They show transactions that affect one customer or one creditor in a single account.** They provide up-to-date information on specific account balances.
2. **They free the general ledger of excessive details.** A trial balance of the general ledger does not contain vast numbers of individual customer account balances.
3. **They help locate errors in individual accounts.** The potential for errors is minimized by reducing the number of accounts in one ledger and by using control accounts.
4. **They make possible a division of labour in posting.** One employee can post to the general ledger while different employees post to the subsidiary ledgers. This strengthens internal control, since one employee verifies the work of the other.

In a computerized accounting system, the last two advantages don't apply. Computerized accounting systems do not make errors such as calculation errors and posting errors. Other errors, such as entry errors, can and do still occur. Internal control must be done using different means in computerized systems since account transactions are posted automatically.

Special Journals

As mentioned earlier, journalizing transactions in a two-column (debit and credit) general journal is satisfactory only when there are few transactions. To help with the journalizing and posting of multiple transactions, most companies use special journals in addition to the general journal.

A special journal is used to record similar types of transactions. Examples include all sales of merchandise on account, or all cash receipts. The types of special journals used depend largely on the types of transactions that occur frequently. While the form, type, and number of special journals used will vary among organizations, many merchandising companies use the journals shown in Illustration C-2 to record daily transactions. The letters that appear in parentheses following the journal name represent the posting reference used for each journal.

Illustration C-2 ▶

Use of special journals and the general journal

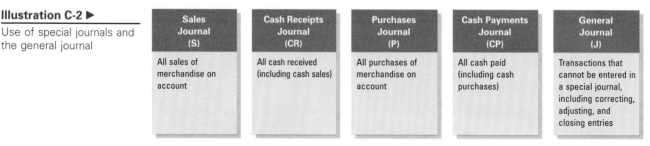

Sales Journal (S)	Cash Receipts Journal (CR)	Purchases Journal (P)	Cash Payments Journal (CP)	General Journal (J)
All sales of merchandise on account	All cash received (including cash sales)	All purchases of merchandise on account	All cash paid (including cash purchases)	Transactions that cannot be entered in a special journal, including correcting, adjusting, and closing entries

If a transaction cannot be recorded in a special journal, it is recorded in the general journal. For example, if you have four special journals as listed in Illustration C-2, sales returns and allowances are recorded in the general journal. Similarly, correcting, adjusting, and closing entries are recorded in the general journal. Other types of special journals may sometimes be used in certain situations. For example, when sales returns and allowances are frequent, an additional special journal may be used to record these transactions. A payroll journal is another example of a special journal. It organizes and summarizes payroll details for companies with many employees.

The use of special journals reduces the time needed for the recording and posting process. In addition, special journals permit greater division of labour because different employees can record entries in different journals. For example, one employee may journalize all cash receipts. Another may journalize credit sales. The division of responsibilities ensures that one person does not have control over all aspects of a transaction. In this instance, recording the sale has been separated from recording the collection of cash from that sale. This may reduce the opportunity for intentional or unintentional error, and is one aspect of a good internal control system.

For a merchandising company, the same special journals are used whether a company uses the periodic or perpetual system to account for its inventory. The only distinction is the number of, and title for, the columns each journal uses. We will use Karns Wholesale Supply to show the use of special journals in the following sections. Karns uses a perpetual inventory system. The variations between the periodic and perpetual inventory systems are highlighted in helpful hints for your information. In addition, special journals under a periodic inventory system are shown more fully at the end of this appendix.

Sales Journal

The sales journal is used to record sales of merchandise on account. Cash sales of merchandise are entered in the cash receipts journal. Credit sales of assets other than merchandise are entered in the general journal.

Journalizing Credit Sales

Under the perpetual inventory system, each entry in the sales journal results in one entry at selling price and another entry at cost. The entry at selling price is a debit to Accounts Receivable (a control account supported by a subsidiary ledger) and a credit of an equal amount to Sales. The entry at cost is a debit to Cost of Goods Sold and a credit of an equal amount to Merchandise Inventory. Some companies also set up Merchandise Inventory as a control account supported by a subsidiary ledger.

A sales journal with two amount columns can show a sales transaction recognized at both selling price and cost on only one line. The two-column sales journal of Karns Wholesale Supply is shown in Illustration C-3, using assumed credit sales transactions.

KARNS WHOLESALE SUPPLY					
Sales Journal					S1
Date	Account Debited	Invoice No.	Ref.	Accts. Receivable Dr. Sales Cr.	Cost of Goods Sold Dr. Merchandise Inventory Cr.
2005					
May 3	Abbot Sisters	101		10,600	6,360
7	Babson Co.	102		11,350	7,370
14	Carson Bros.	103		7,800	5,070
19	Deli Co.	104		9,300	6,510
21	Abbot Sisters	105		15,400	10,780
24	Deli Co.	106		21,210	15,900
27	Babson Co.	107		14,570	10,200
				90,230	62,190

Illustration C-3 ◀
Sales journal—perpetual inventory system

Helpful hint In a periodic inventory system, the sales journal would have only one column to record the sale at selling price (Accounts Receivable Dr., Sales Cr.). The cost of goods sold is not recorded. It is calculated at the end of the period.

The reference (Ref.) column is not used in journalizing. It is used in posting the sales journal, as explained in the next section. Also, note that, unlike in the general journal, an explanation is not required for each entry in a special journal. Finally, note that each invoice is prenumbered to ensure that all invoices are journalized.

If management wishes to record its sales by department, additional columns may be provided in the sales journal. For example, a department store may have columns for home furnishings, sporting goods, shoes, etc. In addition, the federal government, and practically all provinces, require that sales taxes be charged on items sold. If sales taxes are collected, it is necessary to add more credit columns to the sales journal for GST Payable and PST Payable (or HST Payable).

Posting the Sales Journal

Postings from the sales journal are made **daily to the individual accounts receivable accounts** in the subsidiary ledger. Posting **to the general ledger is done monthly**. Illustration C-4 shows both the daily postings to the accounts receivable subsidiary ledger and the monthly postings to the general ledger accounts. We have assumed that Karns Wholesale Supply does not maintain an inventory subsidiary ledger. However, if it did, the procedure is similar to that illustrated for the accounts receivable subsidiary ledger.

A check mark (√) is inserted in the reference posting column to indicate that the daily posting to the customer's account has been made. A check mark is used when the subsidiary ledger accounts are not individually numbered. If the subsidiary ledger accounts are numbered, the account number is used instead of the check mark in the reference posting column. At the end of the month, the column totals of the sales journal are posted to the general ledger. Here, the column totals are posted as a debit of $90,230 to Accounts Receivable (account no. 112), a credit of $90,230 to Sales (account no. 401), a debit of $62,190 to Cost of Goods Sold (account no. 505), and a credit of $62,190 to Merchandise Inventory (account no. 120). Inserting the account numbers below the column totals indicates that the postings have been made. In both the general ledger and subsidiary ledger accounts, the reference S1 indicates that the posting came from page 1 of the sales journal.

Illustration C-4 ▶

Sales journal—perpetual
inventory system

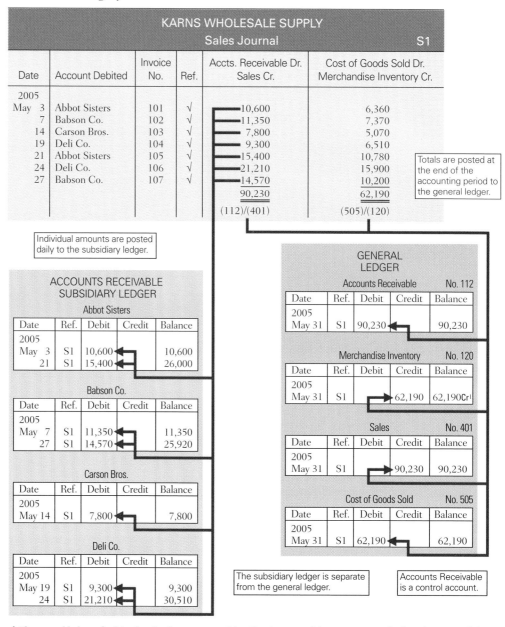

¹ The normal balance for Merchandise Inventory is a debit. But, because of the sequence in which we have posted the special journals, with the sales journal first, the credits to Merchandise Inventory are posted before the debits. This posting sequence explains the credit balance in Merchandise Inventory, which exists only until the other journals are posted.

Proving the Ledgers

The next step is to "prove" the ledgers. To do so, we must determine two things: (1) The sum of the subsidiary ledger balances must equal the balance in the control account. (2) The total of the general ledger debit balances must equal the total of the general ledger credit balances. The proof of the postings from the sales journal to the general and subsidiary ledgers follows:

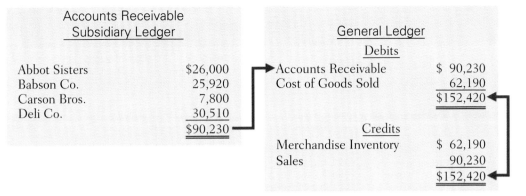

Advantages of the Sales Journal

The use of a special journal to record sales on account has a number of advantages. First, the one-line–two-column entry for each sales transaction saves time. In the sales journal, it is not necessary to write out the four account titles for the two transactions. Second, only totals, rather than individual entries, are posted to the general ledger. This saves posting time and reduces the possibility of errors in posting. Third, the prenumbering of sales invoices helps to ensure that all sales are recorded and that no sale is recorded more than once. Finally, a division of labour results, because one individual can take responsibility for the sales journal alone. These last two advantages help internal control.

Cash Receipts Journal

All receipts of cash are recorded in the cash receipts journal. The most common types of cash receipts are cash sales of merchandise and collections of accounts receivable. Many other possibilities exist, such as a receipt of money from a bank loan and cash proceeds from disposals of equipment. A one- or two-column cash receipts journal would not have enough space for all possible cash receipt transactions. A multiple-column cash receipts journal is therefore used.

Generally, a cash receipts journal includes the following columns: a debit column for cash, and credit columns for accounts receivable, sales, and other accounts. The Other Accounts column is used when the cash receipt does not involve a cash sale or a collection of accounts receivable. Under a perpetual inventory system, each sales entry is accompanied by another entry that debits Cost of Goods Sold and credits Merchandise Inventory. A separate column is added for this purpose. A five-column cash receipts journal is shown in Illustration C-5.

Additional credit columns may be used if they significantly reduce postings to a specific account. For example, cash receipts normally include the collection of sales taxes, which are later remitted to the federal and provincial governments. Most cash receipts journals have a separate credit column for sales tax collections. Other examples include the cash receipts of a loan company, such as Household Financial Centre, which cover thousands of collections from customers. These collections are credited to Loans Receivable and Interest Revenue. A significant saving in posting time would result from using separate credit columns for Loans Receivable and Interest Revenue, rather than using the Other Accounts credit column. In contrast, a retailer that has only one interest collection a month would not find it useful to have a separate column for Interest Revenue.

Illustration C-5 ▶

Cash receipts journal—
perpetual inventory system

Helpful hint In a periodic
inventory system, the Cash
Receipts journal would have
one column fewer. The Cost
of Goods Sold Dr. and
Merchandise Inventory Cr.
would not be recorded.

KARNS WHOLESALE SUPPLY
Cash Receipts Journal
CR1

Date	Account Credited	Ref.	Cash Dr.	Accounts Receivable Cr.	Sales Cr.	Cost of Goods Sold Dr. Mdse. Inv. Cr.	Other Accounts Cr.
2005							
May 1	D. A. Karns, Capital	301	5,000				5,000
7			1,900		1,900	1,240	
10	Abbot Sisters	√	10,600	10,600			
12			2,600		2,600	1,690	
17	Babson Co.	√	11,350	11,350			
22	Notes Payable	200	6,000				6,000
23	Carson Bros.	√	7,800	7,800			
28	Deli Co.	√	9,300	9,300			
			54,550	39,050	4,500	2,930	11,000
			(101)	(112)	(401)	(505)/(120)	(X)

Individual amounts are posted daily to the subsidiary ledger.

Totals are posted at the end of the accounting period to the general ledger.

ACCOUNTS RECEIVABLE SUBSIDIARY LEDGER

Abbot Sisters

Date	Ref.	Debit	Credit	Balance
2005				
May 3	S1	10,600		10,600
10	CR1		10,600	0
21	S1	15,400		15,400

Babson Co.

Date	Ref.	Debit	Credit	Balance
2005				
May 7	S1	11,350		11,350
17	CR1		11,350	0
27	S1	14,570		14,570

Carson Bros.

Date	Ref.	Debit	Credit	Balance
2005				
May 14	S1	7,800		7,800
23	CR1		7,800	0

Deli Co.

Date	Ref.	Debit	Credit	Balance
2005				
May 19	S1	9,300		9,300
24	S1	21,210		30,510
28	CR1		9,300	21,210

Accounts Receivable is a control account.

The subsidiary ledger is separate from the general ledger.

GENERAL LEDGER

Cash — No. 101

Date	Ref.	Debit	Credit	Balance
2005				
May 31	CR1	54,550		54,550

Accounts Receivable — No. 112

Date	Ref.	Debit	Credit	Balance
2005				
May 31	S1	90,230		90,230
31	CR1		39,050	51,180

Merchandise Inventory — No. 120

Date	Ref.	Debit	Credit	Balance
2005				
May 31	S1		62,190	62,190Cr.
31	CR1		2,930	65,120Cr.

Notes Payable — No. 200

Date	Ref.	Debit	Credit	Balance
2005				
May 22	CR1		6,000	6,000

D. A. Karns, Capital — No. 301

Date	Ref.	Debit	Credit	Balance
2005				
May 1	CR1		5,000	5,000

Sales — No. 401

Date	Ref.	Debit	Credit	Balance
2005				
May 31	S1		90,230	90,230
31	CR1		4,500	94,730

Cost of Goods Sold — No. 505

Date	Ref.	Debit	Credit	Balance
2005				
May 31	S1	62,190		62,190
31	CR1	2,930		65,120

Journalizing Cash Receipts Transactions

To illustrate the journalizing of cash receipts transactions, we will continue with the May transactions of Karns Wholesale Supply. Collections from customers are for the entries recorded in the sales journal in Illustration C-3. The entries in the cash receipts journal are based on the following cash receipts:

May 1 D. A. Karns makes an investment of $5,000 in the business.
     7 Cash receipts for merchandise sales total $1,900. The cost of goods sold is $1,240.
    10 A cheque for $10,600 is received from Abbot Sisters in full payment of invoice No. 101.
    12 Cash receipts for merchandise sales total $2,600. The cost of goods sold is $1,690.
    17 A cheque for $11,350 is received from Babson Co. in full payment of invoice No. 102.
    22 Cash is received by signing a 4% note for $6,000, payable September 22 to the National Bank.
    23 A cheque for $7,800 is received from Carson Bros. in full payment of invoice No. 103.
    28 A cheque for $9,300 is received from Deli Co. in full payment of invoice No. 104.

Further information about the columns in the cash receipts journal follows:

Debit Columns:

1. **Cash.** The amount of cash actually received in each transaction is entered in this column. The column total indicates the total cash receipts for the month. The total of this column is posted to the cash account in the general ledger.
2. **Cost of Goods Sold.** The Cost of Goods Sold Dr./Merchandise Inventory Cr. column is used to record the cost of the merchandise sold. (Other columns (e.g., Cash and Sales) record the selling price of the merchandise.) This column is similar to the one found in the sales journal. The amount debited to Cost of Goods Sold is the same amount credited to Merchandise Inventory. One column total is posted to both accounts at the end of the month.

Credit Columns:

3. **Accounts Receivable.** The Accounts Receivable column is used to record cash collections on account. The amount entered here is the amount to be credited to the individual customer's account.
4. **Sales.** The Sales column is used to record all cash sales of merchandise. Cash sales of other assets (property, plant, and equipment, for example) are not reported in this column. The total of this column is posted to the account Sales.
5. **Merchandise Inventory.** As noted above, the Cost of Goods Sold Dr./Merchandise Inventory Cr. column is used to record the reduction in the merchandise available for future sale. The amount credited to Merchandise Inventory is the same amount debited to Cost of Goods Sold. One column total is posted to both accounts at the end of the month.
6. **Other Accounts.** The Other Accounts column is used whenever the credit is not to Accounts Receivable, Sales, or Merchandise Inventory. For example, in the first entry, $5,000 is entered as a credit to D. A. Karns, Capital. This column is often referred to as the sundry accounts column.

In a multi-column journal, only one line is generally needed for each entry. In some cases, it is useful to add explanatory information, such as the details of the note payable, or to reference supporting documentation, such as invoice numbers if cash sales are invoiced. Note also that the Account Credited column is used to identify both general ledger and subsidiary ledger account titles. The former is shown in the May 1 entry for Karns' investment. The latter is shown in the May 10 entry for the collection from Abbot Sisters.

Debit and credit amounts for each line must be equal. When the journalizing has been completed, the amount columns are totalled. The totals are then compared to prove the equality of debits and credits in the cash receipts journal. Don't forget that the Cost of Goods Sold Dr./Merchandise Inventory Cr. column total represents both a debit and a credit amount. Totalling the columns of a journal and proving the equality of the totals is called **footing** (adding down) and **cross-footing** (adding across) a journal.

The proof of the equality of Karns' cash receipts journal is as follows:

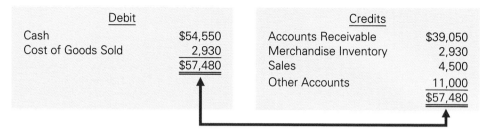

Debit			Credits	
Cash	$54,550		Accounts Receivable	$39,050
Cost of Goods Sold	2,930		Merchandise Inventory	2,930
	$57,480		Sales	4,500
			Other Accounts	11,000
				$57,480

Posting the Cash Receipts Journal

Posting a multi-column journal involves the following steps:

1. All column totals, except for the Other Accounts total, are posted once at the end of the month to the account title specified in the column heading, such as Cash, Accounts Receivable, Sales, Cost of Goods Sold, and Merchandise Inventory. Account numbers are entered below the column totals to show that the amounts have been posted.
2. The total of the Other Accounts column is not posted. Individual amounts that make up the Other Accounts total are posted separately to the general ledger accounts specified in the Account Credited column. See, for example, the credit posting to D. A. Karns, Capital. The symbol X is inserted below the total for this column to indicate that the amount has not been posted.
3. The individual amounts in a column (Accounts Receivable, in this case) are posted daily to the subsidiary ledger account name specified in the Account Credited column. See, for example, the credit posting of $10,600 to Abbot Sisters.

The abbreviation CR is used in both the subsidiary and general ledgers to identify postings from the cash receipts journal.

Proving the Ledgers

After the posting of the cash receipts journal is completed, it is necessary to prove the ledgers. As shown below, the sum of the subsidiary ledger account balances equals the control account balance. The general ledger totals are also in agreement.

Accounts Receivable Subsidiary Ledger			General Ledger	
			Debits	
Abbot Sisters	$15,400		Cash	$ 54,550
Babson Co.	14,570		Accounts Receivable	51,180
Deli Co.	21,210		Cost of Goods Sold	65,120
	$51,180			$170,850
			Credits	
			Merchandise Inventory	$ 65,120
			Notes Payable	6,000
			D. A. Karns, Capital	5,000
			Sales	94,730
				$170,850

Purchases Journal

All purchases of merchandise on account are recorded in the purchases journal. Each entry in this journal results in a debit to Merchandise Inventory and a credit to Accounts Payable. When a one-column purchases journal is used, other types of purchases on account and cash purchases cannot be journalized in it. For example, credit purchases of equipment or supplies must be recorded in the general journal. Likewise, all cash purchases are entered in the cash payments journal. If there are many credit purchases for items other than merchandise, the purchases journal can be expanded to a multi-column format.

The purchases journal for Karns Wholesale Supply is shown in Illustration C-6, with assumed credit purchases.

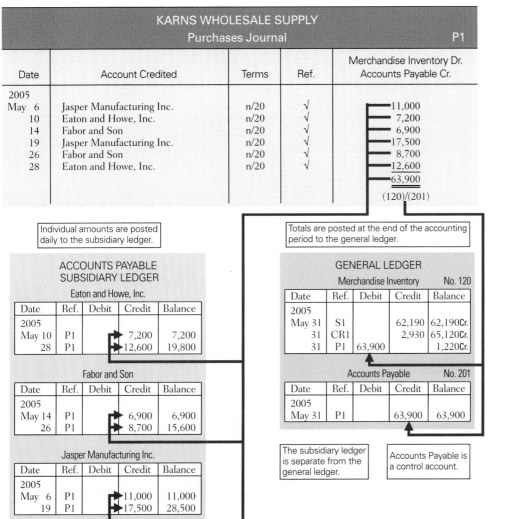

Illustration C-6 ◄

Purchases journal—
perpetual inventory system

Helpful hint   When a periodic inventory system is used, this journal is still known as a purchases journal. The debit to the Merchandise Inventory account is replaced by a debit to the Purchases account.

Journalizing Credit Purchases of Merchandise

Entries in the purchases journal are made from purchase invoices. The journalizing procedure for the purchases journal is similar to that for the sales journal. In contrast to the sales journal, the purchases journal may not have an invoice number column, because invoices received from different suppliers would not be in numerical sequence.

Posting the Purchases Journal

The procedures for posting the purchases journal are similar to those for the sales journal. In this case, postings are made **daily** to the accounts payable **subsidiary ledger** accounts and **monthly** to the Merchandise Inventory and Accounts Payable accounts in the **general ledger**. In both ledgers, P1 is used in the reference column to show that the postings are from page 1 of the purchases journal.

Proof of the equality of the postings from the purchases journal to both ledgers is shown by the following:

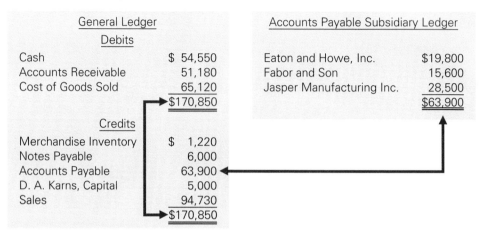

General Ledger		Accounts Payable Subsidiary Ledger	
Debits			
Cash	$ 54,550	Eaton and Howe, Inc.	$19,800
Accounts Receivable	51,180	Fabor and Son	15,600
Cost of Goods Sold	65,120	Jasper Manufacturing Inc.	28,500
	$170,850		$63,900
Credits			
Merchandise Inventory	$ 1,220		
Notes Payable	6,000		
Accounts Payable	63,900		
D. A. Karns, Capital	5,000		
Sales	94,730		
	$170,850		

Note that not all the general ledger accounts listed above have been included in Illustration C-6. You will have to refer to Illustration C-5 to determine the balances for the accounts Cash, Accounts Receivable, Cost of Goods Sold, Notes Payable, Capital, and Sales.

Cash Payments Journal

Alternative terminology
The cash payments journal is also called the *cash disbursements journal.*

All disbursements of cash are entered in a cash payments journal. Entries are made from prenumbered cheques. Because cash payments are made for various purposes, the cash payments journal has multiple columns. A four-column journal is shown in Illustration C-7.

Journalizing Cash Payments Transactions

The procedures for journalizing transactions in this journal are similar to those described earlier for the cash receipts journal. Each transaction is entered on one line, and for each line there must be equal debit and credit amounts. It is common practice in the cash payments journal to record the name of the company or individual receiving the cheque (the payee), so that later reference to the cheque is possible by name in addition to cheque number. The entries in the cash payments journal shown in Illustration C-7 are based on the following transactions for Karns Wholesale Supply:

May 3 Cheque No. 101 for $1,200 issued for the annual premium on a fire insurance policy from Corporate General Insurance.
  3 Cheque No. 102 for $100 issued to CANPAR in payment of freight charges on goods purchased.
  7 Cheque No. 103 for $4,400 issued for the cash purchase of merchandise from Zwicker Corp.
  10 Cheque No. 104 for $11,000 sent to Jasper Manufacturing Inc. in full payment of the May 6 invoice.

May 19 Cheque No. 105 for $7,200 mailed to Eaton and Howe, Inc., in full payment of the May 10 invoice.
    24 Cheque No. 106 for $6,900 sent to Fabor and Son in full payment of the May 14 invoice.
    28 Cheque No. 107 for $17,500 sent to Jasper Manufacturing Inc. in full payment of the May 19 invoice.
    31 Cheque No. 108 for $500 issued to D. A. Karns as a cash withdrawal for personal use.

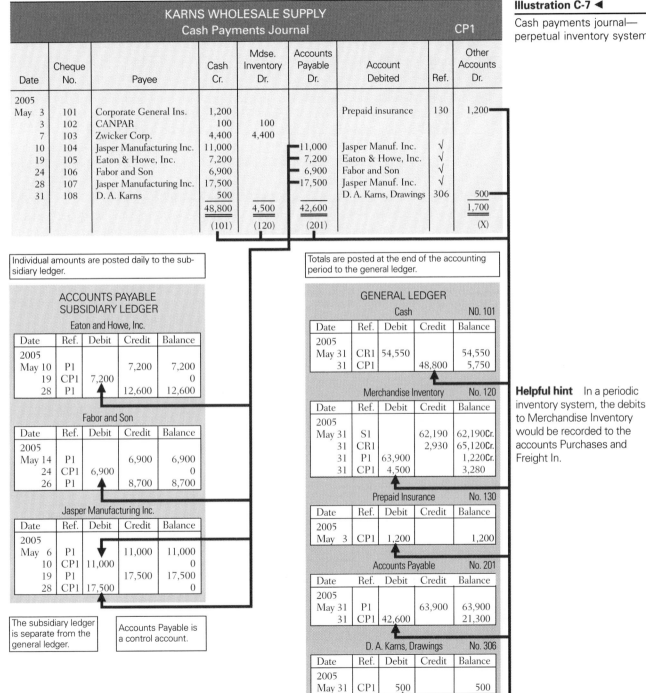

Illustration C-7 ◄

Cash payments journal— perpetual inventory system

Helpful hint In a periodic inventory system, the debits to Merchandise Inventory would be recorded to the accounts Purchases and Freight In.

Note that whenever an amount is entered in the Other Accounts column, a specific general ledger account must be identified in the Account Debited column. The entries for cheque numbers 101 and 108 show this situation. Similarly, a subsidiary account must be identified in the Account Debited column whenever an amount is entered in the Accounts Payable column (as, for example, the entry for cheque no. 104).

After the cash payments journal has been journalized, the columns are totalled. The totals are then balanced to prove the equality of debits and credits. Debits ($4,500 + $42,600 + $1,700 = $48,800) do equal credits ($48,800) in this case.

Posting the Cash Payments Journal

Helpful hint If a company has a subsidiary ledger for merchandise inventory, amounts in the merchandise inventory column would be posted daily in the cash payments journal, as well as in the sales, cash receipts, and purchases journals.

The procedures for posting the cash payments journal are similar to those for the cash receipts journal:

1. Cash and Merchandise Inventory are posted only as a total at the end of the month.
2. The amounts recorded in the Accounts Payable column are posted individually to the subsidiary ledger and in total to the general ledger control account.
3. Transactions in the Other Accounts column are posted individually to the appropriate account(s) noted in the Account Debited column. No totals are posted for the Other Accounts column.

The posting of the cash payments journal is shown in Illustration C-7. Note that the abbreviation CP is used as the posting reference. After postings are completed, the equality of the debit and credit balances in the general ledger should be determined. The control account balance should also agree with the subsidiary ledger total balance. The agreement of these balances is shown below. Note that not all the general ledger accounts have been included in Illustration C-7. You will also have to refer to Illustration C-5 to determine the balances for the Accounts Receivable, Cost of Goods Sold, Notes Payable, Capital, and Sales accounts.

General Ledger		Accounts Payable Subsidiary Ledger	
Debits			
Cash	$ 5,750	Eaton and Howe, Inc.	$12,600
Accounts Receivable	51,180	Fabor and Son	8,700
Merchandise Inventory	3,280		$21,300
Prepaid Insurance	1,200		
D. A. Karns, Drawings	500		
Cost of Goods Sold	65,120		
	$127,030		
Credits			
Accounts Payable	$ 21,300		
Notes Payable	6,000		
D. A. Karns, Capital	5,000		
Sales	94,730		
	$127,030		

Effects of Special Journals on the General Journal

Special journals for sales, purchases, and cash greatly reduce the number of entries that are made in the general journal. **Only transactions that cannot be entered in a special journal are recorded in the general journal.** For example, the general journal may be used to record a transaction granting credit to a customer for a sales return or allowance. It may also be used to record the receipt of a credit from a supplier for purchases returned, the acceptance of a note receivable from a customer, and the purchase of equipment by issuing a note payable. Correcting, adjusting, and closing entries are also made in the general journal.

When control and subsidiary accounts are not used, the procedures for journalizing and posting transactions in the general journal are the same as those described in earlier chapters. When control and subsidiary accounts are used, two modifications of earlier procedures are required:

1. In journalizing, both the control and the subsidiary account must be identified.
2. In posting, there must be a dual posting: once to the control account and once to the subsidiary account.

To illustrate, assume that on May 31 Karns Wholesale Supply returns $500 of merchandise for credit to Fabor and Son. The entry in the general journal and the posting of the entry are shown in Illustration C-8. Note that if cash had been received instead of the credit granted on this return, then the transaction would have been recorded in the cash receipts journal.

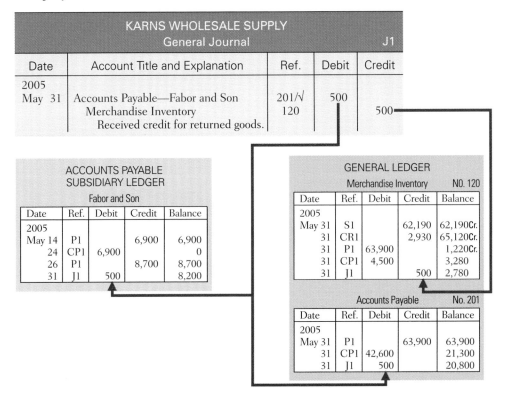

Illustration C-8 ◄
General journal

Helpful hint In a periodic inventory system, the credit would be to the Purchase Returns and Allowances account rather than to Merchandise Inventory.

Notice that in the general journal two accounts are indicated for the debit (the Accounts Payable control account and the Fabor and Son subsidiary account). Two postings (201/√) are indicated in the reference column. One amount is posted to the control account in the general ledger (no. 201) and the other to the creditor's account in the subsidiary ledger (Fabor and Son).

Special Journals in a Periodic Inventory System

Recording and posting transactions in special journals is essentially the same whether a perpetual or a periodic inventory system is used. But there are two differences. The first difference relates to the accounts Merchandise Inventory and Cost of Goods Sold in a perpetual inventory system. In this system, an additional column is required to record the cost of each sale in the sales and cash receipts journals, something which is not required in a periodic inventory system.

The second difference concerns the account titles used. In a perpetual inventory system, Merchandise Inventory and Cost of Goods Sold are used to record purchases and the cost of the merchandise sold. In a periodic inventory system, the accounts Purchases and Freight In accumulate the cost of the merchandise purchased until the end of the period. No cost of goods sold is recorded during the period. Cost of goods sold is calculated at the end of the period in a periodic inventory system.

Each of the special journals illustrated in this appendix is shown again here. Using the same transactions, we assume that Karns Wholesale Supply uses a periodic inventory system instead of a perpetual inventory system.

Illustration C-9 ▶

Sales journal—periodic inventory system

Helpful hint Compare this sales journal to the one presented in Illustration C-4.

	KARNS WHOLESALE SUPPLY Sales Journal			S1
Date	Account Debited	Invoice No.	Ref.	Accts Receivable Dr. Sales Cr.
2005				
May 3	Abbot Sisters	101	√	10,600
7	Babson Co.	102	√	11,350
14	Carson Bros.	103	√	7,800
19	Deli Co.	104	√	9,300
21	Abbot Sisters	105	√	15,400
24	Deli Co.	106	√	21,210
27	Babson Co.	107	√	14,570
				90,230

Illustration C-10 ▶

Cash receipts journal—periodic inventory system

Helpful hint Compare this cash receipts journal to the one presented in Illustration C-5.

	KARNS WHOLESALE SUPPLY Cash Receipts Journal						CR1
Date	Account Credited	Ref.	Cash Dr.	Accounts Receivable Cr.	Sales Cr.	Other Accounts Cr.	
2005							
May 1	D. A. Karns, Capital	301	5,000			5,000	
7			1,900		1,900		
10	Abbot Sisters	√	10,600	10,600			
12			2,600		2,600		
17	Babson Co.	√	11,350	11,350			
22	Notes Payable	200	6,000			6,000	
23	Carson Bros.	√	7,800	7,800			
28	Deli Co.	√	9,300	9,300			
			54,550	39,050	4,500	11,000	

Illustration C-11 ◄
Purchases journal—periodic inventory system

Helpful hint Compare this purchases journal to the one presented in Illustration C-6.

KARNS WHOLESALE SUPPLY
Purchases Journal — P1

Date	Account Credited	Terms	Ref.	Purchases Dr. Accounts Payable Cr.
2005				
May 6	Jasper Manufacturing Inc.	n/20	√	11,000
10	Eaton and Howe, Inc.	n/20	√	7,200
14	Fabor and Son	n/20	√	6,900
19	Jasper Manufacturing Inc.	n/20	√	17,500
26	Fabor and Son	n/20	√	8,700
28	Eaton and Howe, Inc.	n/20	√	12,600
				63,900

Illustration C-12 ◄
Cash payments journal—periodic inventory system

Helpful hint Compare this cash payments journal to the one presented in Illustration C-7.

KARNS WHOLESALE SUPPLY
Cash Payments Journal — CP1

Date	Cheque No.	Payee	Cash Cr.	Accounts Payable Dr.	Account Debited	Ref.	Other Accounts Dr.
2005							
May 3	101	Corporate General Ins.	1,200		Prepaid Insurance	130	1,200
3	102	CANPAR	100		Freight In	516	100
7	103	Zwicker Corp.	4,400		Purchases	510	4,400
10	104	Jasper Manufacturing Inc.	11,000	11,000	Jasper Manuf. Inc.	√	
19	105	Eaton & Howe, Inc.	7,200	7,200	Eaton & Howe, Inc.	√	
24	106	Fabor and Son	6.900	6.900	Fabor and Son	√	
28	107	Jasper Manufacturing Inc.	17,500	17,500	Jasper Manuf. Inc.	√	
31	108	D. A. Karns	500		D. A. Karns, Drawings	306	500
			48,800	42,600			6,200

Brief Exercises

BEC–1 Information related to Bryan Company is presented below for its first month of operations. Calculate (a) the balances that appear in the accounts receivable subsidiary ledger for each customer, and (b) the accounts receivable balance that appears in the general ledger at the end of January.

Calculate subsidiary ledger and control account balances.

Credit Sales			Cash Collections		
Jan. 7	Duffy Co.	$8,000	Jan. 17	Duffy Co.	$7,000
15	Hanson Inc.	6,000	24	Hanson Inc.	5,000
23	Lewis Co.	9,000	29	Lewis Co.	9,000

BEC–2 Identify in which ledger (general or subsidiary) each of the following accounts is shown:

Identify general and subsidiary ledger accounts.

1. Rent Expense
2. Accounts Receivable—O'Malley
3. Notes Payable
4. Accounts Payable—Kerns
5. Merchandise Inventory
6. Sales

BEC–3 Chiasson Co. uses special journals and a general journal. Identify the journal in which each of the following transactions is recorded:

Identify special journals.

1. Paid cash for equipment purchased on account.
2. Purchased merchandise on credit.
3. Paid utility expense in cash.

4. Sold merchandise on account.
5. Granted a cash refund for a sales return.
6. Received a credit on account for a purchase return.
7. Sold merchandise for cash.
8. Purchased merchandise for cash.

Identify special journals—perpetual inventory system.

BEC–4 Swirsky Company uses the cash receipts and cash payments journals illustrated in this appendix for a perpetual inventory system. In April, the following selected cash transactions occurred:

1. Made a refund to a customer for the return of damaged goods.
2. Received payment from a customer.
3. Purchased merchandise for cash.
4. Paid a creditor.
5. Paid freight on merchandise purchased.
6. Paid cash for office equipment.
7. Received a cash refund from a supplier for merchandise returned.
8. Withdrew cash for personal use of owner.
9. Made cash sales.

Instructions

Indicate (a) the journal, and (b) the columns in the journal that should be used in recording each transaction.

Identify special journals—periodic inventory system.

BEC–5 Identify the journal and the specific column title(s) in which each of the following transactions is recorded. Assume the company uses a periodic inventory system.

1. Cash sale
2. Credit sale
3. Sales return on account
4. Cash purchase of merchandise
5. Credit purchase of merchandise
6. Payment of freight on merchandise purchased from a supplier
7. Return of merchandise purchased for cash refund
8. Payment of freight on merchandise delivered to a customer

Exercises

Identify special journals.

EC–1 Below are some transactions for Dartmouth Company:

1. Payment of creditors on account
2. Return of merchandise sold for credit
3. Collection on account from customers
4. Sale of land for cash
5. Sale of merchandise on account
6. Sale of merchandise for cash
7. Credit received for merchandise returned to a supplier
8. Payment of employee wages
9. Revenues and expenses closed to income summary
10. Amortization on building
11. Purchase of office supplies for cash
12. Purchase of merchandise on account

Instructions

For each transaction, indicate whether it would normally be recorded in a cash receipts journal, cash payments journal, sales journal, purchases journal, or general journal.

EC–2 Sing Tao Company uses special journals and a general journal. The company uses a perpetual inventory system and had the following transactions:

Record transactions in sales and purchases journals—perpetual inventory system.

Interactive Homework

Sept. 2 Sold merchandise on account to T. Mephisto, $520, invoice #101, terms n/30. The cost of the merchandise sold was $360.

3 Purchased office supplies on account from Berko Company, $575.

10 Purchased merchandise on account from Miramichi Company, $800, FOB shipping point, terms n/30. Paid freight of $50 to Apex Shippers.

11 Returned unsatisfactory merchandise to Miramichi Company, $200, for credit on account.

12 Purchased office equipment on account from Wells Company, $8,000.

16 Sold merchandise for cash to L. Maillette, for $800. The cost of the merchandise sold was $480.

18 Purchased merchandise for cash from Miramichi Company, $450, FOB destination.

20 Accepted returned merchandise from customer L. Maillette, $800 (see Sept. 16 transaction). Gave full cash refund. Restored the merchandise to inventory.

24 Paid the correct amount owing for the merchandise purchased from Miramichi earlier in the month.

25 Received payment from T. Mephisto for Sept. 2 sale.

26 Sold merchandise on account to M. Christie, $890, invoice #102, terms n/30, FOB destination. The cost of the merchandise was $520. The appropriate party paid $75 to Freight Co. for shipping charges.

30 Paid September salaries, $3,250.

30 The owner, Mr. Sing Tao, withdrew cash for his personal use, $600.

30 Paid for office supplies purchased on September 3.

Instructions

(a) Draw a sales journal and a purchases journal (see Illustrations C-3 and C-6). Use page 1 for each journal.

(b) Record the transaction(s) for September that should be journalized in the sales journal.

(c) Record the transaction(s) for September that should be journalized in the purchases journal.

EC–3 Refer to the information provided for Sing Tao Company in EC–2.

Record transactions in cash receipts, cash payments, and general journals—perpetual inventory system.

Interactive Homework

Instructions

(a) Draw cash receipts and cash payments journals (see Illustrations C-5 and C-7) and a general journal. Use page 1 for each journal.

(b) Record the transaction(s) provided in EC–2 that should be journalized in the cash receipts journal.

(c) Record the transaction(s) provided in EC–2 that should be journalized in the cash payments journal.

(d) Record the transaction(s) provided in EC–2 that should be journalized in the general journal.

EC–4 Argentina Company has the following selected transactions during March:

Record transactions in general journal and explain posting.

Mar. 2 Purchased equipment on account, costing $7,400, from Lifetime Company.

5 Received credit memorandum for $300 from Lyden Company for merchandise returned that had been damaged in shipment to Argentina.

7 Issued a credit memorandum for $400 to Marco Presti for merchandise the customer returned. The returned merchandise has a cost of $275 and was restored to inventory.

Argentina Company uses a purchases journal, a sales journal, two cash journals (receipts and payments), and a general journal. Argentina also uses a perpetual inventory system.

Instructions

(a) Journalize the appropriate transactions in the general journal.

(b) In a brief memo to the president of Argentina Company, explain the postings to the control and subsidiary accounts.

EC–5 Maureen Company uses both special journals and a general journal. On June 30, after all monthly postings had been completed, the Accounts Receivable controlling account in the general ledger had a debit balance of $320,000, and the Accounts Payable controlling account had a credit balance of $87,000.

Determine control account balances and explain posting.

The July transactions recorded in the special journals are summarized below. Maureen Company maintains a perpetual inventory system. No entries that affected accounts receivable and accounts payable were recorded in the general journal for July.

> Sales journal: total sales, $161,400; cost of goods sold, $112,800
> Purchases journal: total purchases, $56,400
> Cash receipts journal: accounts receivable column total, $141,000
> Cash payments journal: accounts payable column total, $47,500

Instructions

(a) What is the balance of the Accounts Receivable control account after the monthly postings on July 31?

(b) What is the balance of the Accounts Payable control account after the monthly postings on July 31?

(c) To what accounts are the column totals for total sales of $161,400 and cost of goods sold of $112,800 in the sales journal posted?

(d) To what account(s) is the accounts receivable column total of $141,000 in the cash receipts journal posted?

Post journals to control and subsidiary accounts.

Interactive Homework

EC–6 On September 1, 2005, the balance of the Accounts Receivable control account in the general ledger of Pirie Company was $11,960. The customers' subsidiary ledger contained account balances as follows: Bickford, $4,820; Cavanaugh, $2,060; Jana, $2,440; Kingston, $2,640. At the end of September, the various journals contained the following information:

> Sales journal: Sales to Bickford, $800; to Jana, $1,260; to Iman, $1,030; to Cavanaugh, $1,100. The cost of each sale, respectively, was $480, $810, $620, and $660.
>
> Cash receipts journal: Cash received from Cavanaugh, $1,310; from Bickford, $2,300; from Iman, $380; from Kingston, $1,800; from Jana, $1,240.
>
> General journal: A $220 sales allowance is granted to Bickford, on September 30.

Instructions

(a) Set up control and subsidiary accounts, and enter the beginning balances.

(b) Post the various journals to the control and subsidiary accounts. Post the items as individual items or as totals, whichever would be the appropriate procedure. Use page 1 for each journal.

(c) Prepare a list of customers and prove the agreement of the control account with the subsidiary ledger at September 30.

Record transactions in sales and purchases journals—periodic inventory system.

Record transactions in cash receipts, cash payments, and general journals—periodic inventory system.

EC–7 Refer to the information provided for Sing Tao Company in EC–2. Complete instructions (a), (b), and (c), assuming that the company uses a periodic inventory system instead of a perpetual inventory system.

EC–8 Refer to the information provided for Sing Tao Company in EC–3. Complete instructions (a) to (d), assuming that the company uses a periodic inventory system instead of a perpetual inventory system.

Problems

Record transactions in special and general journals—perpetual inventory system.

PC–1 Selected accounts from the chart of accounts of Genstar Company are shown below:

101	Cash	201	Accounts payable
112	Accounts receivable	401	Sales
120	Merchandise inventory	412	Sales returns and allowances
126	Supplies	505	Cost of goods sold
157	Equipment	726	Salaries expense

The company uses a perpetual inventory system. The cost of all merchandise sold is 60% of the sales price. During January, Genstar completed the following transactions:

Jan.   3 Purchased merchandise on account from Sun Distributors, $19,800.
        4 Purchased supplies for cash, $280.

Jan. 4 Sold merchandise on account to R. Gilbertson, $8,500, invoice no. 371.
      5 Issued a debit memorandum to Sun Distributors and returned $450 of damaged goods.
      6 Made cash sales for the week totalling $4,650.
      8 Purchased merchandise on account from Irvine Co., $5,400.
      9 Sold merchandise on account to Mays Corp., $5,600, invoice no. 372.
     11 Purchased merchandise on account from Chaparal Co., $4,300.
     13 Paid Sun Distributors account in full.
     13 Made cash sales for the week totalling $5,980.
     15 Received payment from Mays Corp. for invoice no. 372.
     15 Paid semi-monthly salaries of $14,300 to employees.
     17 Received payment from R. Gilbertson for invoice no. 371.
     17 Sold merchandise on account to AMB Co., $1,500, invoice no. 373.
     19 Purchased equipment on account from Johnson Corp., $4,800.
     20 Cash sales for the week totalled $3,400.
     20 Paid Irvine Co. account in full.
     23 Purchased merchandise on account from Sun Distributors, $7,800.
     24 Purchased merchandise on account from Levine Corp., $4,690.
     27 Made cash sales for the week totalling $3,370.
     30 Received payment from AMB Co. for invoice no. 373.
     31 Paid semi-monthly salaries of $13,200 to employees.
     31 Sold merchandise on account to R. Gilbertson, $9,330, invoice no. 374.

Genstar Company uses a sales journal, a purchases journal, a cash receipts journal, a cash payments journal, and a general journal.

Instructions

(a) Record the January transactions in the appropriate journal.
(b) Foot and cross-foot all special journals.
(c) Show how postings would be made by placing ledger account numbers and check marks as needed in the journals. (Actual posting to ledger accounts is not required.)

PC–2 Selected accounts from the chart of accounts of Tigau Company are shown below:

Journalize transactions in special and general journals—perpetual inventory system.

101	Cash		145	Buildings
112	Accounts receivable		201	Accounts payable
120	Merchandise inventory		401	Sales
126	Supplies		505	Cost of goods sold
140	Land		610	Advertising expense

The company uses a perpetual inventory system. The cost of all merchandise sold was 65% of the sales price. During October, Tigau Company completed the following transactions:

Oct. 2 Purchased merchandise on account from Madison & Co., $15,800.
      4 Sold merchandise on account to Petroleum Corp., $8,600, invoice no. 204.
      5 Purchased supplies for cash, $315.
      7 Made cash sales for the week that totalled $9,610.
      9 Paid the Madison & Co. account in full.
     10 Purchased merchandise on account from Quinn Corp., $4,900.
     12 Received payment from Petroleum Corp. for invoice no. 204.
     13 Issued a debit memorandum to Quinn Corp. and returned $260 of damaged goods.
     14 Made cash sales for the week that totalled $8,810.
     16 Sold a parcel of land for $25,000 cash, the land's book value.
     17 Sold merchandise on account to Callebaut Co., $5,530, invoice no. 205.
     18 Purchased merchandise for cash, $2,215.
     21 Made cash sales for the week that totalled $8,640.
     23 Paid in full the Quinn Corp. account for the goods kept.
     25 Purchased supplies on account from Frey Co., $260.
     25 Sold merchandise on account to Golden Corp., $5,520, invoice no. 206.
     25 Received payment from Callebaut Co. for invoice no. 205.
     26 Purchased for cash a small parcel of land and a building on the land to use as a storage facility. The total cost of $35,000 was allocated $16,000 to the land and $19,000 to the building.

Oct. 27 Purchased merchandise on account from Schmid Co., $9,000.
   28 Made cash sales for the week that totalled $9,320.
   30 Purchased merchandise on account from Madison & Co., $16,200.
   30 Paid advertising bill for the month from *The Gazette*, $600.
   30 Sold merchandise on account to Callebaut Co., $5,200, invoice no. 207.

Tigau Company uses a sales journal, purchases journal, cash receipts journal, cash payments journal, and general journal.

Instructions

(a) Record the October transactions in the appropriate journals.
(b) Foot and cross-foot all special journals.
(c) Show how postings would be made by placing ledger account numbers and check marks as needed in the journals. (Actual posting to ledger accounts is not required.)

Record transactions in special and general journals, post, and prepare trial balance—perpetual inventory system.

PC–3 The post-closing trial balance for Gibbs Music Co. follows:

GIBBS MUSIC CO.
Post-Closing Trial Balance
December 31, 2004

		Debit	Credit
101	Cash	$ 49,500	
112	Accounts receivable	15,000	
115	Notes receivable—S. Lava	45,000	
120	Merchandise inventory	22,000	
140	Land	25,000	
145	Building	75,000	
146	Accumulated amortization—building		$ 18,000
157	Equipment	6,450	
158	Accumulated amortization—equipment		1,500
200	Notes payable		–
201	Accounts payable		42,000
275	Mortgage payable		82,000
301	M. Gibbs, capital		94,450
310	M. Gibbs, drawings	–	
401	Sales		–
410	Sales returns and allowances	–	
505	Cost of goods sold	–	
725	Salaries expense	–	
810	Interest revenue		–
920	Loss—damaged inventory	–	
		$237,950	$237,950

The subsidiary ledgers contain the following information:

1. Accounts Receivable—S. Armstrong, $4,500; R. Christof, $3,000; B. Hibberd, $7,500
2. Accounts Payable—Fieldstone Corp., $9,000; Harms Distributors, $16,000; Watson & Co., $17,000

Gibbs Music Co. uses a perpetual inventory system. The transactions for January 2005 are as follows:

Jan. 3 Sold merchandise to B. Rohl, $1,000. The cost of goods sold was $400.
    5 Purchased merchandise from Warren Parts Co., $2,400.
    7 Received a cheque from S. Armstrong, $3,000, in partial payment of its account.
   11 Paid freight on merchandise purchased, $350.
   13 Received payment of account in full from B. Rohl.
   14 Issued a credit memo to acknowledge receipt of $600 of damaged merchandise returned by R. Christof. The cost of the returned merchandise was $250. (*Hint*: Debit Loss—Damaged Inventory instead of Merchandise Inventory.)
   15 Sent Harms Distributors a cheque in full payment of account.
   17 Purchased merchandise from Lapeska Co., $1,900.
   18 Paid salaries of $4,400.
   20 Gave Watson & Co. a 2-month, 6% note for $17,000 in full payment of account payable.

Jan. 23 Total cash sales amounted to $9,600. The cost of goods sold was $3,840.
 24 Sold merchandise on account to B. Hibberd, $7,800. The cost of goods sold was $3,300.
 27 Sent Warren Parts Co. a cheque for $950 in partial payment of the account.
 29 Received partial payment on a note of $35,000 in addition to $175 interest, from S. Lava.
 30 Returned merchandise costing $600 to Lapeska Co. for credit.
 31 Withdrew $800 cash for personal use.

Instructions

(a) Open general and subsidiary ledger accounts and record December 31, 2004, balances.
(b) Record the January transactions in a sales journal, a purchases journal, a cash receipts journal, a cash payments journal, and a general journal, as illustrated in this appendix.
(c) Post the appropriate amounts to the subsidiary and general ledger accounts.
(d) Prepare a trial balance at January 31, 2005.
(e) Prepare a listing to show that the subsidiary ledgers agree with control accounts in the general ledger.

PC–4 The post-closing trial balance for Scholz Co. follows:

Record transactions in special and general journals, post, and prepare trial balance—perpetual inventory system.

SCHOLZ CO.
Post-Closing Trial Balance
April 30, 2005

		Debit	Credit
101	Cash	$ 36,700	
112	Accounts receivable	15,400	
115	Notes receivable—Cole Company	48,000	
120	Merchandise inventory	22,000	
157	Equipment	8,200	
158	Accumulated amortization—equipment		$ 1,800
200	Notes payable		–
201	Accounts payable		43,400
301	C. Scholz, capital		85,100
310	C. Scholz, drawings	–	
401	Sales		–
410	Sales returns and allowances	–	
505	Cost of goods sold	–	
725	Salaries expense	–	
730	Rent expense	–	
810	Interest revenue		–
		$130,300	$130,300

The subsidiary ledgers contain the following information:

1. Accounts Receivable—L. Cellars, $7,400; W. Karasch, $3,250; G. Parrish, $4,750
2. Accounts Payable—Buttercup Distributors, $17,400; Elite Sports, $15,500; Winterware Corp., $10,500

Scholz uses a perpetual inventory system. The transactions for May 2005 are as follows:

May 3 Sold merchandise to B. Simone, $2,400. The cost of the goods sold was $1,050.
 5 Purchased merchandise from Werner Widgits, $2,600, on account.
 7 Received a cheque from G. Parrish, $2,800, in partial payment of account.
 11 Paid freight on merchandise purchased, $318.
 12 Paid rent of $1,500 for May.
 13 Received payment in full from B. Simone.
 14 Issued a credit memo to acknowledge $750 of merchandise returned by W. Karasch. The merchandise (original cost, $325) was restored to inventory.
 15 Sent Buttercup Distributors a cheque in full payment of account.
 17 Purchased merchandise from Lancio Co., $2,100, on account.
 18 Paid salaries of $4,700.
 20 Gave Elite Sports a two-month, 10% note for $15,500 in full payment of account payable.
 20 Returned merchandise costing $510 to Lancio for credit.
 23 Total cash sales amounted to $9,500. The cost of goods sold was $4,450.
 27 Sent Werner Widgits a cheque for $1,000, in partial payment of account.
 29 Received partial payment on a note of $40,000 in addition to $1,600 interest from Cole Company.
 31 Withdrew $1,000 cash for personal use.

Instructions

(a) Open general and subsidiary ledger accounts and record April 30, 2005, balances.
(b) Record the May transactions in a sales journal, a purchases journal, a cash receipts journal, a cash payments journal, and a general journal, as illustrated in this chapter.
(c) Post the appropriate amounts to the subsidiary and general ledger accounts.
(d) Prepare a trial balance at May 31, 2005.
(e) Determine whether the subsidiary ledgers agree with the control accounts in the general ledger.

Record transactions in special and general journals—periodic inventory system.

PC–5 Selected accounts from the chart of accounts on Weir Company are shown below:

101	Cash	401	Sales
112	Accounts receivable	412	Sales returns and allowances
126	Supplies	510	Purchases
157	Equipment	512	Purchase returns and allowances
201	Accounts payable	726	Salaries expense

During February, Weir completed the following transactions:

Feb. 3 Purchased merchandise on account from Zears Co., $9,200.
    4 Purchased supplies for cash, $290.
    4 Sold merchandise on account to Gilles Co., $7,220, invoice no. 371.
    5 Issued a debit memorandum to Zears Co. and returned $450 worth of goods.
    6 Made cash sales for the week totalling $3,950.
    8 Purchased merchandise on account from Fell Electronics, $5,200,
    9 Sold merchandise on account to Mawani Corp., $7,050, invoice no. 372.
    11 Purchased merchandise on account from Thomas Co., $3,100.
    13 Paid Zears Co. account in full.
    13 Made cash sales for the week totalling $4,850.
    15 Received payment from Mawani Corp. for invoice no. 372.
    15 Paid semi-monthly salaries of $14,700 to employees.
    17 Received payment from Gilles Co. for invoice no. 371.
    17 Sold merchandise on account to Lumber Co., $1,600, invoice no. 373.
    19 Purchased equipment on account from Brown Corp., $6,400.
    20 Cash sales for the week totalled $4,900.
    20 Paid Fell Electronics account in full.
    23 Purchased merchandise on account from Zears Co., $8,800.
    24 Purchased merchandise on account from Lewis Co., $5,130.
    27 Made cash sales for the week totalling $3,560.
    28 Received payment from Lumber Co. for invoice no. 373.
    28 Paid semi-monthly salaries of $14,900 to employees.
    28 Sold merchandise on account to Gilles Co., $9,810, invoice no. 374.

Weir Company uses a sales journal, purchases journal, cash receipts journal, cash payments journal, and general journal. Weir uses a periodic inventory system.

Instructions

(a) Record the February transactions in the appropriate journal.
(b) Foot and cross-foot all special journals.
(c) Show how postings would be made by placing ledger account numbers and check marks as needed in the journals. (Actual posting to ledger accounts is not required.)

Cumulative Coverage—Chapters 2 to 6 and Appendix C

Kassam Company has the following opening account balances in its general and subsidiary ledgers on January 1. All accounts have normal debit and credit balances. Kassam uses a perpetual inventory system. The cost of all merchandise sold was 40% of the sales price.

GENERAL LEDGER

Account No.	Account Title	January 1 Opening Balance
101	Cash	$ 35,050
112	Accounts receivable	14,000
115	Notes receivable	39,000
120	Merchandise inventory	20,000
125	Office supplies	1,000
130	Prepaid insurance	2,000
140	Land	50,000
145	Building	100,000
146	Accumulated amortization—building	25,000
157	Equipment	6,450
158	Accumulated amortization	1,500
201	Accounts payable	36,000
275	Mortgage payable	125,000
301	A. Kassam, capital	80,000

Accounts Receivable Subsidiary Ledger		Accounts Payable Subsidiary Ledger	
Customer	January 1 Opening Balance	Creditor	January 1 Opening Balance
R. Draves	$1,500	Liazuk Co.	$10,000
B. Jacovetti	7,500	Mikush Bros.	15,000
S. Kysely	5,000	Nguyen & Son	11,000

Kassam's January transactions follow:

Jan. 3 Sold merchandise on credit to B. Soto $3,100, invoice no. 510, and J. Ebel $1,800, invoice no. 511.

5 Purchased merchandise from Welz Wares for $3,000 and Laux Supplies for $2,700.

7 Received cheques for $5,000 from S. Kysely and $2,000 from B. Jacovetti on accounts.

8 Paid freight on merchandise purchased, $180.

9 Sent cheques to Liazuk Co. for $10,000 and Nguyen & Son for $11,000 in full payment of accounts.

9 Issued credit memo for $400 to J. Ebel for merchandise returned. The merchandise was restored to inventory.

10 Summary cash sales totalled $16,500.

11 Sold merchandise on credit to R. Draves for $1,900, invoice no. 512, and to S. Kysely for $900, invoice no. 513.

15 Withdrew $2,000 cash for A. Kassam's personal use.

16 Purchased merchandise from Nguyen & Son for $15,000, from Liazuk Co. for $13,900, and from Welz Wares for $1,500.

17 Paid $400 cash for office supplies.

18 Returned $500 of merchandise to Liazuk and received credit.

20 Summary cash sales totalled $17,500.

21 Issued $15,000 note to Mikush Bros. in payment of balance due. The note bears an interest rate of 10% and is due in three months.

Jan. 21 Received payment in full from S. Kysely.
  22 Sold merchandise on credit to B. Soto for $1,700, invoice no. 514, and to R. Draves for $800, invoice no. 515.
  23 Sent cheques to Nguyen & Son and Liazuk Co. in full payment of accounts.
  25 Sold merchandise on credit to B. Jacovetti for $3,500, invoice no. 516, and to J. Ebel for $6,100, invoice no. 517.
  27 Purchased merchandise from Nguyen & Son for $14,500, from Laux Supplies for $1,200, and from Welz Wares for $2,800.
  28 Paid $800 cash for office supplies.
  31 Summary cash sales totalled $19,920.
  31 Paid salaries of $6,900.
  31 Received payment in full from B. Soto and J. Ebel on account.

Instructions

(a) Record the January transactions in the appropriate journal—sales, purchases, cash receipts, cash payments, and general.
(b) Post the journals to the general and subsidiary ledgers. New accounts should be added and numbered in an orderly fashion as needed.
(c) Prepare an unadjusted trial balance at January 31, 2005. Determine whether the subsidiary ledgers agree with the control accounts in the general ledger.
(d) Prepare adjusting journal entries. Prepare an adjusted trial balance, using the following additional information:

   1. Office supplies at January 31 total $700.
   2. Insurance coverage expires on September 30, 2005.
   3. Annual amortization on the building is $6,000 and on the equipment is $1,500.
   4. Interest of $45 has accrued on the note payable.
   5. A physical count of merchandise inventory has found $44,850 of goods on hand.

(e) Prepare a multiple-step income statement and a statement of owner's equity for January, and a classified balance sheet at the end of January.
(f) Prepare and post the closing entries.
(g) Prepare a post-closing trial balance.

Company Index

A cumulative index appears at the end of each Part.

Subject Index

A cumulative index appears at the end of each Part.

Photo Credits

All images copyright © Photo Disc, Inc./Getty Images, unless otherwise noted.
Logos are registered trademarks of the respective companies and are reprinted with permission.

Chapter 8
OPENER: Whitehill Technologies. Page 402: Sears Canada Inc.

Chapter 9
OPENER: Southern Alberta Institute of Technology (SAIT). Page 402: Artville.

Chapter 10
OPENER: West Edmonton Mall. Page 494: Corbis Digital Stock.